**LYNE[...]** [...]g You

Prete[...] oauthor

of If Y[...]ses on

Management (with David Baron), and For Mothers of Difficult

Daughters (with Dr. Charney Herst). She lives in Los Angeles.

# Say the Magic Words

## HOW TO GET WHAT YOU WANT FROM THE PEOPLE WHO HAVE WHAT YOU NEED

LYNETTE PADWA

PENGUIN BOOKS

PENGUIN BOOKS

Published by the Penguin Group

Penguin Group (USA) Inc., 375 Hudson Street, New York, New York 10014, U.S.A.
Penguin Group (Canada), 10 Alcorn Avenue, Toronto, Ontario, Canada
M4V 3B2 (a division of Pearson Penguin Canada Inc.)
Penguin Books Ltd, 80 Strand, London WC2R 0RL, England
Penguin Ireland, 25 St Stephen's Green, Dublin 2, Ireland
(a division of Penguin Books Ltd)
Penguin Group (Australia), 250 Camberwell Road, Camberwell, Victoria 3124,
Australia (a division of Pearson Australia Group Pty Ltd)
Penguin Books India Pvt Ltd, 11 Community Centre, Panchsheel Park,
New Delhi - 110 017, India
Penguin Group (NZ), cnr Airborne and Rosedale Roads, Albany, Auckland 1310,
New Zealand (a division of Pearson New Zealand Ltd)
Penguin Books (South Africa) (Pty) Ltd, 24 Sturdee Avenue, Rosebank,
Johannesburg 2196, South Africa

Penguin Books Ltd, Registered Offices:
80 Strand, London WC2R 0RL, England

First published in Penguin Books 2005

1  3  5  7  9  10  8  6  4  2

LIBRARY OF CONGRESS CATALOGING-IN-PUBLICATION DATA
Padwa, Lynette.
Say the magic words : how to get what you want from the people who have
what you need / Lynette Padwa.
p.  cm.
Includes index.
ISBN 0-14-200212-7
1. Customer relations.  2. Patron and client.  3. Professions—Social aspects.
4. Consumers—Professional relationships.  I. Title.

HF5415.5.P33 2005
658.8'12—dc22       2004051364

Printed in the United States of America
Set in Fournier
Designed by Liney Li

TO MY SON, GRANT PALMER

# CONTENTS

## AUTHOR'S NOTE

*Some of the people interviewed for this book requested anonymity.*
*Their pseudonyms appear as first names with last initials.*

# INTRODUCTION
## THE GOLDEN RULE ON STEROIDS

I always believed in the Golden Rule. It made sense that if you did unto others as you would have them do unto you, everybody ought to be happy. There was just one flaw, and it took me a while (years) to figure it out: other people often wanted something different done unto them than I did. Unless I knew what they wanted, it didn't matter how nicely I smiled or whether I said please and thank you. They still viewed me as an outsider, a well-intentioned lame-o, or a mark.

But if I knew what they wanted—what they specifically needed in order to feel as if I understood them and was one of them—ah, the power! And it was even better when I knew the things that irritated them so I could avoid saying or doing those things. With that knowledge, the Golden Rule was elevated from a feeble plea to a magical incantation. It was the Golden Rule on steroids.

This book is the result of my personal quest to get that information from the people who have what we need, whether it is a sandwich, an apartment, or a Maserati. The chapters profile the professionals, tradespeople, and salespeople who make up the supporting cast in the lives of most of us. My goal was to learn about their jobs from their point of view, educate myself about their fields, and ask them point-blank what sort of behavior they appreciated and what really ticked them off. They were delighted to tell me, as nobody had asked them before.

Each of these chapters is a mini-dossier that reveals the standard mind-set of people toiling in a particular field. It gives the lowdown on current working conditions, pay, and general morale. It provides the inside scoop about timing—when to make a hotel reservation or to schedule an appointment with an attorney, a parent-teacher conference, or your child's yearly checkup. The chapters explain behaviors that have mystified common folk for ages, such as why the doctor brushes off your complaints about pain or why the contractor brushes off your half-completed kitchen. You will find out exactly what to say and do to get on these people's good side so they will want to help you. Just as important, you will learn what *not* to say and do. You will know which questions to ask, which to look out for, and when to be quiet.

Nearly every one of these relationships involves an exchange of money (the exceptions are teachers and politicians), yet success rarely depends on the fee. It's about grasping the essence of the jobs, the politics involved, and the forces that push and pull them. If you know these details, you will know that what a teacher really wants at the end of the year is not a two-pound box of chocolates but a letter of thanks with a copy sent to her principal. You will know that asking your lawyer why he got into the law will make you one of his favorite clients. You will realize that the best way to win a nanny's confidence is to grill her mercilessly on the first interview.

Two of the chapters expose the strategies of car salesmen and funeral directors—fleeting players in your daily life, but ones who can ream large holes in your bank account. In those cases, there's not much point in trying to win them over; it's either eat or be eaten. I have provided more in-depth dossiers on these salespeople and their businesses: background information about the industries, where to find the wholesale costs of the items you are buying from them, and most important, how to deflect the psychological ploys they will use to manipulate you. It's so much easier to be civil when you come prepared.

I have to admit that I was hoping the research I conducted for this book would reveal a Platinum Rule that applied to everyone after all. No such luck. There were some basic principles—human beings like other human beings who are polite, appreciative, and free of body odor—but beyond that, only one common theme stood out: people desperately want to succeed at what they do. It's almost as if success equals survival. Doctors want to heal you. Teachers want your child to learn. Car salesmen want to sell you a car. Mechanics want to fix it. Waiters want you to like the service. Lawyers want to win the case. When people are not successful, they become petulant, fearful, and uncooperative. If something about you gives them the impression that you will make them fail, they will be less willing to help you. If they sense that they will succeed with you, they will go out of their way to return your calls, honor their agreements, and save you the booth by the window. The key, then, is to give them the impression that they will succeed. This book will show you how. Ah, the power!

# HAIRDRESSER
## ONE CUT CLOSER TO THE DREAM

Forget the Middle East conflict. What the world really needs is a fact-finding mission between two cultures that have been alienated even longer: hairdressers and their clients. One group is armed with sharp, pointy instruments, the other cowers in the simple black sheath of the condemned. One wants to create art, the other wants to be transformed in 45 minutes. Too often, both sides leave the arena disappointed. Beneath the chirpy "bye-byes" runs an undercurrent of frustration and dashed hopes. The salon that promises peace and pampering instead delivers angst, intimidation, and self-loathing. And I am *not* being overly dramatic—*this is hair we're talking about*.

There is no dynamic quite like the one that exists between hairdresser and client. Cutting hair is technically a service, but the act is so intimate that normal social divisions quickly become blurred. Compare hairstyling to any other professional relationship: Do you worry about insulting your mechanic if he hasn't fixed your car correctly? Or hurting your accountant's feelings if she hasn't prepared your taxes on time? No, because it is a business relationship. With a hairdresser, a personal bond can develop in just a few visits, based on the physical contact and the need to fill the time with chitchat. Suddenly the stylist feels like a friend, and you don't want to criticize her work. You may freely tell her about how you lost your virginity, but when it comes to admitting that you don't like the tint she used, you clam up. After a bad cut or color, chances are you will flee without ever telling the stylist what you didn't like.

There are better ways to handle the disappointment and increase the odds that you will leave the salon thrilled, reborn, looking ten years younger . . . or at least somewhat satisfied.

## Behind the Scenes: Ticklish Territory

The hairdresser's position is simple: he wants to make you happy so you will come back. Most hairdressers are far less sensitive and temperamental than you might think; they understand that not every cut or dye job will be successful. They want you to tell them what you desire and, if you don't like the result, to let them know so they can fix it (usually for free). They won't start crying or storm off in a snit. They value your friendship, yes, but they depend on your business to pay their rent. Honest feedback is preferable to insincere flattery.

Hairdressers get new clients almost exclusively through word of mouth. According to Andrea Knight, who works out of an upscale salon in Santa Monica, California, it takes about three years to build a following. In most salons, stylists rent a stall from the owner. Their income is derived entirely from commissions (usually 50 percent) and tips (anywhere from 10 to 20 percent). The ability to move from salon to salon depends on having a large clientele, because owners want to rent space to stylists who will bring in a lot of new customers.

What makes customers loyal? It's a combination of the stylist's skill and personality, says Knight, adding, "Most of my clients are like me. They're down to earth. I'm not the type to gab for three hours, so the women who want someone like that don't come to me." This concept seems to be fundamental to choosing a hairdresser that you can stick with for a long time. Stylist Ann Reinten writes, "As far as the salon being right for you, look inside and study the staff. Do they have a look that you relate to? If they are completely at odds with what you are looking for, move on until you find one where the staff, decor, and music make you feel comfortable."

Hairdressers are acutely aware that many clients rely on them for friendship and therapy as much as for a cut. Laurence Roberts, who works at Umberto in Beverly Hills, says, "If I have a new client, I always try to open her up a little bit. If I get to know her, it's a way of tying her in with my personality. Otherwise you're just another blow-dryer standing there. What makes you special? What makes you different?" It sounds like an audition, and in many ways it is. Roberts, who has been a hairdresser for 25 years, estimates that client loyalty is based on 60 percent talent and 40 percent personality.

Which brings us to the price-to-talent ratio. Hairdressing salons fall into three basic price categories: economy class, such as Fantastic Sam's and Supercuts, where you can get a haircut for $15 or $20; business class, where a cut will run you $40 or $50; and first class, where you will be pampered and clipped for anywhere from $100–$250. According to Knight, who charges in the middle range, there is a marked difference between the $10 and $40 cut because the bargain salons are proving grounds for inexperienced stylists. The difference between the $50 cut and the $100 cut is not nearly so pronounced.

In the expensive salons you are paying for location, ambience, and, above all, time. Pricey stylists fuss over their clients for two or three hours, says Knight: "They're earning the same amount I am, only the cut takes twice as long. People have a lot of time on their hands if they're paying $100 or $200 for a haircut. It's the kind of wealth that's beyond my imagination—it's hard to believe somebody would really have the stupidity to pay that much for a haircut."

Across town at Umberto, Laurence Roberts reports that he books clients by the half hour and also charges based on the difficulty of the job. "Women are $80, and a top cut would cost $90. If a woman has hair below her bra strap and it's thick and curly and takes forty minutes to blow out, that's going to cost more. I charge one of my clients $65 for a blow-dry."

Roberts also spoke at length about matching a cut to a client's face, which is really what you're paying for with your $80. "I'm not looking at a client's hair as much as the shape of her face. If her eyes are accented, her cheekbones are accented, and her face is looking great by the time I'm done, the cut is right. She doesn't know why, but she thinks, 'God, I look good.' If you're paying $50 and more, your hair will be cut well, technically speaking. But you can have a good haircut that you don't like. If it doesn't compliment your face and features, you won't like it, even though you won't know why."

That's a valid point, but paying more does not automatically buy you artistic ability. According to Roberts, the safest way to check out the talent at a salon is to get a manicure there before you get a haircut. "It gives you a half hour to spy, watch the hairdressers, and get an idea of who would be right for you." You might also ask the manicurist if she knows which stylists are popular and who would be a good match for your hair.

If you are longing for a change but terrified to take the plunge, ask for a shampoo and blow-dry before making an appointment for a cut to get a sense of how the stylist handles your hair. "Most people can tell if a hairdresser is confident or not by the way she works," says Andrea Knight. "Experienced hairdressers are not flimsy with their hands—they have a good, strong, firm touch. If you've got a nervous hairdresser, that is not a good sign."

People who don't have the time or inclination to shop around should make the most of the free consultation salons offer their new clients. This is your best chance to communicate with the hairdresser, before the bond of friendship sets and you become reluctant to speak out.

## The Consultation

The typical salon consultation lasts about fifteen minutes. Call and ask them which days and times are the slowest, and try to book your session then. (Most are busiest on Saturdays and in the evenings.) If you are trying out a new salon rather than a specific stylist, you should volunteer some extra information, according to Laurence Roberts: "Let them know what kind of hair you have so they can book your stylist properly. Is it thin, thick, curly? How long is it—shoulder length, below the bra strap, chin length? What do you want—cut, color, highlights? If you have extra-thick hair, say so; it takes longer to color than fine hair does." Salon receptionists are not trained to ask for this information, but clients who want the best service will offer it.

Come to the consultation prepared to explain yourself, and stay in your street clothes. Once you don the black robe, your personal style will fade away and you'll be just another generic head. The following will help the hairdresser understand what you're looking for.

**PHOTOGRAPHS OF THE STYLE YOU WANT.** "Pictures are the most helpful, not necessarily to follow exactly but just to get a general idea," says Andrea Knight. "There have been a thousand times when somebody has told me they want their hair a certain way and when I get the pictures out and we start looking at them, it's totally different than how they described it." If you happen to have a photo of yourself in a cut you liked, bring that along.

**PHOTOGRAPHS OF THE STYLE YOU *DON'T* WANT.** If you are dead set against a certain look and have a photo of that, bring it. Photos of what you do not want are very helpful to stylists whether or not you have shots of what you do want.

**INFORMATION ABOUT YOUR LIFESTYLE.** If you can't get the hang of blow-drying your hair or don't want to spend more than five minutes on it in the morning, say so. Tell the hairdresser what types of products you like and how much you are comfortable putting on your hair every day. Mention anything you have had problems with in the past, as well as cuts that have worked for you. If you work out a lot, swim, or need to wash your hair frequently, tell the hairdresser. It might affect not only the cut and color but also the products he suggests you use.

After you have shared your vital statistics and photos, ask the hairdresser for his opinion. Even if you're wedded to the same style you have worn for years, hear him out. Says Roberts, "Lots of people have set ideas; for instance, they'll be stuck in a rut from 1972 because the Farrah Fawcett looked good on them then. They could have a variation on that theme and look more current." It's also possible that the style you want won't go well with your face. Rather than asking the hairdresser if he is capable of giving you that cut, ask how he thinks it will look. Make it clear that you welcome his opinion, and if he has doubts about your choice, ask why. Maybe a slightly different style with the same overall feel will work better for you.

There are a few danger signs to watch for in this initial consultation. If the stylist isn't paying attention or asking any questions, be careful. A good stylist will touch your hair, notice how it falls, and visibly concentrate on it for at least a few minutes. Be on the alert for prima donnas who try to convince you they know what's best without hearing you out. According to Roberts, these are the stylists who say, "I'm an artist and I'll make you look gorgeous. I have my way, I have my technique, me, me, me, I, I, I. If someone isn't willing to listen to you and hear about your lifestyle, you probably shouldn't be going to him. Your hair is his hair for forty-five minutes. You're the one who has to live with it for the next five or six weeks."

## No Phrase Book for the Salon

In most transactions it's useful for customers to know some of the lingo so they can establish a bond with the other person and have a better understanding of what he or she is talking about. In the world of hairdressers, the opposite is true. There are so many different terms that a little bit of knowledge can do a great deal of harm. Even innocuous words such as *trim*, *bob*, *layer*, and *feather* may mean something different to you and the hairdresser. In fact, the terms often have different meanings from hairdresser to hairdresser.

The safest route is to stick to plain English and visual aids. To indicate the length you want, show pictures, point, or talk in inches. To indicate the style, photos are the best way to go. If you don't have one and are reduced to using words alone, choose them carefully. For instance, you might say, "I think I want a feathered look on the bangs, but what does *feathered* mean to you?" If you are not absolutely certain she understands you, ask to see some magazines and try to find a photo that approximates the look you want. If the hairdresser starts tossing around terms you are unsure of, stop her and ask her to explain exactly what she is talking about.

## Magic Words and Deeds in the Salon

Hairdressers charge by the hour, the half hour, or (in the case of some children's hairdressers) the quarter hour. Time is always an issue with them, explains Andrea Knight, because, "if somebody is late it can throw off your whole schedule, which means you're apologizing for the rest of the day." Therefore, the first rule of hairdressing etiquette is to be on time or, better yet, five or ten minutes early. After that . . .

**LET THE STYLIST KNOW WHEN YOU ARRIVE.** Then sit where it will be easy for her to find you. "Don't slink past and sit down in the farthest, darkest corner and expect me to know you are here by feeling your presence," writes stylist Cindy Clark in *Snip* magazine.

**SIT UP STRAIGHT IN THE CHAIR AND TRY NOT TO CROSS YOUR LEGS.** It helps the hairdresser cut your hair evenly.

**SPEAK UP IF YOU DON'T LIKE WHAT THE HAIRDRESSER IS DOING.** This is one of the biggest misunderstandings between hairdresser and client. If you see the stylist doing something that looks alarming, say, "Could you stop for a minute?" and ask her to explain. They do not mind this; in fact, they want you to tell them if something is bothering you while the cut is in progress so they can explain it or change it while there is still time. Just don't grab their arm or snatch the scissors out of their hand.

**BE SENSITIVE TO THE HAIRDRESSER'S MOOD.** Although you may crave your hour-long chat, be polite. Getting your hair cut is not a free pass to dump on the hairdresser. Stylists see up to fifteen clients a day and, like all of us, they get emotionally drained now and then.

**LEARN FROM THE HAIRDRESSER.** Your hair will never look as good at home as it does when the stylist plays with it, but if you pay attention during the blow-dry you can eventually master a few of the techniques. Most hairdressers will be delighted to share their expertise with you. They don't get tired of the subject, and they won't be peeved if they have explained it three times before.

**COMPLIMENT THE HAIRDRESSER IF YOU LIKE THE WORK.** This should be obvious, but hairdressers report that not everyone remembers to say, "Thanks, it looks great!"

**TELL THE STYLIST IF YOU DO NOT LIKE THE FINISHED WORK.** As mentioned earlier, hairdressers want to keep your business, so they need to know when you're not satisfied. There are gracious ways to express disappointment, most of which center on that handy concept, *expectation:* "This looks different than I expected"; "The color is lighter than I expected"; "It's not as short as I expected." Don't waste time blaming the stylist. As soon as you tell her how you feel, follow it up with, "Is there anything we can do to adjust this?" Most hairdressers will be happy to comply at no extra charge, although they might suggest you wait a week for the cut to settle and to give yourself a chance to get used to it.

**TIP 10 TO 20 PERCENT.** Although some hairdressers claim that the proper tip is 15 to 20 percent, 10 percent is more typical. "Five to seven dollars for a $40 to $50 haircut—one or two dollars for the hair washer, and five for me, that's about average," says Andrea Knight. Laurence Roberts agreed that the range is 10 to 20 percent, with most of his clients tipping 15. "If your budget doesn't allow for tipping, then say so when you tell us how much you love what we did. We all understand budgets. And we love praise," writes Cindy Clark. If the salon owner charges the same rate as everyone else, tip her. If she charges a lot more, don't.

## Absolute No-No's

It bears repeating: do not be late! If you are unavoidably delayed, call and let the stylist know. Whatever you do, don't pull a no-show. If at the last minute you realize you can't make it, call and apologize. If you're feeling flush, offer to pay for the visit anyway. This remarkable act will earn you the stylist's undying respect and devotion.

Aside from tardiness, the following behaviors will annoy the average hairdresser.

**DON'T GUSH ABOUT OTHER HAIRDRESSERS YOU HAVE KNOWN AND LOVED.** While it is perfectly permissible to tell your stylist about a cut you liked, leave the hairdresser out of it.

**DON'T BAD-MOUTH OTHER SALONS OR HAIRDRESSERS.** This instantly erodes the trust between you and the stylist.

**DON'T STAND OVER THE HAIRDRESSER WHILE SHE IS FINISHING UP WITH THE PREVIOUS CLIENT.**

**DON'T COME IN IF YOU'RE SICK.** With all the physical contact that goes on in a salon, it's easy to catch colds and flus.

**DON'T DIRECT THE STYLIST WHILE SHE IS CUTTING YOUR HAIR.** Says Andrea Knight, "I get distracted when people are very bossy with me. You can't stipulate every single hair being cut. If that's how you feel, cut your own hair. I've said that to people! Cutting hair is what I do. Allow me to do it, and then if you're not happy with it, I'll correct it."

**DON'T PRESSURE THE STYLIST FOR EXTRA SERVICES AT THE LAST MINUTE.** It's fine to inquire if she could fit in a color as well as a cut—maybe her schedule is light that day—but if the answer is no, don't push.

**DON'T BOOK AN APPOINTMENT THAT IS TOO SHORT.** Long hair takes longer, especially if it's curly and you're getting it blow-dried. That is why it's important to tell your stylist or the receptionist exactly what you want and what type of hair you have when you schedule your appointment.

**DON'T HAGGLE OVER PRICE.** Pricing in most salons is straightforward, and the stylists don't like negotiating.

**HELP FOR CURLYHEADS**

Roughly half the population in the United States has curly or wavy hair, but relatively few hairdressers know how to bring out its beauty. One of the biggest challenges with curly hair is shrinkage—it looks entirely different wet than dry, and hairdressers like to cut hair when it's wet. A Web site called naturallycurly.com is a great resource for curlyheads. It features products, articles, and, best of all, a list of stylists who specialize in cutting curly hair, along with testimonials from their clients. The list covers cities in the United States, Canada, the United Kingdom, and a few other locales, such as New Zealand and South Africa.

## The Chair or the Couch?

One of the requirements for becoming a hairdresser is being good with people. Cosmetology schools are very forthcoming about this, and it is obvious to anyone who wants to go into the business. Still, it's doubtful that many hairstyling students are prepared for the level of emotional involvement the job entails. The relationship is so personal that social service agencies have begun tapping hairdressers to intervene with at-risk clients. In Connecticut and Nevada, hairdressing students are being taught how to recognize signs of domestic violence—what to look for, what questions to ask. In San Diego, stylists are encouraged to educate their clients about mammograms. In Nashville, HIV prevention is taught in some salons. All of this is possible because of the uniquely intimate nature of hairdressing. Stylists quickly learn that it is not uncommon for clients they have worked on only once or twice to start confessing very private information and expecting advice in return.

How do hairdressers feel about playing therapist, and how much should you tell them? Karen M. Shelton, a hair specialist for HairBoutique.com, queried a number of stylists and found that many are ambivalent. For one thing, they rarely feel comfortable enough to offer their honest opinion, as it may impact their tip or make a client angry. "While many stylists try to be sympathetic and helpful, just as many stylists don't want the added responsibility of offering advice," Shelton says. "When this is the case the stylist will try to change the topic, finish the styling session as fast as possible, or tell the client they are uncomfortable."

For some reason, a great many clients believe that tales told to a stylist are as classified as those told to a priest. While most hairdressers are discreet, Cindy Clark advises people to use common sense: "Don't tell me private things when you are sitting out in the open salon where thirty other people can hear you—not if you want them to stay private." And Karen Shelton observes, "Stylists can, and are, fair game to be used against you in a court of law"—a warning to all the husbands and wives who confess their affairs while relaxing in the chair. (According to Shelton, men bare their souls to hairdressers as often as women do.)

Umberto's Laurence Roberts concurs. "A lot of people look to you for advice, and sometimes that gets a little wearing. You almost know more about your clients then you do about your friends. Some will sit down and go on autodrive: 'This week I had a big fight with my husband—' and they're off. They get so into their personal lives that it becomes exhausting. I call them energy zappers." The relationship ought to be a two-way street, he says. "At least say hello. Acknowledge another person is standing there."

When hairdressers develop close friendships with their clients, the emotional toll can be high. According to Andrea Knight, "At the end of the day, the hardest thing is when you've had a client you've known and loved over the years, and bad, sad things happen—their husbands are ill, they're ill, or they've been diagnosed. It can really take it out of you." Knight takes her role as friend/therapist seriously and feels guilty if she can't meet her clients' needs. "A lot of people who are very lonely want to come in and spend time and talk, and that's OK if I've got the time. But if I don't, it upsets me because I feel like I'm pushing them away." The stress is balanced by the emotional advantages of the job, however. "I like people. That's a big part of it for me. I love my clients."

## When You Have to Say Good-Bye

There's a saying among hairdressers: "We'd be out of business if everybody loved their hair." The vast majority of folks will always be unsatisfied with their God-given locks, which means that sooner or later they will want to try a different stylist. Hairdressers take this in stride, but clients often feel so guilty about leaving that they vanish without saying good-bye. Stylists will rarely phone to find out why a client has left because they don't want to appear to be soliciting. Yet they do worry, says Laurence Roberts, especially about long-time clients: "Where'd she go? What did I say? What did I do? Is she healthy? Is she dying?"

There are civilized ways to depart. Hairdressers will be appreciative, not insulted, if you call and say, "I've really enjoyed the way you do my hair, and it's nothing personal, but I think I need a change. I may be back." That way, you're leaving the door open if you do want to return. When you disappear and then show up again two years later, it's a little more awkward. If you can't muster the nerve to have the farewell conversation with your hairdresser, tell the receptionist and ask her to pass it on.

"You get that message and feel good about it. You know where you stand; you're not wondering," says Roberts.

After all is said and done, hairdressers are a pretty understanding group. "No matter how my clients have left, I welcome them back with open arms. I'm real easygoing that way," says Roberts. "The key word is respect. If you show your clients respect, they will respect you. You get what you put out." The same thing goes for those of us on the receiving end of the scissors.

## WAITER
## PLAYING WITH YOUR FOOD

Waiters both love and hate their jobs. They love the flexibility and the money that can be made, but the grueling psychological demands of the work can leave them feeling downtrodden and short-fused. They succeed at their work only by acting graciously in the face of humiliation, yet they possess an awesome, unspoken power: they can mess with your food. Like anyone who spends a lot of time with the public, their view of humankind can be rather bleak. For that very reason, the patron who is kind and respectful to a waiter will usually receive stellar service, especially if he or she is also a good tipper (15 to 20 percent, never 10—not even at breakfast).

### Behind the Scenes:
### Be Nice, or Else You Don't Want to Know

If you haven't experienced the serving life firsthand, you can get a good taste of it by logging on to one of the Web sites that have been created solely for the purpose of letting waiters vent. The outrage, black humor, and revenge fantasies you'll find there are eye-openers. Yet Kim Stahler, the creator of the hilarious and enlightening stainedapron.com, says, "I dine out constantly, even knowing what I know. I am a nice patron, of course."

A major source of stress for waiters is the fact that while they are on the front lines with the customer, they have very little power. They don't control what goes on in the kitchen, how many chefs showed up for work that day, or how skillful the chefs happen to be. They don't control how many tables they are required to serve. It is helpful to keep this in mind so that when things go wrong (with the food, not the service), you will ask to speak to the manager instead of taking it out on the waiter.

Restaurants pay waiters between $2 and $3 an hour. This is legal because the government realizes that waiters make tips. In most restaurants, however, the waiters have to "tip out," or pay a portion of their take, to the bussers and bartenders. The tip-out is usually calculated as a percentage of the total checks paid that shift, not as a percentage of the tips the waiter actually collected.

How important is tipping? A particularly blunt waiter on stainedapron.com supplied the following advice: "If you are one of those despicable types who doesn't believe in tipping and who frequents the same restaurants repeatedly, I *guarantee* the servers are doctoring your food or throwing it on the floor and then back onto your plate or worse. . . . People can be really sick, especially after suffering repeated rudenesses without an option of talking back." But you wouldn't get the same waiter every time, right? "Servers pass the word around in the restaurant to other servers when you come in again," the same waiter confides. "Oh yes, they'll be ready for you. You'll just never know it." He may be exaggerating, but there's no way to tell for sure.

On the bright side, most waiters are touchingly grateful for pleasant patrons who tip well. So whether or not you think it's fair, tip that extra dollar or two and you will reap the benefits of both peace of mind and good service.

## The Secrets of Great Service

How do you prefer your service? Fast but not rushed, unless you're going to see a movie (in which case it should be ultrafast) or unless you're having dinner with an old friend (in which case the waiter should be attentive but not pushy)? "We're expected to be mind readers," one waiter complained. The best way to get satisfaction, whether it is regarding dietary preferences, special orders, or your schedule, is to tell the waiter what you want at the beginning of the meal.

To get the fastest service, tell the hostess that you're in a hurry and sit at the table she suggests. If you insist on sitting at a more desirable table that is in a busy section, the service might drag. Let her know your schedule as soon as possible, and don't ask for separate checks—it will slow her down at the cash register. If you must have separate checks, tell the waitress when you place your order.

People often arrive at a restaurant hungry and cranky. Several waitresses mentioned that their anxiety shot up every time an argument broke out between a couple or between parents and children. The uglier the atmosphere at your table, the less you're going to see of your waitress, and not just because she doesn't want to interrupt your squabble: "Every time a kid starts screaming or a couple gets in a fight, it seems the tip goes down." No tip, no incentive to serve you.

If you decide to show off for your date or friends by bossing or belittling the waitress, be aware that all the things that happen to bad tippers' food can just as easily happen to yours. So whatever your mood happens to be when you sit down, for your own well-being stay civil to the server.

One last service hint for bar patrons: give your cocktail waitress a big tip after the first round, not the last one. This will guarantee her benevolence for the rest of the evening.

## How Does It Taste?

Some waiters are quite willing to steer you away from dishes that aren't terrific if you ask for their advice. Kim Stahler says, "I had no problem saying that it was a small portion or that it wasn't the best cut in my experience or that the description was misleading." But coaxing accurate information out of a waiter can sometimes be a challenge, especially at a mediocre restaurant. Here is a sampling of dodges waiters use to get around admitting that a dish isn't very good:

> **YOU:** "How's the blackened salmon?"
> **WAITER:** "I don't know, I've never tried it."

If the dish is good, this comment will be followed by, "But everyone who orders it seems to like it." It is the waiter's job to know the taste and textures of the food whether or not he has personally sampled every item.

> **YOU:** "How's the filet mignon?"
> **WAITER:** "I don't know. I don't eat meat."

There aren't all that many vegetarians in the world, but there sure seem to be a lot of vegetarian waiters. At any rate, consider this: if the waiter really is a vegetarian but the filet is great, he will report that other customers think so.

> **YOU:** "How's the roast chicken?"
> **WAITER:** "It's rubbed with herbs and spices and then roasted in the brick oven. It's served with mini-garlic potatoes and fresh green beans."

Waiters who "misunderstand" your question are trying to get you to order the dish without actually having to endorse it. Their strategy: distract you with juicy descriptions of the meal, which they already know you want to order. You must follow up with a more pointed question, such as, "Yes, but does it taste good?" To which the waiter may respond, "It's a very popular dish." In many cases, this is as close to a thumbs-up as you're going to get.

Of course, there are waiters who insist that everything at the restaurant is delicious. Maybe you lucked out, or maybe you need to probe on. Take the word *fresh*, for example. In some restaurants, fresh fish is fish caught that day. In others, it is a day or two old. In still others, it's "fresh frozen." You have to ask, and that goes for pies, bread, pastries, and so forth. If the waiter doesn't know, he should ask the chef.

## Magic Words and Deeds

Waiters want you to go away happy so that you will leave a generous tip, but after having served so many offensive customers, they tend to make snap judgments about people. If they judge you to be a "good" patron, they will be good to you. Here are some of the words and behaviors that warm their hearts.

- Make eye contact and smile.
- Greet the waiter by saying "Hello," not by barking, "What's the special?" or "Two coffees, two waters."
- Say please and thank you.
- Answer the waiter's questions with words, not grunts or mumbles.
- If you are not ready to order when the waiter comes by, say so. Waiters have no desire to witness your decision-making process. Said one, "Customers will wave at you and then you get to the table and they're reading the menu while you stand there like a fool."

- Be patient: "If they see I'm busy and they're patient, I will go overboard for them. If I could ask just one thing of customers, it would be patience."
- If you have been especially pleased by the service, let the manager know.

## Absolute No-No's

The following behaviors grate on waiters like knives on a china plate. To stay on their good side:

**DON'T TALK WHILE THE SPECIALS ARE BEING DESCRIBED.** Or, as one waitress delicately put it, "When I walk to your table to greet you and tell you the features, *shut the hell up.*"

**DON'T LABOR OVER THE CORRECT PRONUNCIATION OF MENU ITEMS:** "What is up with these Socially-Conscious-Liberal-I'm-So-Educated types who insist on pronouncing everything on the menu with a foreign accent?" wondered a waiter on the stainedapron.com Web site. "I can't tell you how many times I have listened to people pronounce Tequila names with this ridiculous, affected Spanish accent or a fake Japanese accent if they happen to be ordering a dish containing sake. I have yet to hear a person of foreign origin use a fake 'American' accent."

**DON'T USE BRUTISH TECHNIQUES TO GET THE WAITRESS'S ATTENTION.** Snapping your fingers, tugging her apron, whistling, waving theatrically, or yelling, "Hey, waitress" will only annoy her. "I can do a great imitation of not noticing your rude display," said one waitress, thereby answering the timeless question, Do they *practice* ignoring customers?

**DON'T COUGH ON THE WAITER.**

**DON'T LET YOUR YOUNG CHILDREN RUN AROUND THE RESTAURANT, ORDER THEIR OWN FOOD, OR MAKE A BIG MESS AT THE TABLE.**

**DON'T TALK ON A CELL PHONE WHILE THE WAITRESS WAITS TO TAKE YOUR ORDER.**

**DON'T COMMANDEER EVERYONE'S ORDER.** A waitress at a deli reported, "There's one at every table who says, 'Oh, honey, why don't you get this instead.' It's usually the borscht they're suggesting. Or, 'Don't just have a water, try a milkshake.' They won't let their family or friends order for themselves and it messes up my check."

**DON'T LIE TO GET FASTER SERVICE.** "They'll come in and say, 'I'm in a big hurry, I've got to catch a plane.' Two hours later they're still sitting there," said one waitress.

**DON'T CALL YOUR WAITRESS HONEY OR SWEETHEART.** She may not mind, but the odds are against you.

Yes, that is a long list of don'ts. It is a good indication of just how underappreciated and powerless many servers feel. Fittingly, a common fantasy among waiters is one in which the roles are reversed and they get to be nasty, demanding patrons while all the rude customers they have served must wear aprons and serve *them*. So the next time you dine out, speak kindly and leave a big tip.

## RESERVATIONS AGENT AND FRONT DESK CLERK
# POWER TO THE LITTLE PEOPLE

Conventional wisdom holds that online discounters have radically changed the game of hotel reservations. It is true that these Web sites offer low rates for many hotels, but they are by no means the answer for every traveler. If you want a popular hotel, or a particular type of room, or if you are traveling during high season, you may strike out on the Web. For many people, reserving a hotel room still comes down to a phone call and a human being on the other end of the line. And making the reservation is only half of the process—the other half takes place when you arrive. Reservations agents and front desk clerks have the power to give you a glorious room at a great price or to stick you in a shoe box next to the elevator. It all depends on who you talk to, when you talk, and what you say.

## Behind the Scenes: Supply, Demand, and Attitude

To outsiders, hotels appear to be fairly anonymous places. Not true. How long would you guess it takes news of your behavior—good or bad—to reach every member of a hotel's staff? "Twenty minutes to two hours," says veteran hotelier Marion Kukurudz. "And that's true for a bed-and-breakfast with 20 rooms or a hotel with 500." Hotel employees, perhaps more than others, are watching you. To a large degree, your happiness depends on the impression you make.

"A front desk hotel clerk or switchboard person has a tremendous amount of power, but nobody outside realizes it," Kukurudz says. "You rub someone the wrong way and you're not going to get what you want." And these employees can be touchy. Let's say you're staying at a four-star hotel. "The front desk is full of people who don't make nearly as much money as you do and certainly can't afford to stay in the hotel where they're working," says Sean M., director of sales and marketing at an 800-room luxury resort in the South. "If you're nice to them they're going to be nicer to you and you might get a little further. Eye contact is a big factor."

If the biggest mistake travelers make is being rude to the front desk staff, the second biggest is being ignorant about the ebb and flow of room rates. It's common knowledge that hotels change their rates according to season, but few people realize that at many hotels the rates change *daily.* "It's almost like the stock market," says Sean M. "I'm setting rates every day with our director of reservations and once a week with the GM (general manager). It's all based on supply and demand."

The goal of every hotel is a "perfect sell"—100 percent occupancy. To reach this goal, management gives its reservations clerks a certain amount of leeway in negotiating room rates. On-line discounters usually have the best rates, but hotels only release rooms to these discounters if they are desperate to get rid of them. Desirable hotels in popular cities rarely need to use discounters except in the off-seasons, but the hotels are still aiming for a perfect sell, which means they will negotiate with guests rather than be left with too many vacancies. Hotel rooms are a perishable commodity. Once the night has passed, lost revenue for a room that went empty can never be recovered.

Major hotel chains prefer that you call their 800 number and book your room through their central reservations system. Seasoned travelers know better. They realize that a central reservations handler in Omaha, Nebraska, is probably not going to be very knowledgeable about a resort in Park City, Utah. However, dialing the hotel directly will not always solve the problem. "At a lot of hotels, you can dial them directly, ask for reservations, and automatically get popped back to the 800 number without ever knowing it," says Sean M. "You have to ask for *in-house* reservations, but most people aren't savvy enough to do that."

Why is it so important to talk to the in-house reservations agent? Because people working on the hotel premises have first-hand knowledge about the rooms, the occupancy rate, the best times to check in, and the special discounts the hotel is offering. They can also connect you to the director of reservations, who in some hotels has an access code that prevents anyone else from altering the reservations she has made. If you're seriously concerned about your room, ask to speak to the director of reservations and book your stay through her. *Hint:* Do not tell a lower-level person why you want to speak to the director. Just insist on doing so, and once you have her on the line, explain your concerns and make the reservations.

Many hotels now have their own Web sites with pictures of the rooms, floor plans, and so forth. These are useful to peruse before placing your call, but even if you have isolated the floor and room you think will be perfect, ask the reservations agent about it. You never know—it could be located next to a smoking room or facing a construction site.

## Timing Is Everything

There are two timing issues to consider: when to book the reservation and when to arrive at the hotel. Most people make reservations 30–60 days before they travel. That's a prudent move, especially for popular destinations. But no matter when you call, it's essential to ask the reservations agent, "What is your projected occupancy for the dates I'm planning to visit?" *Projected occupancy* means the number of people who will be staying in the hotel. If you're calling a month or two ahead of time, the agent may not have an exact body count. However, in-house reservations staff are often able to make an educated guess because they are aware of events that will be taking place in town that week—conventions, festivals, and so forth. If the agent tells you the hotel will probably be full, you should plan your arrival time accordingly.

Different rules for arrival times apply to business and leisure travelers. Business travelers, especially conventioneers, need to be acutely aware of occupancy levels. In aiming for a perfect sell, hotels frequently overbook. One agent admitted that "a hotel will usually run it down to the wire hoping that it's all going to work out because other people are departing and there might be a snowstorm on the East Coast." If the hotel will be full, arrive and check in as early as you can. Leave your luggage behind the front desk if the room isn't ready and roam the city for an hour or two; just secure that room. Otherwise, you may get "walked"— bumped to another hotel—*even if you have a reservation*. The later you arrive, the greater the likelihood is of this happening.

Leisure travelers rarely get walked because customer satisfaction and good word of mouth are the lifeblood of destination properties. The last thing a resort wants to do is lose your business forever by sending you to a rival. If you are traveling to a resort or other leisure destination, you want to arrive when the front desk is quiet and the employees are relaxed and bored. That way you'll have time to chat them up, forge a bond, and negotiate some perks for yourself (more on that later). If the front desk is busy with a crush of other guests, the staff won't have time to play Let's Make a Deal. The reservations agent can tell you what time the crowds arrive; it's usually the same every day—for instance, around 4:00 P.M. for most Hawaiian destinations. Even if you will be on the same flight as the other guests, you can do a little sightseeing after the plane lands and check in when the crowds have subsided. (If the resort happens to be full, you shouldn't do this. Instead, arrive as quickly as possible to secure a good room.)

## Magic Words: The Reservation

When you're booking a room, you are juggling three things: the price, the quality of the room, and the location. You want a good rate, but not if you're going to be awakened at 5:30 A.M. by the cleaning staff as they greet one another while wheeling their metal carts down the gravel path outside your bungalow. Likewise, if the cheapest rate means you're shoehorned into a former service closet, it's not worth it.

First let's consider quality. In most hotels, there are at least three tiers of rooms. Starwood Sheraton properties, for example, have the Executive Club level, the Sheraton Premiere room, and a regular room. The Executive Club level features large rooms or suites, complimentary hors d'oeuvres in the evening and breakfast the next day, and a separate check-in on an upper floor—no mingling with the masses at the front desk. The Premiere room is a standard-size room with a few special features, perhaps a good view, a coffeemaker, a nicer bath. The regular room is the basic, no-frills room.

Travelers who want no surprises should secure exactly the type of room they desire when they make their reservation.

Those who don't mind a little risk might want to negotiate a price for a basic room, then try to get an upgrade upon check-in. Always specify whether you want a smoking or nonsmoking room when you make your reservation.

What about location? It's a personal decision, but you should be clear about your priorities before you place your call. Some options include:

- upstairs or down
- near the elevator (but never right next to it)
- near the ice machine (but never right next to it)
- tenth floor or below (a fire truck's hook and ladder can reach it should disaster strike)
- near a fire exit
- away from service rooms
- quiet

If you want a quiet room, be adamant about it when you make your reservation. You can't second-guess which rooms are quiet by reading maps on the Web site. Tell the in-house agent to note your desire for quiet on your reservation, but realize that your best hope lies in arriving early so you have your pick of rooms.

Now for the price. The "rack rate" is the official price of a room on a particular day. It is the price you will be quoted when you first ask how much a room costs. *It is a jumping-off point.* From the rack rate you want to work your way down to the lowest available rate. To do this, you have to push every button and hope that one opens a door.

The best approach to take when calling in-house reservations is that of a polite, highly educated detective. Most reservations agents pay close attention to a potential guest's tone of voice and level of sophistication. At the Intercontinental Hotel in Paris, Marion Kukurudz trained new staffers with a course called Assessing Customer Cues. She says that callers who are well-spoken get the best rooms. Why? "The more articulate they are, the choosier they'll be about their accommodations." To avoid having to placate unhappy guests, she instructs her staff to book the people who *sound* picky into the nicest rooms.

Being articulate doesn't mean being snooty. Take a few seconds to greet the reservations agent before beginning your interrogation. Once you've said "Hello, how are you today?" and waited for a reply, you can start the interview. Ask any of the following that apply to your situation:

**WHAT WILL YOUR OCCUPANCY BE DURING THE PERIOD I'M PLANNING TO VISIT?** Mentally file this information and time your arrival accordingly.

**WHAT'S YOUR NATIONAL CORPORATE RATE?** The national corporate rate is set up by hotels to accommodate business travelers. It'll be less than the rack rate. If you work for a large corporation, your company might have negotiated a *volume corporate rate* with certain chain hotels. This is even cheaper than the national corporate rate. Volume and national corporate rates are ostensibly designed for people traveling on business, but the reservations staff is not likely to grill you about it.

**DO YOU HAVE ANY AIRLINE PROMOTIONS?** Airlines sometimes run promotions in tandem with certain hotels. It pays to make the hotel reservations prior to the plane reservations for this reason. You can always cancel the hotel reservations if you can't get a flight on the participating airline.

**WHAT OTHER PROMOTIONS OR DISCOUNTS ARE YOU OFFERING?** Credit card companies often run promotions with hotels, especially destination properties. Some venues offer discounts you would never think to ask for. Hotels near universities, for example, may give special rates to visiting faculty members or performing artists.

**DO YOU GIVE AN AAA (AMERICAN AUTOMOBILE ASSOCIATION) DISCOUNT?** Many hotels do. It's usually 10 percent off the rack rate.

**DO YOU HAVE A BED-AND-BREAKFAST PACKAGE?** Bed-and-breakfast deals are not just for country inns. Most large hotels offer them too. If you know you'll be eating at the hotel, these specials may save you some money.

**DO YOU HAVE ANY OTHER PACKAGES?** Many leisure destinations offer packages to their guests. These typically include a tourist attraction and added benefits such as breakfast and features for children.

**WHAT'S YOUR CANCELLATION POLICY?** These vary widely across the industry, with some hotels insisting on 72-hour notice, others requiring only 24. Some charge one night's stay plus tax for no-shows; others charge first and last night's deposit so that you won't leave early. Small hotels and inns tend to want the whole stay prepaid.

**CAN I HAVE A CONFIRMATION NUMBER AND YOUR NAME, PLEASE?** This is crucial! It's also a good idea to ask the agent to mail or fax you a copy of the confirmation. Hotels used to do this automatically, but they don't anymore.

## Magic Words and Deeds: The Front Desk

If you have timed your arrival well and the hotel isn't too busy, the front desk offers a great opportunity to garnish perks and room upgrades. The emptier the hotel, the better the deal you can make. Don't feel shy about making these requests. Not only are the front desk personnel accustomed to it, they are sometimes told to initiate the bargaining themselves. Management will instruct them to "upsell" customers upon check-in, meaning try to sell you a more expensive room. Don't accept their first offer. They'll probably be flexible if they are initiating the deal.

If they don't make you an offer, simply say, "What would it cost for an upgrade?" They'll come back with a price—for instance, "Forty dollars for a Premiere room." Before you respond, have them list the differences between that room and the one you already have. Unscrupulous hotels have been known to "upgrade" people into the very rooms they were going to get anyway.

When you know what you are bargaining for, make your offer—for example, "How about $10 for the Premiere room?" Back and forth you can go until you hit a price you're comfortable with. While you are bargaining, ask for anything else that might sweeten the deal: vouchers for drinks in the bar, dinner, breakfast, videos, or spa privileges. In the hotel business everything is negotiable. If you don't reach an agreement, you still have your original room.

If you will be staying at the hotel for more than a few days, consider tipping the appropriate staffers when you first check in. Will you be expecting a lot of phone calls or faxes? Will you frequently require the services of the concierge? "Guests will tip the man who brings extra towels to their rooms, but no one thinks to tip the front desk staff or the switchboard operator who's been helping them all week," grumbled one clerk. It may feel odd to offer $10 or $20 at the beginning of your stay, but give it a try. For the price of a few lattes, you'll be treated like a prince.

## Absolute No-No's

Hotels seem to bring out the con artist in people. To get a free upgrade or cheap rate, otherwise honest citizens will tell blatant and foolish lies. Reservations agents and front desk clerks have heard every version of every fib, and they are weary of them.

"Guests will insist that so-and-so promised them a room upgrade," reports a staffer at the Fairmont Hotel in New Orleans, "but they don't have a piece of paper to prove it. Usually you find out that their contact hasn't worked here for three years or you've never heard of the person. Last week a businesswoman faxed us this badly faked 'upgrade voucher'—she had typed a few lines on a piece of hotel stationery and scribbled an unreadable signature. When my boss refused to honor it, she cussed him out and hung up on him." When it comes to free upgrades, tempers can flare no matter how wealthy the guest. One petite desk clerk recalled what happened when a portly, well-known actor didn't get the upgrade he thought he deserved: "He threw his cane at my head."

Here are some lines hotel staffers have heard too often.

**GUEST:** "I'm a travel agent, so I'd like a travel agency discount."
**RESERVATIONS AGENT:** "May I have your IOTA number?"
**GUEST:** "What's an IOTA number?"

All legitimate travel agents have an IOTA (International Organization of Travel Agents) number. To get a travel agency discount, you have to supply the number.

**GUEST:** "How much does your best room cost?"
**AGENT:** "$225."
**GUEST:** "What's the cheapest room?"
**AGENT:** "$100."
**GUEST:** "I'll take the best room for $100!"

"They think they're being terribly funny," says Marion Kukurudz with a sigh.

**GUEST:** "There are 850 rooms at this hotel! I don't believe you don't have any left."

While some hotels always hold a few rooms back for emergencies, many really do sell out every single room. "Just the other week we had to walk someone at 2 A.M. And he had a reservation," confessed one front desk clerk. "I felt really terrible, but it happens." If a few heartfelt pleas don't get you a room, switch tactics and ask for the clerk's assistance in finding you other accommodations. Hotels typically cover one another since they all overbook, and a few kind words from your clerk could get you a good room at the next hotel.

**GUEST:** "I made a reservation but you lost it."

Reservations agents can and do make mistakes, but if you don't remember the gender of the person you talked to, or when you made the reservation, or what credit card you used to hold it, or what the confirmation number was, they'll think you're bluffing.

## See You Next Time

It should go without saying: don't steal. They have your credit card number and will charge you for the towels and robes anyway. You can buy these items in the lobby store if you find them so irresistible. (It's okay to take sample soaps, pens, and stationery.) Remember to tip the maids a dollar or two a night. If you plan to come back, consider telling the manager how much you enjoyed your stay and ask which rooms he thinks are the best. Compliment him on the staff or anything else that impressed you. Although hotel employees are a fairly transient group, managers at the nicer establishments tend to stay put. Leave the manager feeling good, and chances are he will want to return the favor on your next visit.

# LANDLORD
## THE ACCIDENTAL INQUISITOR

No special training is necessary to become a landlord. All it takes is some cash for a down payment and the willingness to work hard. There are a few glitches, however. Housing markets fluctuate, as does the economy, both of which affect the landlord's cash flow. And then there are the tenants. When landlords first begin to buy and manage properties, they are often appalled to discover how many tenants are no-goodniks. The typical landlord has had to endure people who trash the apartment, refuse to pay the rent, call at all hours demanding minor repairs, or let their cats use the bedroom as a litter box. Long-term tenants are becoming rare, which means landlords must screen more people to keep their properties filled and the money flowing in.

As a result of all this, landlords have become near-obsessive about interviewing prospective tenants and checking their backgrounds. The tighter the housing market is, the pickier they can be. If you are married and have a good job, perfect credit, no pets, and several glowing letters from former landlords, you probably don't have to worry. Everyone else may need to be a little creative to win a landlord's heart.

## Behind the Scenes: Once Bitten, Forever Shy

"It's our property and we should be allowed to rent to who we want," declared a landlord on the message board of Mrlandlord. com. A quick perusal of the site offers a stark outline of land-lords' prejudices, and generally speaking they're not about race or culture. They're about pets, kids, and single moms, and it's a toss-up which are less popular. Listen to these comments culled from the site's chat rooms:

> "I had a tenant with a cockatiel and I thought, How bad can it be? Well, the noise [was awful], and they poop out through the cage and knock grain in the carpet. When they left I pulled up the carpet and found grain maggots living on the seed. Oh, and some people get a lung disease from parrot dandruff."

> "I discovered massive holes in the walls made by a dog [the tenants] kept inside. There were also massive holes in the carpet from where it appeared the dog was trying to dig."

> "I'd rather have a dog in one of my houses than kids any day. When I pick up the phone and hear kids screaming in the background before I even say hello, I know I don't want to rent to whoever is on the other end."

> "We just had a single mom move out . . . the place is a disaster and she expects her deposit back."

> "I think all us landlords feel the same way about kids. However, we can't advertise that way. Keep it to yourself, and as you get applicants, choose accordingly. You can always make up excuses when the single female with

four kids calls about her application: (1) I'm still screening, (2) Someone else put up a deposit, etc."

Isn't that illegal? Yes, but try enforcing it. Although federal and
state fair housing laws prohibit discrimination based on race,
color, religion, national origin, gender, disability, and family status (the presence of children), these laws can't force a landlord to
rent to someone he believes will be a poor tenant. Landlords have
the legal right to expect a tenant to pay the rent on time, not disturb other tenants, and keep the unit in reasonable condition. If a
tenant can't meet these standards, the landlord is allowed to reject
him. If a potential tenant can prove he has a history of meeting
the standards, the landlord is still allowed to choose between him
and everyone else who can prove the same thing. That is where
biases come into play. If the single mom with four kids is pitted
against a working couple with one child, and both would be good
tenants, it is purely the landlord's call.

"The government used to, and probably still does, troll for
violations of the discrimination laws by sending overqualified
applicants who happened to have children or happened to be a
minority," one landlord warned his online comrades. "If the
landlord refused to rent to them, or said or did anything that
was against the law, the landlord was brought up on criminal
charges. From the private sector, a qualified tenant who was
turned down for reasons of discrimination can sue you." Perhaps
to avoid such lawsuits, landlords require ever more stringent
background checks. As long as they apply the same criteria
equally to everyone, it's legal. They can even demand that all
their tenants earn a specific minimum yearly income, as long as it
is reasonably related to the rent.

In fairness, landlords have good reason to be careful. Most of
them are small-business people, not real estate barons, and when

a tenant misses the rent, they feel it directly in their pocketbook. Sixty percent of U.S. rental housing is owned by individual mom-and-pop landlords, and that jumps to 86 percent in the central cities. More than half of one- to four-unit properties had negative cash flows in 2000, which means that quite a few mom-and-pops are struggling to make the dream work.

When landlords interview prospective tenants, then, they are on high alert for people who will cause them trouble and cost them money. The thing they fear most is an income gap, that is, a period of time when an apartment is empty and generating no rent. For that reason, landlords are very interested in how long a tenant plans to stay in the apartment—the longer, the better. Landlords are also leery of people who seem as if they will demand a lot of repairs. They want to weed out people and pets who might damage the property or disturb the other tenants. Finally, landlords look for clues that a tenant might be prone to filing lawsuits.

All this is fair and reasonable. The problem for landlords is that they must decide whether or not you meet their criteria based on relatively little information. They can run credit checks and call your employer and former landlord, but, as a 20-year veteran mortgage underwriter observes, "The fact of the matter is, 's——t happens,' folks. And it happens to the 'good' ones nearly as often as the 'bad' ones. . . . For all of the criminal checks, credit reports, criss-cross checking, courthouse checking, reverse number checking, etc., that I see here, much of it means nothing. . . . There's something to be said for 'gut' feeling."

In the end, many landlords (especially those in charge of smaller properties) base their decisions on the gut feeling that someone will be a good tenant. You can inspire a warm and fuzzy feeling by calming the landlord's fears before he ever voices them, and you can do this even if you are not a stellar candidate on paper.

## Magic Words: The Telephone Interview

The process of renting an apartment usually begins when you phone the landlord. Do this from a quiet location, and if you get an answering machine, be careful about the message you leave. Try to arrange the callback for a time when your household will be peaceful. Noisy children, TVs, barking dogs, loud music, or roommates shouting in the background are instant turn-offs to landlords. If you can't be sure what will be going on when the landlord calls your home, have him phone you at work instead.

Some landlords make a practice of letting the answering machine pick up the call because they want to know where you're calling from. Reports one landlord: "If I get [the number of] a really nice hotel, they are moving into the area. If I get a cheap motel or welfare motel, I simply don't return their phone call. I have had people give a neighbor's phone number and the neighbor has to go over and get them (very bad red flag). I have discovered the caller is living with friends (not a good sign). I have found people in a house with many roommates. I have had the person answering the phone sound stoned."

When you finally connect with the landlord, he may try to keep you talking for a while. Maybe he's just being friendly, but more likely he is practicing his detective skills. He might ask you the same question several times, listening for discrepancies in your answers. Another technique is the salesman's strategy of saying nothing so the other person will fill in the silence with nervous and revealing chitchat. "Conveniently, a lot of people flub-up info the first conversation because they are anxious," notes one landlady. Boasts another, "By simply listening, I can extract an awful lot of information and they don't even realize that they have been interviewed." Along the same lines, landlords like to ask open-ended questions that cannot be answered with a simple yes or no. As you're chatting, be prepared for such queries followed by the vacuum of silence. For instance:

> **LANDLORD:** Why are you moving?
>
> **TENANT:** I want a change from my current neighborhood.
>
> **LANDLORD:** Why is that?
>
> **TENANT:** The neighbors are too loud.
>
> **LANDLORD:** (*Silence*).
>
> **TENANT:** They have a lot of company over late at night.
>
> **LANDLORD:** (*Silence*).
>
> **TENANT:** I tried to talk to them about it, but they didn't care. I went to the landlord, and he said they're allowed to do whatever they want until 10 P.M.
>
> **LANDLORD:** What did you do then?
>
> **TENANT:** I called the police a few times, but they couldn't tell them to be quiet until after 10, either.

While this tenant's complaint may be valid, the landlord might also take it to be the griping of a troublemaker who will irritate the other tenants and call the cops at the least provocation. Lesson: Do not offer extra information, and do not fall into the trap of talking just to fill the silence.

The landlord is likely to ask you the following questions, if not during the phone call, then when you meet in person.

- Why are you moving?
- When are you moving?
- Do you have any children?
- What kind of pet(s) do you have? (A trick question designed to catch people who were planning to lie about owning a pet.)
- How many people will be living in the unit?
- Have you had any problems with former landlords?
- Have you ever been evicted?

- Do you have letters from your former landlords, or can I call them?
- How is your credit?
- Where do you work?
- How long have you worked there?
- May I call your employer?

If you must give less-than-ideal answers to some of the landlord's questions, follow them with a brief comment that will allay his fears. For example, if you're self-employed, assure the landlord that your business is doing well and you would be happy to provide him with tax returns, bank statements, and/or recommendations from former landlords. If you're a single parent, you might volunteer information about how you handle your children—where they go during the daytime, who helps care for them, and so forth. The point is to assure the landlord that you run a tight ship and the kids won't be tearing around unsupervised. If you share custody and the children are gone for specific periods each week or month, let the landlord know that as well. Nothing will help your cause as much as a letter or phone call from a former landlord who liked you and your family.

Keep in mind that the landlord *needs* to rent the property. He wants to get the screening process over with and start collecting money again. His ideal tenant may never show up, so as long as you ease his concerns, your chances are as good as the next person's.

As you speak with the landlord over the phone, your tone should be calm, your answers consistent. Don't feel compelled to charm his socks off at this point. It's better to have the long discussion in person, when you can gauge his reactions and get a feel for what is important to him. During the phone call you have two main goals: establishing a level of comfort and trust with the landlord and discovering information about the apartment that might rule it out for you, thus saving you a trip to see it in person. Among the questions you might ask are:

- What floor is the apartment on?
- How many bedrooms and bathrooms does it have?
- How do you access the apartment? (From an interior hallway? An exterior hallway? Directly from the street?)
- What is the parking situation? What about guest parking?
- Is the apartment near public transportation?
- What are the other tenants like? Are they singles, families, young couples, older people?
- Does the unit have many windows?
- Are the building and grounds well-lit?
- Is the neighborhood safe?
- What is your name and phone number (or the name and phone number of the person I will be meeting with to look at the apartment)?

## Magic Words and Deeds: Meeting the Landlord

Just as you would for a job interview, you should dress neatly and conservatively for your meeting with the landlord. The better organized and prepared you are, the better an impression you will make. Most landlords will want to see the following, so have them ready:

- Driver's license
- Social security number
- Letter from or phone number of current employer
- Letters from or phone numbers of current and/or previous landlords
- Copy of a current credit report
- Contact information for your bank

- If you are self-employed, proof that you can pay the rent. A letter from your current landlord may be enough, but some landlords may ask for bank statements or tax returns.
- A photo of your children. Landlords won't demand to see these, of course, but a winning photo may help your cause. *Winning* means the child looks clean, calm, and happy.

Don't be surprised if the landlord asks for an application fee. They do this to weed out tenants who are not serious. One landlord testified, "I have literally had over 100 phone calls and no more than 6 people show up to look." Fill out the application legibly and complete all the questions, even if some of the information is already in your other documents. The landlord could be sloppy and misplace those papers.

During your visit, ask the following questions. They will give you the basic information you need to evaluate the apartment.

- What is the rent?
- How much is the security deposit?
- When can I move in?
- Is the unit rent-controlled or stabilized? If not, how often will the rent be raised, and by what percentage?
- How many people live in this building or complex?
- Where are the laundry facilities? How many washers and dryers are there?
- Are there any other facilities attached to these apartments (community room, workout room, pool, playground, etc.)?
- Is there a security guard on duty? What are his hours?
- Am I allowed to paint the apartment? What other modifications can I make?
- How long have the tenants in the other apartments been here?
- What types of tenants live in the adjoining apartments?
- Would you mind if I speak with some of the tenants?

There are other questions landlords listen for, questions that mark you as a grade-A candidate. Says one landlord, "'What are the heating bills?' means they are actually serious lookers and are really going to rent a house." The following questions will send the right signals. You can learn the answers to some of them by reading the rental agreement, but asking the landlord directly will work in your favor.

- What are the terms for renewing the lease?
- Which utilities will I be responsible for? How much are they, on average?
- What maintenance will I be responsible for?
- Is there a public library nearby?
- Is it all right if I do some gardening out front?

For extra credit, you can make a few comments that indicate you understand the landlord's challenges and are going to be a model tenant. Maybe you've known someone who was a landlord and have listened to her litany of troubles. If so, a brief recollection might be in order, along the lines of, "My cousin managed some apartments, and I'll never forget how she'd have to get up at all hours to go deal with leaky toilets or a blown fuse. I just want you to know that I'll try to be reasonable about calling you for repairs."

Anything you can say that will indicate your desire to stay in the unit a long time will warm the landlord's heart. Maybe you've always wanted to live in that particular neighborhood, or in a high-rise building, or near a certain park that's within walking distance of the apartment. Go ahead and tell the landlord about it. Give him every reason to believe this is your dream home and you will never want to move.

## Absolute No-No's

Landlords expect you to ask questions, and you have a right to know the details about the place where you intend to live. However, certain questions will set off alarms. In some cases, it's a matter of timing. Said one landlord, "When a mom asked me if the house had lead paint, I got nervous. Not because of my lead paint, but because she asked that before she asked about bedrooms or parking."

Many of your questions will be answered on the lease or rental agreement, which you can read after you meet with the landlord. If the agreement does not tell you what you need to know, you can always ask about it later, after you have established a bond with the landlord (but before you sign anything). In the meantime, your mission during the interview is to earn the landlord's trust and make him think you plan to stay in the apartment forever. To that end:

**DON'T BRING OTHER PEOPLE WITH YOU TO THE FIRST MEETING.** Since there is no way of telling what the landlord's biases are, it is best to arrive alone unless you are going to rent with roommates or a spouse.

**DON'T BRING YOUR CHILDREN OR PET IF YOU CAN AVOID IT.** A cute picture is safer; it can't start whining halfway through the interview.

**DON'T ASK QUESTIONS THAT HINT YOU COULD HAVE CASH FLOW PROBLEMS.** For example, "What happens if I'm a little late with the rent? Is there a grace period?"

**DON'T ASK QUESTIONS RELATING TO LEAVING THE APARTMENT.** No point in arousing suspicion with queries such as, "What are the rules about subletting? What are the penalties for breaking the lease? How soon do I get my deposit back when I move out?"

**DON'T BEGIN THE INTERVIEW WITH NEGATIVE QUESTIONS.** Save those until the end. Included would be questions about the safety of the apartments, lead paint, loud neighbors, and so forth. At some point before you sign the lease, check with the local police department to verify what the landlord tells you about crime in the area. Landlords who are desperate to rent are not above lying.

**DON'T OFFER TOO MUCH INFORMATION.** It's a fine line to walk, because you want to establish a rapport with the landlord. However, be aware that he will still be playing detective as he escorts you through the unit: "They will spill everything if I just keep nodding and looking pleasant. I tell them a few nice features about the house and then give them time to react," reported one landlord.

## Make Him an Offer He Can't Refuse

Perhaps you don't have a perfect credit record, don't earn a lot of money, or can't get a good reference from your current landlord. How do you prove you're not a risk? Or maybe you're an A+ candidate, but so are three other people and the competition for housing is fierce. How do you pull ahead of the pack? The following strategies are based on giving the landlord more of what he wants: an unbroken income stream, a well-maintained property, and a reasonable tenant.

- Most landlords ask for first and last month's rent plus a security deposit. Offer more—for example, three months' rent—to convince the landlord of your passion for the place. If he is worried about your income, offering an extra month will give him peace of mind and a longer period of time in which to get a new tenant should you be unable to pay the rent.
- In a tight housing market, you might offer to lease the unit for two years instead of one. This way the landlord is guaranteed at least two years of unbroken income and two years without having to screen more tenants.
- If the lease is for one year and the landlord seems worried

about your income, offer to rent on a month-to-month basis. That way he'll know he can boot you out quickly if you can't come up with the rent.

- Offer to do chores or gardening, either in lieu of a portion of the rent or in addition to it. If you are an avid gardener, you will probably end up beautifying the outdoor space anyway, so you might as well use it to your advantage.

- Promise the landlord that if you should ever have to leave, you will give him extra advance notice—for example, three months instead of two. Offer to write this into the lease.

- If you are handy around the house, tell the landlord. One of the biggest complaints landlords have is that tenants call them about petty problems such as replacing light bulbs or squirting graphite into a sticky lock.

## The Truth about Pets

If you own a pet, you are already familiar with the challenges of finding pet-friendly rental housing. According to the Humane Society of the United States, nearly 50 percent of U.S. renters have pets, yet only 5 percent of rental housing anywhere allows them. Obviously, many people are lying to their landlords about owning pets. This is not a wise move. The Humane Society also reports that about 25 percent of the pets in animal shelters around the world are put there because their owners were forced by a landlord to either get rid of the pet or move out.

The biggest objection landlords have to pets is that they destroy floors and carpets. Replacing the ruined flooring is expensive, and any odor is hard to remove. Pets that are kept indoors all day tend to do the most damage, sometimes chewing on molding and walls in addition to soiling the floors. Then there's the issue of barking, howling, or squawking, which bothers the other tenants. Unfriendly animals that bark at neighbors and scare the mailman are another problem. Finally, there are liability issues should your pet bite somebody.

It's usually futile to try to talk a no-pets landlord into making an exception for you. And the larger the apartment complex, the less likely he is to bend the rules, because he is legally required to treat all tenants equally. If he allows your pet to move in, everyone else must be allowed to have pets as well. People who manage properties of fewer than five units are easier to sway. If you can offer a big deposit and lots of evidence that your animal is friendly and well-behaved, you might get lucky.

Landlords who are willing to take a chance on pets will usually require you to sign a special lease agreement, pay an extra security deposit, and perhaps pay a higher monthly rent. Regarding the deposit, "Most of my tenants have pets, and I charge $150 for one and $200 for up to two pets," writes one landlord. "Half a month's rent per pet," writes another. A third charges "$35–$50 per month per pet, plus an $800 deposit." Nationwide, most landlords charge about $15 a month for pets with a $100 security deposit (the rates are generally higher for large dogs). That amount doesn't come close to covering the damage a pet may inflict: "It cost me $3,000 to have carpet and padding removed, subfloor cleaned and sealed and carpet replaced," reported one landlord.

In addition to money, landlords may want additional information and personal guarantees about your pet. Their rental agreement may include statements such as "My pet has/has not injured any person/property." To put the landlord at ease, come to the interview equipped with:

- A copy of your pet's health and immunization records from your veterinarian.
- A letter from your current landlord stating that the pet has been well-behaved and has not caused any damage or problems with the neighbors.

- A copy of your pet insurance policy, if you have one.
- Information about the breed, if it will help your cause.
- Flattering photos of your clean, calm, friendly pet.

A landlord can set any standard he wants regarding pets, as long as he applies it to everyone equally. Thus, one landlord decided there would be "no puppies, no dogs over 25 pounds, usually. They have to be neutered, friendly and trained. Especially friendly. I don't want them taking the handyman's leg off—a good handyman is even harder to find than a good tenant."

## Your Current and Future Landlords

The landlord you have right now is probably your best guarantee of future success in the rental arena. All else being equal, landlords rely on the recommendations of other landlords. So pay the rent on time, stay civil with your neighbors, and don't hassle your landlord about minor repairs, especially in the middle of the night. When you are ready to move, give him as much notice as possible so he can rent the unit to someone else and avoid an income gap. Keep the place clean when you know he's going to show it to prospective tenants and your accommodating nature will be fresh in his mind when your new landlord calls to check on you.

There is one other step you can take to foster goodwill between you and the landlord: read the rental agreement carefully before you sign it. Most landlord-tenant disputes involve timely payment of rent, privacy rights, and security deposit refunds, so make sure the specifics of these are clear. Work out any compromises before you sign the agreement, and don't assume you can trick or cajole the landlord later on. Do not try to sneak kittens into your no-pets apartment. And around Christmastime, it couldn't hurt to bake him a batch of brownies.

## 5

## DOCTOR
# SEE ME, HEAR ME, TAKE ME SERIOUSLY

No matter what your age, gender, or position, you are the weaker sex in the doctor's office. The whole operation reeks of inequity. You're naked under a paper sheet, he's dressed. You call him "doctor," he calls you by your first name. You speak English, he wields a technical vocabulary that's impenetrable to all but those of his own tribe. You have the power to take your business elsewhere, he has power over sickness and health.

We want to trust our doctors and believe they are superb at what they do. The alternative is too unnerving to consider. Yet the thriving medical malpractice industry proves that our doctors don't always deserve our devotion. Sometimes they disappoint us, endanger us, treat us like children, and ignore our input. Or do they? Maybe the problem is with us. Maybe we just don't know how to talk to them. Whoever is to blame for the miscommunication, both sides pay dearly in health and money: 70 percent of all medical malpractice suits are filed not because of technical negligence but because the patient misunderstood the doctor.

Medical schools have been paying more attention to this problem lately, and the new generation of doctors is supposedly trained to listen, be empathetic, and look beyond the most obvious diagnosis to see if a patient's problems might be more complex. But while doctors are trying improve their bedside manner, reality is undermining them. Doctors today have far less time to spend with patients than they did twenty years ago, mostly because of the paperwork demanded by HMOs and insurance companies and the patient load required to make ends meet. In the typical practice, a visit with the doctor lasts 7 to 15 minutes—and is interrupted within the first 27 seconds by a nurse or a telephone call.

Meanwhile, doctors who think they are improving their communication skills are often mistaken. One study asked physicians how much time they spent educating their patients. "Nine to ten minutes" was the most likely response. In reality, it was about one minute. And patients clearly need the education. Another study highlighted the sorry state of patients' "medical literacy": more than 40 percent couldn't understand instructions that indicated they should take a certain medication on an empty stomach.

Even the most well-meaning doctors regularly fail their patients by overestimating their knowledge of medical terminology and rushing through the exam. Patients complain that doctors don't ask their opinion, don't explain the side effects of drugs, don't take an adequate medical history, don't warn them properly about the difficulty of recovery, don't take their pain seriously, and discourage questions—and that's just a short list of grievances.

Complaining is useless. Waiting for your doctor to change is futile. Your only choice when it comes to dealing with doctors is to change your own behavior in order to influence theirs.

## Behind the Scenes:
## We're Not Gods, We're Overworked Humans with Godlike Powers

As a group, doctors don't inspire much sympathy, yet in order to get the best treatment you must be able to see things from their point of view. Like all of us, doctors have feelings and fears that influence their work.

First, consider your doctor's mission: to heal you. If he can do it, he is a success. If he cannot, he thinks he is a failure—and doctors hate to fail. You may feel powerless in his presence, but in fact his self-esteem depends on you. Will you heed his advice or ignore it? Will you refuse his treatment? Lie to him about your symptoms? Snub him for another doctor? Occasionally, even if you follow the doctor's instructions, you won't get well. His skills will fail you. This is a doctor's greatest fear and a source of constant anxiety.

Next, contemplate the typical doctor's training. Doctors are schooled to diagnose illnesses and prescribe treatments as quickly as possible. With most internists logging about 150,000 office visits in their careers, speed and accuracy are highly valued. Being right is important, but being right *fast* is the mark of a real pro. In surveys, medical literature, and interviews, doctors repeatedly admit to diagnosing the typical patient within just 30 seconds of walking in the examining room. "It is subsequently quite easy to go on autopilot," writes Victoria Maizes, M.D., in *American Family Physician*. Instant diagnoses, followed by formulaic, half-interested questions, thus become their normal mode of operation. Maybe it's not the way Marcus Welby would have done it, but it effectively propels them through their overpacked days.

Another more troubling aspect of doctors' training is the well-known desensitization that takes place in medical school and during a physician's internship. It is a grueling trial by fire as the student is thrust into a world of pain, suffering, and death with very little emotional support. Barbara M. Korsch, M.D., who has devoted much of her career to studying doctor-patient communication, wrote a book on the topic: *The Intelligent Patient's Guide to the Doctor-Patient Relationship* (Oxford University Press,

1997). In it she explains that in medical school the emphasis is on anatomy, chemistry, and other hard sciences, with little or no attention paid to the human aspect of attending to the ill. "When third-year students have their first intense encounter with real patients, they are faced with sickness and death in very large doses." As the years of training continue, "students' inner conflicts with facing illness and death become more and more acute. Their role models, the attending physicians, often behave toward them (and their patients!) in ways that are not very human. . . . One of the goals in the education of physicians is to 'professionalize' them, to toughen them up."

When the training is finally over, relatively few doctors emerge with their empathetic equipment intact. Korsch says that doctors "turn away from emotion. They are not trained to deal with feelings." This detachment is very hard to unlearn. It doesn't have anything to do with a doctor's talent, but it does affect the way he treats his patients and the success of his practice. On the one hand, doctors with lousy people skills have trouble keeping clients and attract more lawsuits; on the other, doctors who aren't emotionally tough are likely to burn out and become unable to function.

Today's physicians, then, are constantly grappling with opposing forces. They want to solve your problem but must do it quickly, which automatically increases the likelihood that they will make a mistake. They depend on your compliance but you can defy them at will, which undermines their chances of success. Theirs is a people-oriented profession, yet they learn few social skills and have much of their natural empathy squeezed out during medical school. They must operate within ever-shrinking time and money constraints, even as patients are becoming more proactive and demanding more attention. They are expected to take control but are constantly being second-guessed by insurance companies, HMOs, and the patients themselves.

The result is that doctors are under a lot of stress. The power, respect, and money that once compensated for the tensions of the job are eroding. They spend more on insurance and keep less for themselves than they once did. Some doctors are even forced to change specialties because they can't afford the malpractice insurance. These healers, who at one time held themselves above the fray of commerce, are now neck-deep in it— resentful, frustrated, and concerned about the level of care they are able to provide their patients. So when the doctor walks into the examining room and you're laid out on the table like a piece of pastry, remember: underneath the trappings of power, he too may feel anxious and vulnerable.

## Good Patient, Bad Patient

Most doctors genuinely want to help you. "There's a difference between treating people and caring for people. I'd like to think I do both, and that I do the latter well," says Los Angeles oncologist Barry Rosenbloom. Many doctors do empathize with their patients, and there is no question that the issue of bedside manner is getting more attention these days. Hospitals sponsor seminars on the topic and medical journals publish papers on how to master, as Sir William Osler put it, "the kindly word, the cheerful greeting, the sympathetic look." Still, according to Rosenbloom, "Some patients' expectations are way beyond anything the doctor can deliver." In truth, both doctors and patients bring plenty of unspoken (sometimes unconscious) expectations into the examining room.

The first time you meet a doctor, it is fair to assume that he is hoping you will turn out to be a "good" patient, one who listens to him, follows his orders, and promptly gets well. Put another way, doctors have a hard time dealing with patients who don't improve. Patients return the favor—they like doctors who can heal them and dislike those who cannot. Naturally, doctors are aware of this.

In 1995, *Consumer Reports* published a survey of 70,000 readers who were asked about their experience with medical care. Patients with chronic headaches or back pain reported the greatest amount of dissatisfaction with their doctors. Not surprisingly, the doctors who treat these conditions "may not even want to see these patients come in the door," according to psychologist Judith Hall. The patients who were *most* satisfied with their medical care were those who had glaucoma, cataracts, or were pregnant—conditions that require a single or easily understood course of treatment that is usually successful. Patients were also generally satisfied with their oncologists (cancer doctors) because, although the outlook may be grim, the illness is always taken seriously. Additionally, cancer patients understand that their condition might be impossible for any doctor to cure.

Patients who get better quickly affirm the doctor's skill, whereas "chronic, insoluble problems are very, very frustrating to doctors," says Barbara Korsch. "Doctors are success-oriented; they can't see a failure. They dislike anything they can't diagnose and cure; they hate fibromyalgia, chronic fatigue syndrome. Those poor patients really suffer because doctors tend to think that if they can't find any objective signs it's probably all in the head, and if it's all in the head, instead of feeling sympathetic they become contemptuous and say, 'That's not my problem.'"

This doesn't mean you must give up hope of finding a caring doctor if you have a chronic condition. It means that, by being aware of the doctor's bias, you can take steps to overcome it. You can begin by voicing what the doctor is probably thinking, advises Korsch: "You can say, 'I realize nobody knows what fibromyalgia is and there is no cure, but I'm hoping you'll find something that will help me.' Build up the good side, the Dr. Jekyll side of the doctor. You might also say, 'I don't expect any magic. I know this is a very complex, long-standing, and partly psychological issue we're dealing with, but I'm hoping you can help with some of the most incapacitating symptoms.'"

People who are overweight also aggravate doctors, because the condition sets them up for almost certain failure. Sooner or later, one of the many diseases associated with obesity will probably show up. Like most of society, many doctors are inclined to feel scorn rather than empathy for people with a weight problem. "Curbside Consultation," a page on *American Family Physician*'s Web site, offers advice and a place for doctors to vent anonymously. One physician confessed, "My opinion of some of these [overweight] patients has been that they are lazy, lack willpower and like being sick. At times I felt that they wanted me to give them a magic pill to cure their problem, when they were the ones who actually needed to do the work."

How do you overcome this prejudice? Korsch advises overweight patients to be candid and at the same time practice a little reverse psychology: "If it's there and real, you have to deal with it. If you're heavy, say, 'I know everybody thinks fat people are just sloppy and overeat and are self-indulgent, but I hope you won't consider me that way because I've really tried and I do want your help with it.' You can sometimes detoxify the particular stigma by bringing it out into the open, because that enables the doctor to say, 'I don't really think that.'"

The point is that the experience you have with your doctor has a lot to do with what's ailing you. Both you and the doctor will bring preconceived notions into the examining room. Both of you will be waiting to see if the other is "good" or "bad." Understanding this dynamic improves your chances of success.

Let's say you have an illness that is not life-threatening and is fairly mundane. How do you solidify your standing as a "good" patient? According to one study cited in *Consumer Reports*, doctors described good patients as those who appear to understand what the doctor is saying, ask few questions, and respect their time. Sadly, these are exactly the traits that keep patients in the dark. Most people have difficulty understanding the doctor's terminology, so they ask questions, which takes time.

Physicians also agree that "good" patients follow doctors' orders. Noncompliers are the bane of the profession, but the reasons patients don't comply can often be traced to bad communication with the doctor. A man might be told to take a prescription medicine he can't afford and be too embarrassed to admit it. It's common for people to be instructed to change their lifestyle—to diet, exercise three times a week, give up caffeine, and so forth—but often they just aren't up to the challenge. They fear being judged by the doctor, so they put off scheduling a visit or they lie about their progress. Are they bad patients, or are the doctors at fault for not knowing their patients well enough to advise a course of action they might actually follow?

As a patient, you have your work cut out for you. You want to be a "good" patient, one whom the doctor will want to spend time with and help. Yet you must speak up and make sure you understand what the doctor is talking about. It's like downhill skiing: the course is fast, skill is essential, and you must be sure of the terrain before you push off. The first stop on the journey is inside your own head.

## Patient, Know Thyself

Physicians constantly complain that patients don't share crucial information about their symptoms and lifestyle. This is ironic, since patients' number-one complaint is that doctors don't seek their opinion. It seems as if patients are forever waiting for the doctor to ask just the right questions, while doctors are waiting for their patients to go ahead and spit out the facts already. It is up to you to break the impasse and start speaking up in the doctor's office whether or not he asks you the right questions. In fact, speaking up is the single most powerful thing you can do for your health. About 70 percent of correct diagnoses depend *solely* on information the patient tells the doctor, according to an analysis done by the American Society of Internal Medicine.

Why do patients find it so difficult to talk to their doctors? Some common reasons include:

- **I DON'T WANT TO WASTE THE DOCTOR'S TIME.** This is a natural reaction to the hurried, no-nonsense atmosphere in most doctors' offices. What you need to do is come prepared with a list of questions and concerns so that you won't ramble and lose focus. (See "Getting Prepped," page 61.)

- **I DON'T WANT TO SEEM WEAK.** Lots of people were taught to bear their pain silently, even in a doctor's office. They don't want to seem like wimps. Yet pain is often the first signal your body sends when things are going wrong. You could seriously jeopardize your health by hiding or downplaying your symptoms.

- **I AM AFRAID OF WHAT THE DOCTOR MIGHT FIND.** If this is the case, talk your symptoms over with a friend before you go to the doctor. It will get you more comfortable with saying the words out loud, and your friend will give you moral support and encouragement.

- **I AM AFRAID THE DOCTOR WILL TELL ME TO CHANGE MY LIFESTYLE.** Instead of fibbing to the doctor about your lifestyle, try asking him to give you a range of options for making changes. Request that he help you devise a plan that's broken down into small steps so you will be more likely to comply.

- **I AM INTIMIDATED BY MY DOCTOR.** It's not unusual for people to be so fearful of their physician that they simply tell him what they think he wants to hear. This is especially true if they have not been following the doctor's orders concerning medications, diet, and/or behavior. If you're too afraid of your doctor to be honest, you should consider changing doctors.

- **I DON'T SPEAK THE SAME LANGUAGE AS THE DOCTOR.** Bring along a friend who can translate or ask the doctor's office if they can provide a translator.

- **I DON'T FULLY UNDERSTAND WHICH INFORMATION IS IMPORTANT.** No matter how unrelated it seems, tell the doctor anything you think might have influenced your condition. Pain in the body is often "referred"—that is, an injury or ailment in one part will result in pain somewhere else.

- **I DON'T WANT THE DOCTOR TO KNOW EVERYTHING.** Some patients deliberately withhold information to protect a third party (such as an abusive spouse) or for some sort of gain, such as qualifying for disability or an insurance claim. This is a pretty dangerous game to play with your health.

## Will the Doctor Think I'm Dumb?

Of all the reasons patients clam up in the doctor's office, the most common is that they're afraid the doctor will think they are stupid. Doctors' intimidating terminology is to blame for this. If you're like most people, you may walk into the office fully prepared to state your case only to have your mind go blank the moment the doctor opens her mouth. Doctors often ask questions that require a simple "yes" or "no" response, so you answer those and forget everything else you were going to say.

To set the record straight, no one except other doctors understands what doctors are talking about. Doctors know this, but they tend to forget. "The situation is like trying to talk in English to a Japanese speaker who has studied one year of English," according Dr. Terry S. Ruhl. "[The patient] will understand many of the simple words but will miss much of the complex meanings. . . . Likewise, many patients lack the basic anatomy and physiology concepts to understand our explanations. They are starting with no frame of reference."

Ruhl suggests that doctors use analogies to explain how the body works, and you might ask your doctor to do the same. Although some of the examples he provides seem a little preschoolish—"The heart is like a pump that pushes blood around the body. . . . The spine is like a pile of blocks"—you have to start somewhere.

No layperson can be expected to grasp medical terminology, and most doctors are not adept at translating it. To resolve this problem:

- Bring a notepad and pencil, or, better yet, a tape recorder.
- When the doctor totally loses you, politely interrupt: "Excuse me, but I don't understand what you're saying. Can you explain it in layperson's terms?"
- Don't expect to understand everything, even if the doctor tries his best to explain. Tape record everything or take notes and plan to research it later. Then, with a little more knowledge, you can call him back for a phone consultation or schedule another visit.
- Ask the doctor where to go for more information. The office may have brochures about your condition, but they are usually very brief or published by drug companies who have their own priorities. Ask the doctor for specific Web sites, books, or magazines that would be helpful.

## Getting Prepped

If you have read anything at all about preparing for a visit to the doctor, you know that you're supposed to bring a list of health concerns with you. What you may not know is that although doctors recognize a need for "the list," most of them cringe inwardly when you pull one out. In *Patient Care* magazine, Frederic W. Platt, M.D., writes that doctors resent patients who bring long, poorly organized lists that waste their time and (some feel) challenge their authority. French doctors even have a nickname for what's ailing the list-bearers: *"la maladie du petite papier"* (the sickness of the little paper).

Don't let this stop you from bringing your list, however. Just make sure it is brief, specific, and prioritized. Platt recommends bringing a copy for the doctor, too, so she will feel included. For each item, provide the following information:

- What are the symptoms?
- When did you first notice them?
- What times of day or night do they occur?
- How long do they last?
- Are they getting better, worse, or remaining constant?
- How do the symptoms affect your daily activities?

## Magic Words and Deeds in the Doctor's Office

Once you understand the mind-set of doctors, you can choose behaviors that will put them at ease while you draw information out of them. The most important strategy is to keep your voice steady and calm. Doctors are afraid of emotion, so the less you show, the more comfortable they will feel. Barbara Korsch explains: "If you put drama in your voice, it will turn the doctor off. Be quantitative and objective instead of saying how you feel. This is unfortunate; doctors shouldn't be that way, but in my studies we've learned that they are." When you seem desperate or panicky, when your voice is trembling with anxiety, the doctor's first reaction will be to try to tone it down. "Your emotional reactions engage doctors less than describing what it is you're reacting to," says Korsch.

In addition to using a neutral tone of voice, the following words and deeds will keep you in the doctor's good graces.

- **USE NEUTRAL WORDS TO DESCRIBE FEELINGS.** Be *concerned* instead of *scared*. Be *apprehensive* instead of *a nervous wreck*. In everyday life we tend to exaggerate to get results, but with doctors you have to go to the opposite extreme. Even if you are *in agony*, try not to use those words. Instead say, "I have a lot of discomfort." (More on pain later in this chapter.)

- **USE SPECIFIC WORDS TO DESCRIBE SYMPTOMS.** "I haven't slept a wink," doesn't tell a doctor much. Instead say, "I've been averaging only four hours of sleep a night, and I usually get seven. I've been waking up every hour or so, and it takes me at least 20 minutes to fall asleep again."

- **TALK ABOUT THE MOST IMPORTANT THINGS FIRST.** Doctors are very time-sensitive and will (understandably) be annoyed if you wait until the end of your visit to bring up a problem that requires some time to address.

- **MAKE YOUR EXPECTATIONS CLEAR.** At the beginning of the visit, tell the doctor exactly why you are there and what you hope she can do for you.

- **ACKNOWLEDGE THE DOCTOR'S SITUATION.** If the office is jam-packed and everyone seems stressed out, let the doctor know you're on his side: "It must be hard for you today, so I'll try to be concise."

- **BE CLEAN.** Personal hygiene does matter. If you smell bad, the doctor will want to get away from you, just as anyone else would.

- **KEEP AN OPEN MIND.** "Patients have a tremendous amount of misunderstanding about medicine," says Barry Rosenbloom. "It's vague or distorted or based on what they've heard from a friend or read in a magazine." As a result, some people arrive at the doctor's office expecting a certain response, and when they don't get it, they go on the offensive. "They may not like what the doctor says, and that's OK," says Rosenbloom. "But if they're going to challenge the doctor at every turn, the doctor, like any other human being, is going to be put off by it. If people want a valuable experience with a physician, they have to be open-minded."

## Absolute No-No's

Certain behaviors are like fingernails on a chalkboard to doctors. Some of these you can control, others you cannot. As mentioned earlier, if you are overweight or have a chronic health problem, you will need to strategize to overcome the doctor's possible bias against you. Beyond that, here are a few behaviors to avoid:

**DON'T ACT ENTITLED.** No matter how lofty your position in the outside world, when you are on the doctor's turf, resist ordering him around. "[Patients] seemed to think my job was to write them referrals," groused one doctor anonymously in "Curbside Consultation." "At their jobs . . . [they] were used to aggressive, confrontational relationships and they continuously challenged me into arguments." Control is extremely important to doctors. If you challenge them or overstep the bounds of typical patient behavior, you will raise their hackles. If you need to question their decisions, ask politely; never demand or confront.

**DON'T PLAY DOCTOR WITH THE DOCTOR.** "Patients often arrived at the office armed with complex and marginal information from the Internet that was inconsistent with standards of care," the same "Curbside Consultation" physician complained. Oncologist Barry Rosenbloom voiced similar concerns. "I personally feel good when people are educated about the disease. They ask intelligent questions. But the thing I've got over the patient is experience and judgment and the ability to take care of sick people. Breast cancer is a good example. Patients come with literature; they're aware of the various chemotherapy regimens. But they have no idea what they mean, whether one is better than the other."

**DON'T TEST THE DOCTOR.** Doctors are aware that many people seek second opinions, and that is fine with them. What they object to are patients who see several physicians for the same problem but don't reveal what the other doctors have discovered. This type of blind testing undermines all the doctors.

**DON'T BLAME THE DOCTOR FOR HIS STAFF.** Doctors are often as frustrated with the front office staff as you are. Bring your complaints to the office manager, not your doctor. It's not worth wasting 5 minutes of your 15-minute visit. If you get no satisfaction from the office manager (or if she herself is the problem), call, write, or e-mail the doctor explaining the situation. If the staff is so wretched or disrespectful that you are considering dropping the doctor because of them, it's only fair to let him know.

**DON'T ASK THE DOCTOR TO DO SOMETHING UNETHICAL.** People commonly ask their doctors to write false reports so they can get out of work, get on disability, get handicapped parking permits, and so forth. Although it might seem like a harmless request, you are in fact asking the doctor to lie and possibly jeopardize his career.

**DON'T BAD-MOUTH OTHER DOCTORS.** If you disliked a former doctor's care and must explain your concerns to your new doctor, keep your tone and language neutral. Talk about the treatment itself rather than the doctor who provided it. If the doctor asks why you changed physicians, simply say that you and he didn't communicate very well.

## Stoicism Is for Wimps

Talking about pain makes doctors experience significant discomfort, to use their own dainty jargon. "They don't care to think anything is painful, especially if they've had something to do with it, like perform the surgery," says Barbara Korsch. Pain is nothing if not emotional, yet here again, "If doctors think you're exaggerating and being very emotional, they'll say, 'There,

there, it can't be that bad. I've taken care of a lot of patients who have that.'"

Most of us are encouraged to be stoic about pain, which makes two people in the examining room who don't want to talk about it—the patient and the doctor. According to the American Pain Foundation, this approach is not only pointless, it is dangerous. Ignoring pain can make a condition worse, so that when you do finally treat it, the cost and disability are far greater than if you had dealt with it early on. Chronic pain (lasting six months or longer) impairs your mood, sleep, sexual appetite, friendships, energy, and overall lust for life. Both the Joint Commission on Accreditation of Healthcare Organizations and the Department of Veterans Affairs have requested that pain be treated as a fifth vital sign, to be assessed along with pulse, temperature, breathing rate, and blood pressure.

Whether your pain is chronic or not, don't be ashamed to speak up about it. Make an effort to stay calm. The doctor needs precise information about the nature of your pain, and the more specific you are, the more she will be able to help you. If she attempts to brush off your concerns by comparing you to other patients or insisting that it can't be that bad, bring the focus back to you: "I realize other patients may have reacted differently, but I have a very low tolerance for pain and I need you to take this seriously." Approach the conversation with the attitude that *of course* she wants to help you alleviate the pain (even if she has tried to brush you off). Do not blame the doctor for the pain. Keep it neutral. The American Pain Foundation suggests the following tips for talking about pain with your doctor:

- Tell him where it hurts and when you first noticed the pain.
- Describe what it feels like, using specific words such as stabbing, aching, radiating, throbbing, sharp, dull, burning, tingling, deep, pressing, and so forth.

- Describe how badly it hurts on a scale from 1 to 10, 10 being worst.
- Describe what makes the pain better or worse.
- Explain how the pain affects your daily life. Has it impaired your work, exercise, sleep, sexual activities, mood, ability to concentrate, state of mind?
- Tell the doctor about pain management techniques and medications you have used in the past, and explain what worked and what didn't.

Despite their best intentions, some doctors don't have much to offer in the way of pain management. Few are trained in it, and many simply don't give it much attention. If you are not getting satisfaction with your doctor, ask her to recommend a pain specialist. If she doesn't know of any, shop for one on your own. The American Pain Foundation (www. Painfoundation.org; 888-615-7246) can help.

## The Biggest, Baddest Communication Gaps

Medical malpractice insurance is often blamed for the mess in our current health-care system. There are undoubtedly some rotten doctors out there who deserve to be sued for their bad work, but in nearly three-quarters of malpractice lawsuits, the core reason for patients' unhappiness is their doctors' bad communication skills, not their technical ability. In most cases the patients did not understand the procedure, or what the tests meant, or how long the recovery would take. The lack of understanding, coupled with the doctor's poor bedside manner, left them feeling betrayed and cast aside, and those basic human emotions are what fuel most lawsuits. This is good news, because it means that despite all the scary stories about malpractice lawsuits and incompetent doctors, you actually have a lot of control over your health care.

You just need to be aware of the points at which communication most often breaks down.

Barry D. Lang, M.D., of Boston, has particular insight in this area. Lang practiced orthopedic surgery from 1975 until 1996 and then did an about-face: he went to law school and became an attorney specializing in medical malpractice. "I think doctors are their own worst enemies," he says. "I believe that many of my clients, or at least some, would not come to see me even if the doctor did something wrong, if there had been better communication. This is one reason chiropractors are rarely sued. Chiropractors listen to their patients and doctors don't, and I can say that because I'm a doctor."

Many of Lang's lawsuits involve surgery, and the problems are concentrated in a few key areas. First, there is the "complete and unfettered trust" some patients place in their doctor. "They assume the doctor has more education, knows what he's doing, and will do the best for the patient—and most times this is true. Sometimes, unfortunately, it's not. If somebody goes in for a complicated hip procedure, for instance, he may be reluctant to ask the doctor, 'Have you done this before?' And the doctor is not going to tell him unless he asks."

Dr. Lang also warns patients to ask about the *specific* complications of their surgery, and to get it in writing. A great many of his cases involve arguments about informed consent. "The patient says, 'Gee, the doctor never told me that my foot could drop off in this operation'; the doctor says, 'Of course I did.' Many times the doctor has not even approached the subject. They give the patient a general, generic release that that says, 'My doctor has informed me of every complication,' and the patient signs it. The release is made up by the hospital. The hospital isn't privy to what the doctor and patient discussed."

Patients should also ask how long it will take them to recover from surgery—meaning a complete return to normal functioning—and how traumatic or painful the recovery period will be. Says Lang, "Doctors have a well-meaning tendency to tell a patient, 'I've done this a thousand times and everything's going to be super.' When everything isn't super, guess who the patient is angry at? The doctor." Another malpractice lawyer, Evelyn W. Bradford, attempted to educate physicians about this problem in an article for *Medical Economics*: "Don't gloss over surgery's effects. I hear this lament again and again in my office: 'If that doctor had told me what to expect, I wouldn't have gone through with the surgery.' . . . Orthopedists, I've found, are the most guilty of poor communication."

The message to the patient is clear. "Ask questions," says Barry Lang. "There is no such thing as a stupid question. Your doctor wants to help you, but he is not able to look into your mind."

If you are considering any type of surgery or treatment, be sure to ask the doctor:

- Have you done this procedure before? How many times?
- Exactly what are you going to do?
- How necessary is this procedure?
- What are my chances of being completely cured?
- What are the possible complications?
- What is the least and most amount of time it will take for me to fully recover?
- What will the recovery period be like? Is the recovery painful?
- What is your pain-management plan for this procedure and the recovery period?
- What will happen if I do *not* have this procedure?

Don't feel pressured to make a decision right then and there in the doctor's office. Go home and think about it. If you aren't satisfied with the doctor's answers or don't understand them, research the issues yourself, call the doctor and ask her to clarify them, or get a second opinion.

## Speak Up and Stay Well

Health care is truly in a state of flux, not just because of stingy HMOs and flip-flopping insurance practices but also because so many extraordinary medical breakthroughs are being made every year. Gone are the days when you could find one good, trustworthy doctor and rest easy. You will probably deal with many doctors over the course of your life, so the person you need to trust is you. You have to trust yourself to ask the right questions, speak up, and stand up for yourself. You have to trust yourself to judge the doctor instead of worrying about the doctor judging you. Luckily, this is a skill guaranteed to pay off in a big way as you get older. If you teach yourself to speak up when you're thirty, by age eighty you'll be a master—just when the whole machine is starting to sputter and you really need that expertise.

**PHRASE BOOK**

The Internet is a lifesaver when it comes to researching medical terms. The "Glossary" page on Patientsguide.com links you to glossaries for specific conditions and diseases. Patientsguide also has a "Medical Terminology" page that briefly explains how those long Latin names are constructed. FamilyDoctor.org, hosted by the American Academy of Family Physicians, has a somewhat limited but very easy to understand "Dictionary." This site also features information in Spanish on a wide range of common health problems.

## 6

**PEDIATRICIAN**

# DOCTOR, TEACHER, THERAPIST, FRIEND

Pediatrics is probably the happiest branch of medicine. Medical students choose it because they love children, and most seasoned pediatricians will tell you that the joy of working with youngsters still holds up 30 years into their careers. In addition to being cute and generally endearing, children tend to recover quickly and come down with serious illnesses far less often than adults. If doctors like to succeed, the chances of doing so are much greater in pediatrics than in any other field of medicine. Perhaps because of this, 69 percent of all medical residents plan on becoming pediatricians. What this means for parents is that there are a lot of enthusiastic, talented pediatricians who would love to serve your family.

## Behind the Scenes: Multitasking and Loving It

Children's health care used to be about treating severe communicable diseases such as polio, scarlet fever, diphtheria, and smallpox. All that changed during the last half of the twentieth century, when vaccinations for most of these diseases were developed. Today, health issues are only a part of the pediatrician's territory.

"So much of what we do is, for lack of a better term, social work/ mental health care," says Margaret Fitzgerald, a family nurse practitioner in Lawrence, Massachusetts, and founder of Fitzgerald Health Education Associates. Parents count on pediatricians not just for health matters but also for advice about discipline, learning disabilities, social problems, sibling rivalry, custody conflicts, and much more. Writer and pediatrician Perri Klass notes that "parents these days often look to pediatricians to provide the sort of expertise that once was given by a resident grandparent or neighboring aunt." While an adult wouldn't dream of asking her doctor how to solve a problem she was having at work, parents rely on pediatricians to help them solve problems with school bullies, homework, testing anxiety, and a whole range of other school issues. Guidance counselor, grandma, physician, behavioral therapist, and education specialist—today's pediatrician is expected to fill all these roles, and for the most part she cheerfully complies.

Parents aren't the only ones who expect a lot out of pediatricians. The police expect them to be on the lookout for physical and sexual abuse. Schools expect them to help educate teenagers about substance abuse and sex. The American Academy of Pediatrics expects them to provide "anticipatory guidance" for parents, which means informing them about every conceivable childhood safety issue, including but not limited to seat belts, bike helmets, sleep position, nonflammable pajamas, scooters, drowning, lead screening, gun safety, television viewing, and of course, sex, drugs, and smoking. Finally, pediatricians are under pressure from HMOs and insurance companies to provide rapid, cost-effective services. The typical pediatrician sees 28 children a day; the average yearly checkup lasts 15–20 minutes, and a sick-child visit lasts 10.

Despite all the demands, pediatricians are for the most part a willing and passionate group. They readily acknowledge that they aren't just treating children, they are treating families, and they seem eager to step up to the plate even though medical school rarely prepares them for the challenge. Says pediatrician Andrew Baumel of Framingham, Massachusetts: "Training in mental health is definitely deficient. You learn a lot on the job." Most of that learning has to do with how to talk to parents. Baumel's biggest surprise when he became a pediatrician was that "everyone has an advocate. In other areas of medicine, you're dealing with one person who has a problem, but in pediatrics we always have two people for every issue: the patient, who is frequently over two and verbal, and the parent, stepparent, grandparent, et cetera. So we're always dealing with at least two people, and sometimes four or five." Twenty years ago, doctors often resented parents who asked too many questions. Today, everyone agrees that children's health is a family affair, and for pediatricians that means knowing how to talk—and listen—to parents. More than other doctors, they welcome your input and are tolerant of your anxieties.

However, even the most virtuous pediatricians can be pushed to their limits by overly demanding, careless, or inconsiderate parents. And because pediatricians receive the same basic medical training as all doctors, they have some of the same biases: they value calm voices, clarity, and facts, and are turned off by too much emotion and vague information. (First-time mothers get a free pass on neurotic overworrying and general cluelessness until the child is about two; then most pediatricians expect them to calm down.) To get the best out of your pediatrician, begin by learning the basics they wish every parent understood.

## What Pediatricians Really Want You to Know

There are plenty of things pediatricians would like parents to do and say while they are in the office, and we'll get to those shortly, but there are also a few key concepts they wish all parents were clear on before they called or scheduled an appointment.

**VACCINATIONS ARE SAFE.** Unbelievably, pediatricians now have to sell some parents on the benefits of vaccines! In the late 1990s a wave of suspicion about vaccines began to spread across North America and Europe, fueled by rumors that they could cause autism, attention deficit disorder, diabetes, fever seizures, polio, and even AIDS. Ignorance about the diseases themselves compounded the problem. A study done in 2001 found that 90 percent of parents of school-age children didn't know that chicken pox can have deadly complications. Half of those parents said they would rather their kids catch the disease than vaccinate them against it.

Pediatricians were aghast at these developments. Fortunately, new studies confirm the safety of most vaccines, including those protecting children from measles, mumps, rubella, hepatitis B, diphtheria, and polio. The chicken pox vaccine is relatively new so there are no long-term studies of it, but it is recommended by the American Academy of Pediatrics, and studies done thus far show the vaccine to be safe and effective for most children. If you have any doubt at all about vaccinating your child, ask your pediatrician for the most recent information.

**ANTIBIOTICS DON'T CURE EVERYTHING.** Doctors themselves are partly to blame for parents' love affair with antibiotics, since they are the ones who have prescribed them too often in the past, sometimes just to keep parents pacified. In a recent study, one-third of the pediatricians surveyed admitted to caving in to parents' demands for antibiotics whether or not they were called for. As a result, some strains of bacteria are becoming resistant to antibiotics—a very alarming development.

Antibiotics are only effective against bacterial infections.

They cannot cure colds and flu, which are caused by viruses. However, colds and flu sometimes develop into bacterial infections, in which case antibiotics *can* help. It's a tough call to make, and that's what the pediatrician is there for. As a general rule, antibiotics can cure strep throat, some ear infections, some cases of chronic coughs or bronchitis, and some severe sinus infections lasting longer than two weeks. Antibiotics cannot cure most sore throats and most coughs.

**FEVERS ARE GOOD.** Pediatrician Andrew Baumel's views about fever are shared by the overwhelming majority of doctors: "Fever helps the body fight infection. Our immune system works better and quicker at a higher temperature. For a low-grade fever of 100° or 101°, you don't have to use antifever medication, depending on whether or not the child is uncomfortable."

Fever is a symptom, not an illness. A fever can get higher if an illness gets worse, but it won't rise just because you don't treat it. Brain damage can occur only if a fever reaches 107.6°F and stays there for an extended period of time. Untreated fevers usually peak at around 105° unless the child is in a hot room or overdressed.

Infants do need special handling when it comes to fevers. If they are younger than 60 days old, any fever of 100.4° or higher signals the need for a visit to the doctor. From 60 days to three years of age, call the doctor if the fever is 102° or greater. In infants and young children, low-grade fevers that have no obvious source can be a sign of serious bacterial infection. Febrile seizures (convulsions that are brought on by fever) can occur in children whose temperatures rise rapidly. The number itself doesn't matter so much as the speed at which the temperature rises. Although they are frightening for parents, febrile seizures are brief and have no lasting effect on the child.

For children older than two years, call the doctor any time a fever is 105° or greater. Call the doctor after 48 hours about a fever of *less* than 105° if your child seems healthy and active—an infection could be brewing. If she has cold or flu symptoms, you can wait 72 hours to call. If she is uncomfortable, vomiting, dehydrated, or having problems sleeping and the fever is less than 105°, try to lower it—but only to 100° or 101°, so that it can still fight the infection.

**SICK CHILDREN NEED TO TAKE *ALL* THEIR MEDICINE.** One unnerving development in this age of miracle drugs is that parents frequently do not bother to follow through on the regimen. For instance, instead of receiving the complete 10-day course of penicillin for treatment of strep infections, 56 percent of children do not receive the drug by day three, and 71 percent don't receive it by day six. Often this is because the parent either doesn't believe it's really important to follow through or doesn't understand the directions. Doctors want parents to realize that if a child does not take the complete cycle of a medication, the original condition may come back stronger than before. If you are confused about administering the medicine but feel foolish asking the doctor to repeat the instructions, talk to the nurse. You are not alone; many people find the directions confusing.

**YOUR CHILD'S HEALTH CARE DEPENDS ON WHAT YOU TELL THE DOCTOR.** "Ninety percent of our diagnosis is made by the history, by just talking. Ten percent is made by physical exam and lab studies," says Andrew Baumel. Parents, then, aren't just advocates in the pediatrician's office; their observations are the raw data doctors rely on most to treat children.

Yet even the most devoted parents are sometimes reluctant to be forthcoming with the pediatrician, for many of the same reasons adults cite. They may be embarrassed by a problem their child is having or afraid of what the doctor will discover. Many parents become distracted during the visit and forget to relate the most important information. Some don't want to appear ignorant, while others don't want to take up too much of the doctor's time.

It may be tempting to think that a really good pediatrician will uncover any serious problem with your child whether or not you are forthcoming. That is not how pediatricians view things. Good doctors will take a comprehensive history during the yearly checkup, but ultimately they depend on you to tell them anything you think might be relevant to your child's well-being.

## Magic Words and Deeds in the Pediatrician's Office

The well-child checkup is where your most in-depth conversations with the pediatrician will take place. The best time to schedule one is April through September, on any day other than Monday. October through March is flu season, and Mondays are loaded with kids who got sick over the weekend. Parents tend to schedule a yearly checkup around the child's birthday because it's easy to remember, but that is not necessary. You will get a more relaxed doctor and possibly more time if you schedule during the slow months. If you want an extra-long visit or have special issues to discuss, ask the front office if taking the last appointment of the day will assure you more time.

Before your visit, take a few moments to think about your child's health, behavior, and development. Pediatricians expect you to report anything out of the ordinary, even if it doesn't seem to relate to health care. For instance, a child who suddenly starts getting into trouble in school and whose work takes a nosedive may be having social problems, but it's also possible that he is having difficulty with his vision or hearing.

Next, prepare a list of topics you wish to discuss with the

doctor—and be sure to prioritize them. With only twenty minutes for the average visit, you may not get to discuss everything. Be sure to take paper and pencil along to jot down the doctor's advice. The *Merck Manual* reports that within 15 minutes after an office visit, some parents have already forgotten half the information. Parents tend to recall the first third of the visit best, and to remember more about diagnosis than treatment.

Doctors will usually run through a series of questions relating to your child's health and development, and of course you should answer these as specifically and clearly as you can. Keep your list of topics handy so you won't forget your own agenda when the doctor starts talking. For a smooth, satisfying office visit:

**GET YOUR CHILD UNDRESSED BEFORE THE EXAM, IF YOU ARE SO ASKED.** Lots of kids resist taking their clothes off, so their parents wait until the doctor comes in to start wrestling with them. This is a waste of time and a major irritant to doctors. "Skin can tell you so much about what's going on," says Andrew Baumel. "The child really needs to be undressed to be examined properly."

**GREET THE DOCTOR AS IF SHE IS AN OLD FRIEND.** It will put your child at ease, particularly if she sees the doctor infrequently. If the doc doesn't greet your child by name (a good doctor will), casually reintroduce them: "Chloe's grown a lot since last time, Dr. Harmon." Your friendliness toward the doctor signals confidence in her, which will make your child more cooperative.

**KEEP YOUR TONE OF VOICE CALM AND CHEERFUL.** If your voice is important when you visit your own doctor, it is doubly so at the pediatrician's office. "The child picks up all the parent's cues," says Baumel. "When parents are nervous, the child feeds off it. Parents can make the child much, much more anxious than he would be on his own." Your tone is more important than the words you say, so if you can't keep the anxiety out of your voice, say nothing at all.

**ASK THE PEDIATRICIAN WHAT SHE WILL BE DOING DURING THE EXAM.** This is for your child's peace of mind. Sometimes the doctor will volunteer the information, but often they just start right in questioning you or examining your child.

**TELL THE PEDIATRICIAN GOOD NEWS AS WELL AS BAD.** Progress is just as important as problems in helping the doctor assess your child's development. If your son is getting along better with his older brother, excelling at reading, or playing an instrument, let the doctor know. It provides a more balanced view than when you simply list all the problem areas.

**SEPARATE FACT AND OPINION, AND BE SPECIFIC.** When describing problems, make a distinction between your worries and what has actually taken place. For example, say, "I'm concerned that Cindy may be backsliding in her toilet training. She has an accident about once a week," not, "Cindy's backsliding on her toilet training—she has accidents all the time."

**BRING HELP IF YOU'RE BRINGING OTHER KIDS.** If it's noisy, the doctor will not be able to give his full attention to the child who is there for the checkup. She needs to listen to the heart and lungs, talk to you without interruptions, and focus on your child. You need to focus on the child, too. It's best if only the two of you are in the examining room.

**STAY CALM AND STEADY DURING SHOTS.** Your attitude will keep the tension low and help your child deal with the pain. Do not apologize, grimace, or in any way indicate that there is a choice about this procedure. You can be mildly sympathetic, but the moment you start looking anxious your child will get even more upset. If the child really puts up a struggle, follow the nurse's directions to restrain him, and be kind but firm. After the shot, thank the nurse, hug your child, and congratulate him on a job well done. That's the end of it—no big deal.

## Absolute No-No's

Pediatricians are very consistent about what annoys them in the examining room. That's because they hear the same irritating comments from parents day in and day out. Avoid these and your doctor will love you for it.

**DON'T USE THE DOCTOR AS A THREAT.** Says Andrew Baumel, "Every day I hear, 'You better be good or he's going to give you a shot.' What message does that send? You're putting up more barriers."

**DON'T TALK TO THE PEDIATRICIAN WHEN SHE HAS THE STETHOSCOPE ON.** She can't hear you, so she's not going to answer. If you speak loudly, she can't hear the heartbeat.

**DON'T TRY TO SQUEEZE A GENERAL CHECKUP INTO A SICK-CHILD VISIT.** The doctor probably won't do it, and even if he did, you would be getting a rushed, substandard checkup.

**DON'T TRY TO PIGGYBACK ONE CHILD ONTO ANOTHER CHILD'S VISIT.** With an average of 28 patients a day, the pediatrician's schedule is usually very tight. They dislike being pressured into seeing children they have not made time for.

**DON'T DIAGNOSE THE PROBLEM FOR THE DOCTOR.** You may be correct, but it's best to phrase it as a suspicion rather than as a foregone conclusion. Rather than announcing, "Brenda has strep again; she needs more Augmentin," say "Brenda seems to have the same symptoms she did last time she had strep," and let the doctor take it from there.

**DON'T BE RUDE TO THE PERSON AT THE FRONT DESK.** It will get back to the doctor, the nurse practitioner, and the rest of the staff, and they will think less of you no matter how well-behaved you are with the doctor. If you want these people on your side when an emergency comes up, be nice to them now.

**VITAL STATISTICS FOR AN EMERGENCY PHONE CALL**

When it's four A.M. and you've been up all night with a vomiting child, things can get a little blurry. To help the doctor determine what is wrong when you call, be prepared to provide the following information:

- Your name.
- Your child's name (and age and weight, if you don't see the doctor often).
- Your child's ailment, or what you think it might be.
- Your child's temperature. Take it before you place the call.
- The length of time your child has been ill.
- The symptoms—be as precise as possible. If your child has been vomiting or having diarrhea, how frequently? For example, how many times has it happened in the past 12 hours?
- A brief history: Are the symptoms getting better, worse, or holding steady? How much have they varied over the past 12 hours?

## Covert Operations

As children grow older and less likely to confide in Mom and Dad, parents often turn to pediatricians for help in ferreting out the details of their lives. They routinely ask pediatricians to test their teenagers for drugs or sexually transmitted diseases, or to confirm that their daughters are still virgins. "I won't do it," states Margaret Fitzgerald about the latter issue. "It is truly impossible to tell. It's unfair because there's this assumption that you could examine a girl and say yes or no, but there's no expectation that you would examine a young man and come up with an answer." Fitzgerald also refuses to test for drugs or STDs without the adolescent's permission.

Confidential care for minors is a slippery slope for health-care providers. Each state has its own laws as to what kind of information about an adolescent can be kept confidential from a parent, and under what circumstances. The Allan Guttmacher Institute Web site, at www.agi-usa.org, lists confidentiality laws by state. But even if it were legal to attain details about your child's life without the child's knowledge, many pediatricians would be reluctant to cross that line. "I will use the issue as a way of facilitating a dialogue between the child and the parent," says Fitzgerald. She offers this somewhat world-weary observation for parents concerned about their teenagers' sex lives: "The idea of two fifteen-year-olds having sex does not warm my heart, but at least in all likelihood they're equally unempowered. It is more likely *not* to be an exploitative relationship at that age. Fourteen- and fifteen-year-old girls are rarely pregnant by fourteen- and fifteen-year-old boys. Usually it's by twenty-one- to twenty-five-year-old men."

## Bidding Farewell to the Exam Room

When your child is eleven or twelve years old, it's time to introduce the idea of seeing the doctor alone. "Part of growing up into a young adult is the kid's responsibility to participate in his or her own health care," says Fitzgerald. "I generally start saying that to parents and children at an age when you couldn't surgically extract the parents from the exam room. The child wants the parent there, the parent wants to be there." When the children are twelve or thirteen, Fitzgerald will ask the child if she wants the parent to stay or leave. By the age of sixteen, a child should definitely be accustomed to going it solo at the doctor's office. That might be a great time to point him or her toward chapter 5 of this book. The sooner they learn how to talk to effectively communicate with the doctor, the better.

---

### HEALTH WEB SITES FOR PARENTS AND KIDS

There are a number of excellent Web sites that provide parents, children, and teenagers with health-care information. A few of the most widely used are:

**KIDSGROWTH.COM.** An extremely comprehensive site that covers health, parenting, and behavioral and development issues.

**DRGREENE.COM.** Dr. Greene and his colleagues offer chatty, very informative pages on a wide range of children's health issues.

**KIDSHEALTH.ORG.** This site is divided into user-friendly categories for parents, kids, and teens.

**COOLMD.COM.** Geared toward teenagers, this site contains information they may be too shy to talk about with their doctors.

**FAMILYDOCTOR.ORG.** An easy-to-search site sponsored by the American Academy of Family Physicians.

**APA.ORG.** Sponsored by the American Psychological Association, this site is a great resource for mental health information.

# NANNY
## LOVE FOR HIRE

Suppose you could create the ideal nanny. Chances are it would be someone who sat down for her interview and announced, "I have really enjoyed being a nanny. I honestly don't believe there is a better job out there. My days are spent exploring the world through the eyes of children, where everything is a great new adventure. Most days start and end with a great big hug and kiss! The last days with each one of my old 'families' have all been very difficult and teary." Too perfect to be true? Not at all. Of the many people interviewed for this book, nannies were probably the happiest with their jobs. The enthusiasm of Lisa B., quoted here, isn't unusual. It's typical of the women who choose this modestly paid but tremendously rewarding career.

Odd, then, the horror stories you hear about neglectful and incompetent nannies, or the tales of households that go through nannies like so many disposable diapers. How can you avoid their fate? There is no lack of compassionate nannies looking for work, but finding one who is the right match for your family can take some time. Using a nanny placement agency is no guarantee that the person you hire will stay with your family longer or be superior to someone you hear about through the grapevine. And although a placement agency can weed out poorly qualified, inexperienced nannies and provide criminal background checks, there is a limit to their usefulness. Ultimately, your success will depend on more than background checks and gut feelings. It will also require some honest reflection about yourself and your expectations. The clearer you are about those, the better your chances of recognizing the right nanny for you and being able to forge a lasting bond with her.

## Behind the Scenes: The Parent Trap

"I love children. It's their parents that make the job so hard!" confessed a nanny on the nannynetwork.com bulletin board—an excellent place for parents to browse for insight into the attitudes of nannies. You'll get to eavesdrop as they gush, brag, and fret about their charges, whom they usually refer to as "my baby" or "my boy" (or girl). No hidden video camera could reveal as much as these candid postings do. On the downside, the site is full of nannies' rants about their employers. Their frustration provides a crash course in nanny-parent relations.

There is no reliable profile that describes the type of woman who chooses to become a nanny. Their only common thread is that they love children. No matter how desperate for work a woman might be, she simply won't survive in the field if she doesn't genuinely like kids; there are too many kind and capable nannies out there willing to take her place. In 2000, the U.S. Department of Labor reported that three million mothers leave their children in the care of a nanny or other individual while they work outside the home. The nannies' level of training and education varies widely: some have college degrees in child development while others have only the experience they have acquired over years of caring for children. Their pay varies as well. At the bottom end of the pay scale are nannies earning less than minimum wage, and at the high end are those earning $15 an hour or more. Nannies for the very wealthy command as much as $1,500 a week, with perks such as a separate dwelling with all expenses paid, cell phone, use of a car, health benefits, gym membership, paid vacations, and more.

For a great many nannies, especially live-ins, exploitation in the form of unpaid overtime is common. Most of the nannies' problems stem from the informal, unregulated nature of the work. "She's just like a member of the family" often translates into the nanny being taken advantage of as if she were an indulgent aunt—or Cinderella. Nannies report not getting reimbursed for children's toys, food, or treats; not being paid for gasoline on work-related trips; not being paid if the family goes on vacation; not being paid on time; and having parents reduce their hours at will, changing them every week. Leah H., a nanny in San Francisco, recalled how her former employers' requests spiraled out of control: "They had me doing things that were not child related—they once had someone come over and watch the baby so I could clean the house (8,000 square feet, four floors). Then there were the outside errands—buying the dad cigarettes in the middle of the night, going on candy runs for the mother, delivering unmarked envelopes to people. . . . Toward the end, I discovered that I had, in fact, been working for old-school members of the Italian Mafia. I quit shortly after." An extreme example, perhaps, but only the part about the envelopes.

Whether a nanny likes her employers or has problems with them, her affection for the children, especially if she has cared for them since they were babies or toddlers, tends to trump all other concerns. "I have always been astounded by what I can and will put up with when I feel a child really needs me," wrote one nanny. And a nanny in Westchester, New York, confessed her grief at having to leave a child who was about to enter preschool:

"My baby's a big boy now. . . . I rock him at night now when we read stories and think how I'll miss his head against my chest, or the way his hair smells, or the sound of his laugh, or the dimple in his chin, the way he chases his dog, or smiles after a frustration and manages a new skill. . . . I can't stand it, only four more days with him. That's it. Four days. . . . I will and do miss him terribly already and he's not even gone yet."

## Finding a Nanny

Nanny placement agencies claim that it takes four weeks to find a nanny if you use their services and eight weeks if you do it on your own. Most parents use the agencies or the grapevine to find a nanny, but there is a third option for those who have the time: the park observation method. Go to your nearest park at midday, any time between 11:00 and 2:00. Observe the group of nannies and children you see there. After several days, you may notice one who seems particularly good with the children in her care. Approach her and ask if she happens to be looking for a job. Although this may seem underhanded—you'll be taking her away from her current employer—it is an excellent way to prescreen a nanny. You'll be able to see how affectionate she is with the children, how quickly she runs to them if they get hurt, whether she is attentive and playful with them or more interested in chatting with her friends. It's also instructive to observe a group of nannies together and get a sense of the general level of attention they pay to the children.

If the nanny you approach is open to working for you, you will need to ask for references and do a background check just as you would for any candidate. As for stealing her from someone else, it's no different than when someone is called by a corporate headhunter from a competing company. If the nanny is happy with her current employers, she won't leave. Also, the nanny's job may be ending soon anyway—many nannies must look for work when the child they are caring for enters preschool.

The grapevine is an even better way to locate a nanny because the person you hire will have already been employed by someone you know. However, good nannies tend to stay with the same families for several years, so unless you have a very wide circle of acquaintances you may come up empty with this method. That leaves nanny placement agencies, a generally reliable, if pricey, way to find candidates. Just be sure that the agency itself is reputable. It should belong to an organization such as the International Nanny Association, which maintains a list of approved agencies. It's also wise to choose an agency that has been in business at least a few years. When you're calling around to various agencies, ask them:

**HOW MANY NANNIES DO YOU PLACE IN A MONTH?** A good agency will place at least three to six nannies every month.

**HOW DO YOU SCREEN YOUR NANNIES?** The agency should be able to provide you with information about the nanny's previous employers, her references, and the general impression she made on the people she has worked for. The screener who works for the agency should also offer her own impression of the nanny. Ask also about the screener's background; top-notch agencies and some nanny training schools employ screeners who have degrees in social work and/or child development. Most agencies will not do criminal background checks until you have selected a nanny and she has agreed to work for you.

**WHAT ARE YOUR FEES?** They vary dramatically across the country, from around $500 to more than $3,000. If you hire a nanny through a placement agency that is part of a nanny training program, such as the English Nanny and Governess School in Chagrin Falls, Ohio (the Big Kahuna of nanny programs), the fee may be calculated as a percentage of the nanny's yearly salary.

Whatever the fee, get it in writing. Most agencies offer a 90-day replacement policy, but few will agree to refund your fee if the nanny doesn't work out.

**HOW DO YOU SUPPORT AND TRAIN YOUR NANNIES?** If the agency is part of a nanny training program, they will have a comprehensive description of the training each nanny receives and will provide her with plenty of books and other reference material to take on the job. Other agencies give their nannies a package that includes child-rearing information, daily logs, food and nutrition tips, and toilet-training strategies.

**DO YOU FOLLOW UP AFTER THE NANNY IS PLACED?** One great advantage to using an agency is that they can help facilitate a good relationship between you and the nanny after she begins working for you. The agency should call you the first week and check in periodically thereafter. Ask about their policy in this regard. If you are having trouble with the nanny or if she has concerns about you, the agency can serve as middleman and help iron things out.

## What's Your Nanny Style?

The decision to hire a nanny is almost as gut-wrenching as the decision to have a child in the first place. Intense emotions are attached to the act (guilt and fear, primarily), and those emotions can override your intellect to the point that you end up choosing the first person who makes you feel comfortable and comes with a good recommendation. This can work out fine, especially if you know the family for whom the nanny previously worked and have had a chance to see her in action. If you're hiring a stranger, however, you will need to choose carefully and with much forethought. Having a rapport with the person counts, but it is equally important to think objectively about the type of nanny who would work well with your family.

The main reason this decision is so crucial is that you will want the nanny to stay with your family a long time. Your children will become very attached to her, and they will suffer if she leaves. When they suffer, so will you. The trick is to make sure that the woman who seems so perfect cuddling your infant son will have the imagination to keep him entertained when he's two, as well as the patience and will to discipline him and the energy to chase him around the park.

Before you start interviewing, take stock of your values and parenting style. The following questions may help.

**DO YOU WANT AN AUNTIE OR AN EDUCATOR?** Any nanny you hire should be warm and affectionate toward your child, but beyond that, do you expect her to be actively involved in teaching him or are you more concerned that she be a loving, consistent presence in his life? If you plan on enrolling your child in preschool, it may not matter to you that the nanny does not speak flawless English. However, if you will be relying on her until your child enters kindergarten, you may want someone with enough English proficiency to teach him basic reading (ABCs, numbers, colors) and other pre-K skills.

**ARE YOU LOOKING FOR A "MEMBER OF THE FAMILY" OR AN EMPLOYEE?** In truth, the nanny *is* an employee, no matter how much time she spends in your home or how much you and your children grow to love her. She will always remain aware of her status even if you tend to forget it. Some families spend a lot more time with their nannies than other families do, however. In those cases it's nice if you enjoy her company and can communicate easily with her in a common tongue. Will you be sharing family meals with the nanny? Will you be shopping with her and taking her on family outings or vacations? Bear in mind that there are wonderful nannies who are perfectly suited to caring for young children but with whom you might not want to spend a lot of time yourself.

**IS YOUR PARENTING STYLE STRUCTURED OR RELAXED?** Is it important to you that the nanny stick to prescribed routines for mealtime, play, and naps, or do you feel comfortable with a more flexible schedule? How clean do the kids have to be? Can they eat in front of the TV or must all food be consumed at the kitchen table? If you are first-time parents, you may discover that you and your spouse have different views on structure (oh, the fun is just beginning). Take a stab at forming a consensus now, before you start interviewing nannies. You can always adjust your rules later on.

**WHAT SORT OF DISCIPLINE DO YOU WANT THE NANNY TO ENFORCE?** Discipline is a huge issue for nannies because their bottom line is keeping the child happy and quiet, especially when the parents are around. This usually means placating a child rather than enforcing rules. The more specific and supportive you can be with the nanny about discipline, the more confident and consistent she will be about providing it. Methods of discipline evolve throughout the early years of childhood, so you will need to keep the nanny informed if you change tactics.

**DID YOU HAVE ANY DIFFICULTIES WITH PAST NANNIES?** If so, do those problems form a pattern? What have you learned about yourself and your parenting style from those experiences?

**HAVE YOU HAD A PARTICULARLY GOOD EXPERIENCE WITH A NANNY?** If so, can you identify what it was about that person that made her work so well with your family?

**WHAT ARE YOUR BIGGEST FEARS ABOUT LEAVING YOUR CHILD IN THE CARE OF A NANNY?** If you can determine these, try to imagine the traits the nanny would need to possess in order to make you feel at ease.

Reflecting on these issues will give you a reference point from which to evaluate the nannies you will be interviewing. In addition, there are several other elements that are must-haves in a nanny.

First, the nanny must be reasonably intelligent. She doesn't need a college degree, but she should possess a good deal of common sense. Many intelligent women choose to become nannies, but there are also people who end up in the field because it is unregulated and requires no formal training whatsoever. These women can be very sweet and perhaps work wonders with babies, but babyhood is brief and caring for a child is extremely challenging. There is nothing more nerve-wracking than leaving your toddler in the care of someone who you suspect is not bright enough to do the right thing in an emergency.

Second, you must choose someone who has both the emotional maturity and the physical stamina to care for small children. No age is ideal in this regard: a very young woman might have loads of energy but lack the patience to calm a furious toddler, while a woman in her fifties might have tremendous experience but tire out too easily. The interview questions later in this chapter should shed some light on these issues.

Third, the woman should be a career nanny rather than someone who is only doing it until she has completed night school or found a "real" job. A career nanny should have a solid knowledge of child development, either through formal education or from experience. The interview questions on page 99 are designed to help you gauge the nanny's knowledge.

Finally, the nanny should have recommendations from at least two previous employers who can confirm her commitment to caring for children. (The more references, the better. Call all of them.) If she has letters of recommendation, you should still call to check. Many parents also hire a service to check for a criminal background. Mind Your Business, Inc. (www.mybinc.com; 888-758-3776) and American International Security (703-691-1110) are two such services; the Web site 4nannies.com also offers a background checking service.

## What Nannies Want

Chances are, the nannies you interview will be more focused on impressing you than on telling the truth about what they prefer in a work environment. The following issues are at the top of all nannies' lists when it comes to a desirable job. You should discuss them at some point in your interview and include the specifics in a written contract (Nannynetwork.com and 4nanny.com have contracts you can download; they are very comprehensive and you can edit them as you see fit).

**DECENT PAY.** Starting pay is about $300–$500 a week for a live-in nanny and $400–$600 for a live-out, but it can go higher. Pay generally depends upon the nanny's child-care skills, experience, and English proficiency; it is also determined by the number of hours she will be expected to work and the number of children who will be in her care. Nannies who can drive and who own their own car command higher wages. Realize that if you pay the least amount you can get away with, the nanny will probably be on the lookout for a better job from the moment she enters your household. Ask your neighbors and friends what the going rate is in your area and match it or go a little higher if possible.

**VACATION AND SICK-PAY POLICY.** When your children are small, it can be wonderful to take the nanny with you on vacations. In fact, that may be the only way you and your spouse will get to relax. However, your nanny deserves a vacation, too—a paid vacation. It's a good idea to think about this before hiring the nanny. For instance, if you know you'll be visiting your in-laws over Christmas, you might tell the candidates, "You'll get one week paid vacation at Christmas this coming year and another paid week of your choice." The nanny should also be paid for days she is sick, within reason.

**FAIR WORKING CONDITIONS.** Every child-care situation is unique.

Some families want a live-in nanny who is available 24 hours a day, five or six days a week. Other parents need someone to arrive at 7 A.M. and leave at 5 P.M. The parameters you require should be spelled out to the nanny during the interview, and once she is hired you should respect those parameters. Don't expect your 7–5 nanny always to be available for last-minute nighttime babysitting jobs, and don't expect your live-in to work on her days off. If you do need extra help, pay the nanny for her time.

**CLEARLY DEFINED RESPONSIBILITIES.** Write down all the things the nanny will be responsible for in addition to the usual feeding, diapering, dressing, bathing, and playing. Do you want your child to visit the park every day or to do a certain amount of arts and crafts each week? Will the nanny be doing the child's laundry? Would you like her to prepare special foods for your child? If this will be your first nanny, ask around to find out what other parents are having their nannies do. While you may at first be reluctant to sign off on various duties, the more you trust the nanny, the more work you will want her to do. In the beginning she might only be required to do a few of the items on your list, but it's best for both of you if she understands that eventually her duties will expand.

**A METHOD FOR RESOLVING CONFLICTS.** Even the most agreeable parents and most intuitive nanny will have occasional misunderstandings. A weekly parent/nanny meeting (it need only be 15 minutes or so) can relieve the nanny's anxiety about how or when to deal with these bumps. It's also a good time to catch each other up on the child's life—funny things he said or did, first bites of a particular food, or new friends made.

**A CLEARLY DEFINED SCOPE OF EMPLOYMENT.** How many years do you anticipate needing the nanny? Are you planning on having more children? Will you be sending your child to preschool? Will anyone's schedule be changing in a way that will impact the nanny's job (for instance, Mom returning to full-time work)? Is your family planning on moving within the next year or so? The more you can tell the nanny the better, so that neither of you will be surprised or feel exploited later on.

## What Nannies Fear

Once the nanny is ensconced in your house and your child's heart, she will probably be very reluctant to quit, even if she is dissatisfied. However, every nanny has her breaking point. The following are emotional land mines that nannies particularly dread. If you bring them up during the interview, it will put her at ease.

**LACK OF RESPECT.** "I want to be treated as an adult and a professional, not like one would treat a teenage babysitter," says Leah H. "Respecting the contract is huge. Things should never just be changed without some notice or discussion." During the interview, you can show respect by behaving as you would if you were interviewing someone for an office job and by assuring the nanny that she will get a written contract if she is hired.

**LACK OF SUPPORT FROM PARENTS FOR DISCIPLINING THE CHILD.** A good way to tackle this topic during the interview is simply to acknowledge it: "We want to be consistent with discipline, and we want you to feel supported in what we ask you to do. Our tactics will probably evolve over time, but we will always keep you in the loop." If you already have a system of discipline in place, you should describe it to her and ask if she feels comfortable with it.

**MICROMANAGING THE NANNY.** Looking over a nanny's shoulder and second-guessing her decisions will make her tense and resentful. "One mom left me a note every day (sometimes 10 pages long) picking apart everything I did wrong," recalls April Mirabile, a Massacheusetts nanny. This seems to be a particular problem for stay-at-home moms who employ nannies. If you can honestly assure the nanny that you won't micromanage her, do so.

**INVASION OF PRIVACY, PARTICULARLY VIDEOTAPING WITHOUT TELLING THE NANNY.** Secretly videotaping a nanny is a horribly invasive thing to do. Most nannies will quit if they find out you've done this. Some will put up with being videotaped if they know about it, but they won't like it. There are less abrasive ways to check up on the nanny, as we will discuss later in this chapter. Live-in nannies should be assured that their rooms will be off-limits to children and other household members unless they are specifically invited in.

**EXPECTING THE NANNY TO PERFORM EXTENSIVE HOUSECLEANING DUTIES.** Some parents, especially those who are at work all day, don't realize how much time it takes to keep a house clean. Bear in mind that every half hour the nanny spends with a vacuum cleaner is a half hour your child is spending alone or in front of the TV.

---

### YOUR LEGAL RESPONSIBILITIES

Some people pay their nanny cash under the table and entirely ignore their tax obligations, but they do so at their own risk. Once you are an employer, you are legally required to pay:

- **SOCIAL SECURITY AND MEDICARE TAXES.** These apply when the nanny's annual wages exceed $1,100 and are currently equal to 15.3 percent of the nanny's pay. In theory the amount is split between nanny and employer, but since so many nannies earn very little money, many employers pay 100 percent of these taxes themselves.

- **FEDERAL AND STATE UNEMPLOYMENT-INSURANCE TAXES.** These apply when the nanny earns more than $1,000 in a calendar quarter. Federal tax is minimal—less than $100 a year—and state taxes vary.

In addition, the nanny must file income taxes quarterly (except in California). If she doesn't want to do this, you can withhold taxes from her paychecks.

The IRS will provide you with information about getting an employer ID number and setting yourself up. Call them at 800-829-3676 and ask for Form SS-4 and Publication 926. Then you'll need to call your state tax authorities or your accountant and ask which forms your state requires. In general these taxes must be filed quarterly, and federal and state deadlines often don't coincide. If it's all too much of a hassle, you can hire a service to handle the paperwork for you. Home/Work Solutions (800-626-4829; 4NannyTaxes.com) and Breedlove and Associates (800-723-9961; breedloveinc.com) are two that specialize in "nanny tax" compliance.

## Interview Questions

The key to interviewing anyone, including a nanny, is to frame most of your questions in an open-ended way. The questions should prompt the nanny to explain her reasoning, experience, judgment, and preferences. Before you begin interviewing her, briefly describe the parameters of the job (ages of the children, whether both parents work, whether she'll need to drive), but don't go into detail. You'll only do that if you're satisfied with the nanny's responses during the interview.

The following list covers issues that are fundamental for any family. Before your interview, think about additional questions that would address your family's specific needs.

- Is being a nanny your primary career goal right now?
- What made you decide to become a nanny?
- Have you had any formal training in child development?
- How many nanny jobs have you had in the past?
- Describe some of those jobs. What did you like about your employers? What did you dislike about them?
- Describe some of the children with whom you have worked.
- What types of activities do you enjoy doing with children?
- What are some problems you have had to resolve in your other positions?
- How would you spend a typical day with a child the age of ours?
- What types of discipline have you found to be effective?
- What do you enjoy doing on your time off?
- Do you smoke?
- Do you have any allergies?
- Do you have any health restrictions we should know about?
- Are you trained in first aid and CPR?
- Have you been tested for TB?
- The baby has been crying for twenty minutes and doesn't appear to be hungry, tired, or wet. What would you do?
- The two-year-old is thirty minutes into a tantrum. How would you handle it?
- The toddler has fallen and hurt her arm. Both parents are at work. What would you do?

And, if applicable:

- Do you have a driver's license?
- Do you own a car?
- Do you have auto insurance?

- Are the safety features on the car current and in working condition? (You should double-check this yourself and instruct the nanny on how to properly attach the child seat.)
- Have you ever been in an automobile accident?

## Magic Words and Deeds

Experienced nannies are veterans of many interviews and have learned to look for certain words and behaviors that bode well for them. The following will raise your value in the eyes of the nanny.

**TELL HER THAT YOU CARE A GREAT DEAL ABOUT YOUR CHILDREN'S HAPPINESS AND WELL-BEING.** Don't assume the nanny already knows this. Nannies experience a great deal of anxiety when they must care for children whose parents neglect them, and they look for reassurance on interviews that this isn't the case. Says Leah H., "Some people just want a nanny so they can get away from their kids. I want to know that the people I'm working for are not like that."

**APPROACH THE INTERVIEW IN A PROFESSIONAL MANNER.** Be prepared to discuss hours, compensation, overtime, sick pay, and vacations. "I want to know that they are looking at this as an employer/employee relationship," says Leah H. "A lot of families expect you to just fall in love with them and not consider the financial portion of the arrangement."

**TAKE YOUR TIME.** The list of questions in the previous section may seem long, but good nannies expect to be queried closely about their child-rearing views and experience. Rushing through the interview signals that you don't value your child's welfare or the nanny's job.

**ASK THE HARD QUESTIONS.** "Parents never ask if I am CPR or First Aid certified," says nanny Jennifer Sibre. "They should ask if I know where the nearest hospital is, how would I react in an emergency, and can I stay calm under pressure. Parents rarely ask about my driving record or if I have ever been involved in a car accident. They tend to ask the 'safe' questions." Tough questions don't insult a good nanny, they reassure her that you are a caring, conscientious parent.

**GIVE HER A GLIMPSE OF YOUR RELATIONSHIP WITH YOUR CHILDREN.** "I always pay close attention to how parents interact with their children," says April Mirabile. "I also like to see if the parents and the children have manners."

Suppose the nanny you are interviewing appears to be a perfect candidate. You delve into the issues discussed earlier in the chapter, and she seems to be on your wavelength. What can you say to make your job offer especially appealing? Salary is the biggest carrot, but there are other perks that might persuade a nanny to say yes. You could offer to:

- Supply a credit card in her name for child-related expenses. A common complaint among nannies is that they must foot the bill for their charge's expenses and then nag the parents to reimburse them. A credit card erases that worry and will make a big difference to the nanny.
- Pay for her airfare home once a year.
- Provide automatic raises every six months.
- Provide her with a cell phone.
- Pay for a gym membership.
- Let a live-in nanny have some say in the design of her quarters—for instance, let her choose the paint color and linens.
- If the nanny has children, pay for their yearly medical checkups.
- Supply incentives for long-term employment. One family promised a car to the nanny if she stayed two years. If you

don't have that kind of money, you might offer an all-expenses-paid vacation (even a three-day vacation is a nice perk) after two years of service, tickets to a theme park after each year, or a sizable gift certificate to a department store.

## Absolute No-No's

Because most of the middle-class people who employ nannies aren't used to hiring household "help," things can get a little unfocused during the interview. The more prepared and professional you are, the more confident the nanny will feel about working for you. To that end:

**DON'T TALK TOO MUCH.** Ask questions, then listen. The time to talk about your family at length is after you have decided that the nanny might be a good match.

**DON'T BE SO DESPERATE THAT YOU GET SLOPPY.** Deborah B., a nanny in Georgia, says, "I think a lot of times the pressure of having to find child-care ASAP makes parents less discriminating than they might be otherwise. If they seem desperate for someone to start, if they won't say specifically why the previous nanny left, and if they seem unsure about job specifics, I know I won't want to work there."

**DON'T DISAGREE WITH YOUR SPOUSE DURING THE INTERVIEW.** "Sometimes if I ask what methods of discipline they use or plan on using, they realize they do not agree with their spouse," says Leah H. All parents have disagreements, particularly when it comes to discipline, but if those disagreements erupt during the very first interview it doesn't bode well for the nanny.

**DON'T GET TOO PERSONAL.** "Questions about boyfriends, when I plan to marry or have children, or my religious beliefs—these make me wary because I feel they may try and control other aspects of my life," says Jennifer Sibre. The boyfriend issue is important, but rather than querying the nanny about it you might simply explain your house rules regarding boyfriends.

**DON'T DRESS OR BEHAVE INAPPROPRIATELY.** "The most alarming thing was when a mom lit up a cigarette while holding her baby and then offered me a drink," recalls Leah H. "I guess that can be summed up as being too open. There are other things that fall into that category as well—doing the interview in boxers or pajamas, swearing, or telling personal information. I don't mind these things after taking a job. I'm working in people's homes and expect to see some intimate parts of their lives, but there should be a certain level of professionalism to start."

## On Probation

Even if you fall in love with your prospective nanny, make sure to tell her during the interview that there will be a two-part probation period. Part one will last one week. That way, you can sever the relationship quickly if it becomes obvious that you have made a mistake. Part two can last two or three months. In that time you should be able to ascertain whether you can live with this woman and entrust her with the care of your children.

After your initial interview, you will probably want to have the nanny back to your home for one more meeting, when you can introduce her to your children if she hasn't yet met them and present her with a written work agreement. Your agreement should include:

- Days and hours of employment
- Salary
- Probation periods
- General duties
- How overtime and vacations will be handled

- Dates when performance will be evaluated (usually every six months)
- Dates when raises will be given (usually every six months or once a year)
- Dates when the agreement will be reviewed by nanny and parents (this can occur at the same time as performance reviews)

The diligent parent will use the probation period not only to get to know the nanny but also to check up on her. This friendly surveillance doesn't need to involve video cameras. Instead, use the element of surprise. If possible, check on the nanny in person, unannounced, at various times during the day. Have your friends or neighbors stop by, too. When the weather is warm, nannies often congregate at a local park during lunchtime; if you or your spouse works nearby, you might join them every now and then. (It's quite lovely to chat with the ladies and watch the toddlers play in the sand.) Call at different times during the day and listen for the background noises. Is the TV always on? How about the radio? Is the baby crying? Do the toddlers sound out of control? What about the nanny—does she sound cheerful and relaxed, or stressed out?

It's best if you can be home with the nanny for the first few days or a week. While you are showing her your daily routine, you'll see how capable she is and whether your child is bonding with her. You will also get a sense of her personal life, not only by chatting with her but also by noticing how often she gets phone calls and the nature of those calls. If she appears to be involved in an ongoing feud with someone, especially a boyfriend or husband, the safest move is to let her go.

Allow the nanny some time on her own during this first week, and if she is from another country, make sure she knows how to operate your appliances. Controls for the thermostat, washer/dryer, toaster oven, and microwave may not be obvious to someone who hasn't spent much time in the United States. You can also use this week to introduce the nanny to neighbors, friends, and family members—anyone who may drop by when you're not home. Whether she will be driving or not, you will want to show the nanny around the neighborhood.

## As Time Goes By

All parents eventually realize that there is no reliable learning curve when it comes to raising children. The years you spend figuring out how to coax child number one to sleep at night might be entirely wasted on child number two, who sleeps easily but refuses to eat anything but white foods. Your child will undoubtedly present the nanny with unique challenges, no matter how experienced the woman is. That's why it is so crucial to keep the lines of communication open. The nanny needs to feel that if she makes a mistake she can confide in you, and if you have a problem with something she's done you will tell her about it and let her make the necessary changes. A 15-minute meeting at the end of each week is enough to accomplish this.

As the months and years progress, how can you make your nanny feel appreciated? Little things count more than you might imagine. "I love the fact that my current employers give my dog presents during the holidays and celebrate my birthday with me," says April Mirabile.

"Offer little bonuses, not just cash but something that shows you pay attention to your nanny's hobbies," suggests Jennifer Sibre. "Once a parent bought me tickets to a local show and I was really blown away that she remembered I loved *Les Mis*. She also left little notes around saying how much she appreciated things I did."

"Say thank you!" says Deborah B. "Financial incentives

are always good, but verbal appreciation, small gifts, occasional chances to leave early, and acknowledgment that you do your best for them and they appreciate it can make my day." Movie passes, restaurant or bookstore gift certificates, even a box of Girl Scout cookies will go a long way toward making your nanny feel loved and valued. When she finally leaves, as one day she must, your eyes may be teary but your heart will be at peace. For if you've treated her right, she may still be willing to babysit.

**TEACHER**

BIG FUN IN LITTLE CHAIRS

In many ways, a parent-teacher conference is like a bad date: The gnawing anxiety as you wait for the door to open. Your pounding heart as the teacher offers you a pint-sized chair. Then the conference itself, which consists of a few hurried pleasantries followed by a rote performance—she flashes a few tests, flips though some of your child's work, and rattles off the upcoming curriculum. You nod attentively, but all the while your mind is racing: *Does she like me? Does she like my child? How do I compare to all the other parents?* And then, *Wow! That was over fast*.

Many parents see their child's teacher only at the conference, so there is no denying that one should attempt to wring the maximum benefit from it. It's just as important, however, to know how and when to move beyond the conference.

## Behind the Scenes: "No, Really, We *Love* Parents"

Parent-teacher conferences are designed to help you and the teacher join forces for the sake of your child's education. The cause is noble, but teachers have very mixed feelings about these meetings. They are often just as nervous as you are, and some are downright intimidated by parents. The younger the teacher, the more nervous she is likely to be, but the great majority of teachers feel at least some trepidation about conference week.

They have lots of reasons to resist. For starters, there is the extra paperwork they must crank out for the occasion. During conference week, the typical teacher assembles individual folders of test results, written work, drawings, and progress reports for 20–35 children. The conferences are also emotionally draining for teachers, who must navigate the psyches of six or seven sets of parents every afternoon. Some mothers and fathers have unrealistic expectations and blame the teacher if their child isn't labeled "gifted" by the first grade. Others seem oblivious to their children's schoolwork. Some spouses are on the warpath with each other and try to force the teacher to pick sides. A good number of parents are well-meaning but so ill-informed that the teacher spends most of the conference explaining basic teaching methods and grading systems. A few parents are outright hostile. In some regions, there is a language barrier between the teachers and many of the parents.

Underlying these frustrations is another, deeper conflict. Until fairly recently, the feeling among many teachers was that they knew what was best for a child's education and that parents should, for lack of a better term, butt out. Studies done over the past ten years, however, have shown that parental involvement is an important factor in students' success. It is no longer acceptable for teachers to merely tolerate parents or brush aside their input. Some schools even have programs specifically designed to foster parental involvement. Your child's teacher may welcome this new togetherness or she may harbor resentment about it.

Teachers, then, bring a fair amount of baggage to the parent-teacher relationship. Parents who want to get the most out of the conference need to be aware of this and plan accordingly.

## Timing

During conference week you're likely to be meeting with an exhausted teacher who offers you a canned presentation designed to answer only the most basic questions. Therefore, the ideal time for a parent-teacher conference is any time *except* conference week. There are several ways to accomplish this.

When the conference notice comes, you can simply ask to reschedule. Putting a week or two between your meeting and conference week will give the teacher time to recover. Don't worry about imposing on her—with so many parents working these days, it's not unusual for some to ask to reschedule. If your life is very hectic and you might only get this one chance to meet with your child's teacher, it is vital that the conference be leisurely and the teacher fresh and focused on your child.

Another approach is to meet during conference week but plan on asking the teacher for a follow-up meeting several weeks later. This way, you can use the twenty minutes to get a general sense of your child's progress without feeling pressured. Concentrate on establishing a rapport with the teacher, take notes if you like, and save your important questions for the follow-up meeting.

Finally, you can jump-start the process by scheduling a "get-to-know-you" meeting with the teacher four to six weeks after the school year begins. At this point, the teacher will have had some time to observe your child. When conference week arrives, you will already know which issues are most important to your child and will be able to zero in on those.

Do not wait until the conference to tell the teacher if anything unusual is going on in your home, however. Let her know immediately if there is a new baby, a serious illness, if the parents are separating, or if the child has allergies or any other medical conditions that could affect her behavior in school.

**THE LIST**

Most teachers advise parents to write down the questions they want to ask at the conference. The following list covers most of the basics you will need to know about your child's development.

- Is my child performing at grade level?
- Does she pay attention in class?
- What part of the curriculum does my child like most? Least?
- Does my child participate in class discussions?
- Does she attend to task? ("Attend to task" means to work on class assignments steadily without getting distracted or giving up.)
- Have you noticed any special behavior problems?
- How does my child get along with the other children in class?
- Does my child express herself artistically? Does she enjoy drawing, painting, dance, or music?
- Is there anything I can do to help my child do better?

## Mastering Grade-Speak

The biggest waste of time in the parent-teacher conference occurs when the teacher has to explain the grading and testing systems. The exact meaning of terms like *rubric*, *stanine*, and *standardized test* confound many parents and frustrate quite a few teachers as well. Grading systems differ from state to state and even from district to district, but most use variations of the following.

**RUBRIC.** A rubric is a list of the skills needed to master a subject at a particular grade level. It is meant to clarify to both the child and the teacher exactly what is expected of the child by the end of the school year. Rubrics are usually broken down into four scoring levels:

1 = **NOT PROFICIENT**

2 = **PARTIALLY PROFICIENT**

3 = **PROFICIENT**

4 = **ADVANCED**

Sometimes the rubric score is used as a grade, especially in early elementary years. For older children, rubrics are used as "scoring devices" that are a partial basis for letter grades. There is no nationwide standard for rubrics—sometimes the school district provides them and sometimes teachers devise their own. In public schools, the district's rubrics for each grade level are usually available from the teacher or the front office.

**STANDARDIZED TEST (STANFORD 9, IOWA, AIMS, TAAS, CAT, ETC.).** Standardized tests assess how well a student is learning. There is no national test; each state is free to select or devise its own. States also differ as to which grade levels must be tested. At the parent-teacher conference you can ask whether your child will be tested and if there is anything you should do to help him or her prepare.

**PERCENTILE RANK.** Percentile rank is a way of comparing a child's scores to those of children in a "norm group" who took the standardized test when it was being developed. If your child has a percentile rank of 80, it means that 80 percent of the children in the norm group got a lower score than your child. Being in the eightieth percentile does *not* mean that your child answered 80 percent of the questions correctly.

**STANINE.** Stanines are the most baffling of the scoring systems. The word is short for "standard nine" and refers to the nine sections of a bell curve into which a child's test results may fall (see illustration). A stanine of 1, 2, or 3 is below average; 4, 5, or 6 is average; and 7, 8, or 9 is above average. Each stanine number indicates a range of performance, not a specific score.

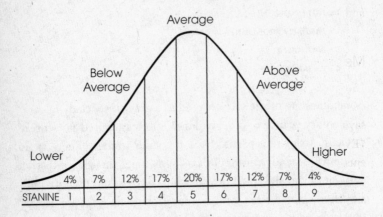

Entrance into G.A.T.E. (Gifted and Talented Education) programs often depends on a child's stanine score. You can ask the teacher what the rules are in your school district, but don't squander too much of your conference time on the topic. You can squander time later when you research it online or compare notes with other confused parents.

There is much controversy about the value of yearly standardized testing, particularly in the early grades, because young children learn at vastly different rates. A 1999 study conducted by the Michigan Association for Early Childhood Teachers found that only 58 percent of teachers believe test scores are useful when conferring with parents. The scores remain a focal point of parent-teacher conferences because parents expect to see them and because it's more time-efficient to show a list of a fourth grader's scores than it is to dissect his essay. If test scores, class work, and your child's behavior are all worrisome, the teacher will certainly give you a heads-up. However, if only his test scores are problematic, it may simply be that he is stressed out about taking standardized tests. Many young children are. Ask the teacher how other children are doing in comparison to yours, and ask if she thinks your child needs extra help.

## Magic Words and Deeds: The Conference

"Sometimes parents come to the conference with their own agendas and misinterpret what I say, and that can put up barriers," says Karen Ivy, who teaches fourth grade at a private school. "Even veteran teachers get very defensive if they don't know parents well and feel like they're being blindsided." When teachers get defensive, they close up. You are there to get their perspective, and you want them to be as candid as possible. Although you are in their territory, it is up to you to make them feel comfortable enough to tell you the whole truth about your child. The following strategies will help.

**FLATTER FIRST, ASK QUESTIONS LATER.** Every teacher wants to know she is making a difference. Therefore, if the first words out of your mouth are a compliment, you'll instantly gain her goodwill. Karen Ivy explains, "If a parent comes in and says, 'We showed your progress report to both sets of grandparents,' that just makes me glow. It makes all the effort and strain and anxiety worthwhile, to know that I've mattered."

"Positive feedback is very important for teachers because we certainly don't get it monetarily," observes sixth-grade teacher Marna Biederman.

**TELL THE TEACHER HOW MUCH YOUR CHILD TRUSTS HER.** Trust is a big issue for teachers. They like to know not only that you trust them with your child's education, but that your child trusts them, too. You can get this across by relating something your child has said about the teacher's skill, such as, "Hillary says you explain math better than any other teacher she's had." If you need ammunition, ask your child to tell you a few positive things about the teacher before you go to the conference.

**VOICE YOUR RESPECT.** Equality with parents is another major issue for teachers. "You wouldn't tell your dentist how to fill your tooth, but some parents who are not educators find it very comfortable to tell a teacher how she should be teaching," says Karen Ivy. "Some people forget that we're professionals, that we have degrees and credentials." Since this is such a sore spot, it pays to mention that you've noticed the teacher's expertise. Be as specific as you can: "I've been really impressed with the science curriculum this year, especially the rain forest section."

**GIVE FEEDBACK ABOUT YOUR CHILD.** "Both parties need to present positive ideas," says Maureen Van Evenhoven, who teaches kindergarten at an inner-city public school. She reports that some parents sit mutely, too tired or uninterested to contribute to the conversation. And the problem isn't unique to working-class moms and dads. At the private school where Karen Ivy teaches, some parents have a similarly passive attitude: "The tuition here is frightfully expensive. Parents think that because they're paying so much, everything should be taken care of for them."

The fact is that your child is competing with at least twenty others for the teacher's attention. She may know his academic strengths and weaknesses, but other information can help her see new ways to inspire him. You might mention his favorite books, computer games, TV programs, movies, sports, hobbies, music, his schedule, and household obligations such as caring for a sibling. The more information the teacher has about your child, the better she'll be able to teach him.

**USE POSITIVE LANGUAGE TO DESCRIBE YOUR CHILD, EVEN IF YOU ARE DISCUSSING A PROBLEM.** The way you perceive your child will have a great impact on the way the teacher perceives her. For instance, if the teacher reports that your daughter has been rowdy and undisciplined in class, you can respond honestly but put a positive spin on it: "Jenny is really enthusiastic, and that's one of the things we love about her. But we're trying to get her to learn some self-control at home, too. Do you have any suggestions?" Enlisting the teacher's help reinforces your faith in her. If you reply, "She's a handful, isn't she?" you are giving the teacher tacit permission to label your child *difficult* instead of *enthusiastic*. If that happens, the teacher may relax her efforts to work with your child.

**KEEP AN OPEN MIND.** "Put away your judgments of the teacher, the situation, and the school," advises Maureen Van Evenhoven. Don't assume that the teaching staff isn't committed just because the campus doesn't have a large grassy field, a new library, or lots of computers. Some of the most dedicated teachers work their magic in unlovely classrooms. Van Evenhoven, for example, spearheaded an innovative reading program at her inner-city campus.

**USE POSITIVE BODY LANGUAGE.** Yes, the chairs are small. But most people can manage to sit in them for twenty or thirty minutes without squirming. Teachers like it when you stay in your chair, look them in the eye, and pay attention to what they are saying. They resent it when parents stand and hover over them or wander around the room during the conference, scanning the walls for their child's artwork or essays. In other words, teachers want the same type of attentive behavior from you that they expect from your child.

## Absolute No-No's

When parents walk into the classroom for a parent-teacher conference, teachers instantly scan them for clues about their attitude. Will they be friendly or hostile? Open-minded or rigid? Throughout the meeting, the parents' words and behavior paint a picture that will follow them throughout their child's career at the school. "Parents don't think about the fact that teachers talk to one another," explains Marna Biederman. "You get your new class and other teachers will say, 'Oh, that father is so critical,' or, 'They're phonies.'" To foster warm relations with the teacher and avoid getting a bad reputation:

**DON'T ENTER THE CLASSROOM CLUTCHING A STACK OF YOUR CHILD'S PAPERS.** "When you see them with the child's papers in their hands, it means they're going to challenge you," notes Biederman. "Even if they only mean to come in and say, 'How lovely—he got a C,' that's not what's coming across when they walk in with those papers." If you must show the teacher your child's papers, keep them in your purse or otherwise concealed until you've established some rapport with her.

**DON'T CRITICIZE OTHER TEACHERS, THE PRINCIPAL, OR THE SCHOOL.** Why should a teacher feel greater allegiance to you than to the people she works with? Your criticism will probably make her feel defensive or mistrustful of you.

**DON'T CRITICIZE OTHER PARENTS OR CHILDREN.** Keep your questions focused on your child. If you believe a particular student is giving your child a hard time—for instance, bullying or teasing him— broach the subject calmly and give specific examples and the names of witnesses, if you have any. There are two sides to every conflict, and the teacher may be able to fill you in on the side you are unaware of.

**DON'T ACCUSE THE TEACHER OF PLAYING FAVORITES OR PICKING ON YOUR CHILD.** "We've heard the whole nine yards," says Ivy. "You don't like my child. You have it in for her. You have favorites. You like boys more than girls." Biederman recalls what happened when she told one mother that her daughter needed to raise her hand in class instead of blurting out the answers. The girl's mom retorted, "Well, I know something about *you*. Another parent told me, 'If Mrs. Biederman likes your child, you're golden, but if not, watch out!'" Outbursts such as this won't help your child. On the contrary, they will make teachers want to avoid you, which may mean avoiding or neglecting your child.

**DON'T FIB ABOUT YOUR CHILD.** No child is perfect, and most parent-teacher conferences include at least a few minutes' worth of criticism about the child. Unfortunately, some parents can't handle bad news. Their response, perhaps out of fear, is to deny any knowledge of their child's shortcomings. "This is a very common complaint in the teacher's lounge," says Biederman. "A parent will look at you with wide-open eyes and say, 'This is the first time anyone's ever said anything!'"

If your child has been in the school for more than one year, you can assume that prior to your meeting, his teacher has conferred with teachers from the previous years. If you feign ignorance about poor past performance or behavior, she will probably know you are lying. Your denial and lack of support may put a damper on her efforts to work with your child. Biederman elaborates: "You begin to think, 'I'm not really going to get anywhere with this parent.' In a funny way, it makes me stop trying to solve the problem, although I'll never stop trying to make the child's year happier."

## For Your Child's Future, Control Yourself

Your behavior at your child's school can have far-reaching effects on his education, especially if you plan to enroll him in a private school at some point. Says Marna Biederman, "Very often parents are not aware, even though I know my superiors have told them, that the middle schools to which their sixth-graders are applying really consider what the parents are like, not just what their pocketbooks are like. And there are some parents who are totally unable to control themselves when they come in to talk about their child."

A teacher at an exclusive girls' high school put it even more bluntly: "The admission interviews are to check out the parents, not the children. The staff wants to weed out the bullying parents who are going to cause everyone a lot of grief." Parent-teacher conferences are wonderful practice for those interviews.

## What If the Teacher Really Is a Monster?

First of all, she is not a monster. She is simply a "bad fit" with your child. This is the acceptable jargon at most schools, where your avenues for conflict resolution are few: the teacher and the principal. However, there are several strategies that can help you improve an unhappy situation. One cardinal rule is that the sooner you voice your concern, the more likely it is that your child can be moved to a different classroom. The first two weeks of the school year are usually considered to be flexible; after that, the principal will be less willing to accommodate you. If your child seems extremely distressed from the get-go (and doesn't make a habit of complaining about her new teacher every year), it may be shrewd to ask for a change right away.

If the problems don't bubble to the surface until later in the semester, try your best to work things out with the teacher and your child before speaking to the principal. Says Marna Biederman, "When [parents] go to the head of the school without talking to you, you just feel like killing them." There isn't much the principal can do anyway, aside from moving your child to another class. She certainly can't change whatever it is that's not working between your child and the teacher; only the teacher (and your child) can do that. Before you meet with the teacher, talk with other parents whose children had her in previous years.

They might be able to shed some light on her personality and give you suggestions about how best to deal with her. If your attempts fail, you can always insist that your child be moved after the winter break. Taking a child out of a class in the middle of the semester should be a last resort.

## Unsung Heroes

Most teachers are in the classroom because they feel a calling to be there. How many other professions inspire such a high level of commitment for such modest pay? Remember this when you are at the parent-teacher conference and throughout the school year, and tell the teacher she's doing a great job whenever you honestly can. In June, write a letter expressing your thanks. "If it's sincere, a letter means a great deal more to a teacher than a two-pound box of chocolates," says Biederman. Send a copy to the principal as well, so it becomes part of the teacher's record. From these small acts, your great reputation will be made.

# THERAPIST
## NO SLOUCH ON THE COUCH

Any one of us, regardless of background or intelligence, may experience bumps along the road of life that leave us feeling overwhelmed, powerless, or deeply unhappy. Our friends are getting glassy-eyed listening to our endless tales of woe and irritated that we haven't taken steps to remedy what ails us. One more weepy mug of beer and they might start charging for their time . . . and yet we delay calling a therapist. Although therapy is a common experience these days, some people still think it is an admission of failure. The vulnerability of the relationship strikes fear into our hearts: Will you be forced to confess your most intimate struggles to a stranger who does nothing but nod quietly and mumble, "Hmmm"? Will the therapist secretly think you're an idiot? How would you know?

Take a breath. Times have changed. Therapy itself has changed from the traditional psychoanalytic model (months or years of analysis intended to uncover the deep-seated roots of your dilemma) to a more goal- and results-oriented process. In part, the change has been driven by insurance companies, who usually expect therapeutic goals to be met in ten to twenty sessions or the patient picks up the tab. The revolution in pharmacology has also radically altered our views of the human mind and personality. The time-honored theories of inner conflict and neurosis have given way in great part to the ebb and flow of our neurotransmitters. If taking a mild antidepressant can significantly improve the way you feel and function in the world, most therapists see no problem with your trying it.

Therapy "patients" have changed as well. Today, someone seeking therapy is as much consumer as patient, a person who selects the best therapist for her needs, decides for herself if progress is being made, and determines when it is time to end the therapy. You may feel like a sick puppy, but the power is always in your hands.

## Behind the Scenes: Feeling for You

Abandon any lingering stereotypes of the bespeckled, goatee-scratching patriarch with x-ray vision into your soul. Therapists are mortals, subject to all the emotions and angst the rest of us feel. Many are motivated to become therapists by a desire to help others, and some are fueled by their own personal history of problems. There is a higher percentage of depression, anxiety, substance abuse, and inner turmoil among therapists than in the general population, yet that may not be an entirely bad thing. Many in the field believe that therapists with a history of personal problems are more sensitive to those types of issues in others and may be better therapists in the long run. It makes sense that people who have suffered are more sensitive to the suffering of others.

When a client trusts a therapist enough to truly open up, the relationship that develops between them provides a level of emotional satisfaction for the therapist that few other enterprises can match. "What they teach you in graduate school is such a fraction of what the relationship really becomes," says Seattle psychologist Linda Pietrafesa. "For example, in graduate school they say,

'Never become attached to your clients.' Well, that's BS. You become attached. . . . They say you'll learn how to leave it at the office and you do, you get better at that. But for that moment, that 50-minute hour, the person is profoundly influencing you."

The dynamic that occurs between therapist and patient was recognized by Sigmund Freud, who termed it *transference* and *countertransference*. According to Freud, transference occurs when a patient's response to a therapist reflects feelings about people who were important to the patient in childhood, especially parents. Countertransference is when the therapist's responses to the patient reflect feelings about important people in the therapist's life. In traditional psychoanalysis, the therapist was trained to maintain a completely neutral façade, letting the patient regress into a "transference neurosis" that supposedly would lead to a breakthrough about the roots of the patient's problems. That's where the stereotype of the infuriating, noncommittal, "Ahhh . . . so," analyst comes from. Today, many therapists reject such strict definitions of transference and countertransference. What the terms mean in a practical sense is that therapists are human and will have human reactions to you, just as you will to them.

Countertransference can be a problem for young, inexperienced therapists because they are often slow to recognize what's happening. Los Angeles psychologist Wendy Mogel recalls her own introduction to the dilemma, which occurred during the 1970s. "I had this older woman at the clinic. One of the first things she said was, 'I hate those damn Beatles and all these young people who listen to this trash music.' I was just beginning my training, and *I* hated *her*." Mogel's supervisors helped her clarify her countertransference: being young herself, Mogel was stung by her client's words. "I came to see how all this was the client's defense against being rejected, against feeling old—how much she hated being old, and her unconscious envy. We got to love each other by the end, but she was a big challenge for me."

A good therapist is a professional and will control his own emotions appropriately, but in a revealing survey reported in a 1993 article in the *New York Times*, a third of 285 therapists admitted hating or fearing at least one of their patients. More than 80 percent confessed to having feelings of anger toward patients, feelings of sexual attraction or arousal, or worry that patients might physically harm them. The biggest fear was that a patient might commit suicide.

Fortunately, therapists also develop a deep regard for most of their patients. This bond is perhaps the most rewarding aspect of the therapist's job. "Your patients change you," says Linda Pietrafesa. "I'm very grateful for that. When someone reveals a very dark secret and trusts that I will not judge them but listen to them—listen to their side, how it's influenced their life—it has a profound effect on me. I love my work. I really look forward to my days and my clients."

"It's a real privilege to hear the stories and have that level of trust," says Wendy Mogel. "Whatever is going on outside, it's wonderful to be in the consulting room."

## Credentials Are Essential

It's not hard to find a therapist. A recommendation from a trusted friend or your doctor is often the most reliable source, but you can also use the yellow pages or referral services to help you sort through the lengthy list of possibilities. Once you begin perusing the pages, you'll notice that the therapists' names are followed by letters, sometimes lots of them. These represent various credentials, and it's important to know what they stand for. Although each state has a licensing requirement for practicing therapists, states vary widely as to who is legally allowed to hang out a shingle. Some states require only a Master of Education, a degree with literally no psychotherapeutic training at all.

Therapists' fees can vary greatly. The more education the therapist has, the higher the cost will be. Credentials are not the only predictors of skill, however. There is an art to the practice of therapy, and people with relatively modest credentials are sometimes extremely effective. Experience is always an asset in a therapist. According to Linda Pietrafesa, "I personally wouldn't see anyone who didn't have at least 10 or 15 years at it."

The following credentials are those you are most likely to see on your search.

**PSYCHIATRIST (M.D.).** A psychiatrist is a physician who has gone through medical school as well as training in psychology. They are the most expensive practitioners, with hourly fees of $100 or more. In the old days, all psychiatrists were trained in the traditional psychoanalytic method: delving into your subconscious and analyzing your conflicts. You can still find a psychoanalyst if you want that type of therapy, but today psychiatrists are primarily prescribers and monitors of medication. They often work in conjunction with other types of therapists who provide the hands-on therapy for people who are using both medications and psychotherapy. This two-pronged approach is much more cost-effective for the consumer and insurance company.

**PSYCHOLOGIST (PH.D.).** A psychologist is a clinical practitioner with a doctorate in psychology. They are usually well-educated in the various theories of personality and human development and have extensive training in the different types of treatments. Psychologists cannot prescribe medications but should be able to tell you if they think you would benefit from them. If so, the psychologist can refer you to a psychiatrist for the prescription you need.

**CLINICAL SOCIAL WORKER (M.S.W.; L.C.S.W.).** A clinical social worker is a master's-level counselor who has done postgraduate work with a focus on a particular discipline such as marriage counseling, grief counseling, family counseling, or individual counseling.

Many work for hospitals and large nonprofit agencies; many also do freelance work. If you open the yellow pages to *psychotherapists*, the majority of individuals listed will be M.S.W.'s (Master of Social Work) or L.C.S.W.'s (Licensed Clinical Social Worker). Experienced clinical social workers can be an excellent choice for your counseling needs and are more affordable than psychologists or psychiatrists.

**PSYCHIATRIC NURSE PRACTITIONER (R.N.; M.S.).** A psychiatric nurse practitioner has attended both nursing school and an additional two years of postgraduate work to earn an M.S. in mental health. Many of these R.N.'s practice individual counseling, and their medical training gives them insight as to the biological roots of mental illness and emotional problems. Some states allow them to prescribe medications. Their fees are similar to those of clinical social workers.

**MARRIAGE AND FAMILY COUNSELOR.** These counselors must have a master's degree, but it can be in one of a variety of disciplines, such as education, social work, or psychology. They should have extensive training in this type of therapy and should have a license.

---

### BEFORE YOU REACH FOR A PILL . . .

Dozens of medications are available for major mental illnesses such as chronic depression, chronic anxiety, bipolar disorder, and schizophrenia. A psychiatrist is the best person to oversee these medications. He will understand how various drugs interact with one another and which can safely be used to treat a condition the drug is not traditionally prescribed for. Although your regular M.D. could write a prescription for you and may be willing to do so, it is safer to consult a psychiatrist. You might need to get the medication adjusted or try a different one before you are entirely satisfied, and chances are your M.D. won't have the expertise to fine-tune these medications.

If you are seeking therapy from a community mental health center, there is another issue to consider. Many of these centers can't get reimbursed by insurance companies unless you have been diagnosed with a major mental health disorder and are taking medication for it. That means you could be incorrectly diagnosed and overprescribed by the health center's psychiatrist.

Whether you see a psychiatrist in private practice or at a community health center, try to do a little research on the medication before you start taking it. If you feel too overwhelmed, ask a friend or one of the health-care workers at the center to assist you.

## Magic Words and Deeds: Interviewing a Therapist

You are about to call a therapist for the first time. Even if you're feeling weak, miserable, and one step away from flinging yourself off the nearest bridge, you still control the process. It's standard practice to interview therapists over the phone, and some even offer a free face-to-face session that lasts about twenty minutes. If you are depending on insurance to cover the cost of your therapy and won't be able to continue if you have to pay out of pocket, these interviews are especially important.

Just as you want to make certain you're selecting the right person, the therapist will want to be reasonably sure she can help you. To that end, she will expect you to ask questions that reveal the type of help you need. The more specific you are, the better.

If factors such as the age, gender, or race of the therapist matter to you, try to select accordingly. Many people feel more comfortable with someone of a similar background or life experience. Even if you like someone immediately, it's a good idea to compare that therapist with at least one other before making a commitment.

In your first conversation, ask the therapist:

- What are your credentials?
- Where were you educated?
- How many years have you been practicing?
- Are you licensed? (You can easily verify that with the state licensing entity.)
- How much do you charge?
- Do you have a sliding scale?
- Do you accept my insurance?
- What is your treatment philosophy? (If you don't understand some of her terms or the philosophy in general, ask her to rephrase it.)
- How much experience do you have treating people with my type of issues? How many such patients are you currently treating?
- Can you give me a ballpark figure for how much time people with my problem generally stay in therapy?
- How do you set therapy goals with your patients?
- How do you handle it if it appears the goals are not being met?

You will get the most useful responses by asking questions that elicit specific information rather than just a "yes" or "no" answer. For example, if you ask, "Do you do family therapy?" a therapist could answer yes when, in fact, she has no families on her caseload but is simply *willing* to do that type of therapy. Instead ask,

"What percentage of your practice is family therapy?" You want someone with actual, hands-on experience with your specific issues.

A good therapist should answer all your questions directly, willingly, and objectively. Beware of any beating around the bush or glib answers such as, "All my patients meet their treatment goals." She should not try to hustle you into therapy, but leave the decision completely up to you.

As you are gathering information, you will notice that you feel more rapport with some therapists than others. Because therapy is such a vulnerable relationship, you want the person to be more than experienced and knowledgeable. Is she warm and animated when she speaks? Does she sound interested in you? Is she vague or distracted? Do you feel intimidated by her? Does she have a sense of humor? Does she seem to be answering your questions thoughtfully, or is she just repeating a canned rap? It may be hard to evaluate all these things during a fifteen-minute conversation, but try to keep them in mind before you call. When you hang up, take a minute to pause and reflect. Do you feel optimistic after the conversation?

Expect some questions from the therapist as well. She will want to know what problems have brought you to seek therapy, what you expect out of the experience, and, briefly, what your goals are. She may want to know if you've had therapy before. Try to think about these things ahead of time so your answers are as succinct and articulate as possible. You don't want this brief conversation (trust me, she is looking at her watch) to *be* therapy nor do you want to relinquish control of the conversation to the therapist. Although it is fair for her to gather information that will help guide you both to a good decision, you are still the consumer purchasing a service. Make sure you get all the information *you* need.

## Absolute No-No's: Interviewing a Therapist

Interviewing a therapist over the phone is not like interviewing any other professional. These people are highly attuned to the nuances of human behavior and will be the first to admit that certain attitudes on the part of the client make their job harder. "If the therapist has too much countertransference, she can't be of help to the patient because it crosses the boundary between a useful source of data and prejudice," says Wendy Mogel. Translation: If she senses that you will be a client who triggers many negative feelings in her, she may suggest that you look for help elsewhere.

Which clients come off poorly in that first phone call? "Help-rejecting complainers," says Mogel. "That's a standard term. It's a person who says, 'I've had six therapists before seeing you and they have all let me down in one way or another, or exploited me, or failed me, and I know you're going to be the one who can save me.' Beginning therapists have what's called rescue fantasies, so they imagine they're going to be the one. They are seduced into that delusional thinking." Experienced therapists rarely welcome clients who admit to having a long history of disappointment with other therapists.

Linda Pietrafesa points to ambivalence as a turn-off. "A woman left a message saying, 'My friends said I really need to see you, so I guess I do, so I guess you should call me back.' She did all this guessing and qualifying." In Pietrafesa's opinion, a client's motivation to change is a fundamental part of successful therapy. People who hem and haw in the very first phone call are rarely motivated, and she advises them to wait before taking the plunge. "If you're not ready, don't waste your time and money."

## Magic Words and Deeds: The Sessions

Once you have made the decision to begin therapy, there are certain rules of etiquette that will keep the process professional and focused. Psychologists call this the *frame*. The two most important rules are to be on time for your appointments and to pay your therapist promptly. The therapist is responsible for the frame as well, by beginning and ending the sessions on time and billing you on a regular schedule. If the therapist is chronically late, the client won't feel secure in the relationship. If the client is often late for appointments or in paying bills, the therapist will feel resentful. Either way, it damages the trust that is necessary for therapy to succeed. Clients should also give the therapist at least 24 hours' notice if they need to cancel an appointment.

Beyond the rules of the frame, Linda Pietrafesa cites motivation and curiosity as key attributes of people who gain from therapy: "Curiosity about themselves, about what's getting in the way of their having a more effective life. Also, a willingness to trust the therapist."

Trusting the therapist is essential, but good therapists realize that it may take some time. "It's influenced by an individual's experiences either with other therapists or their family," says Pietrafesa. "If they couldn't trust others—like their parents—because of abuse, it will take longer to build the trust with me. That's reasonable. That's something I totally expect."

Most people go to therapy once a week, every other week, or once a month. After the first few sessions, where you and the therapist get to know each other and you acquaint her with the basic plot, characters, and conflicts of your story, you may find yourself scheduled for a session and having very little to say. Given the cost of therapy, it's tempting to cancel. Try to resist this. Seeing your therapist on a "good" day can be extremely rewarding.

"What I do as a patient myself is write things down during the week," says Wendy Mogel. "Then I come and dump it all out, and a pattern I haven't seen is revealed to me by the therapist." Feeling as if you have nothing to say might also be a clue that you're having some resistance to the therapy. "Part of the frame is the consistency," says Mogel. "Seeing the therapist every week at the same time, completely unrelated to the level of crisis you're in, is how deep levels of structural change in character and emotions will get made. Also, when you're feeling stronger you can do a different kind of work than you might be able to do when you're feeling more emotional or upset."

Finally, it's a good idea to establish goals early on and check frequently to make sure you are on track. During the first session, you might ask the therapist to help you prioritize your issues and set milestones for each goal. This structure will help you focus your efforts on the good days.

## Absolute No-No's: The Sessions

Being late, not paying the therapist on time, or canceling at the last minute are the most obvious barriers to a good relationship. If you're motivated to be there in the first place, these are easy to avoid. More difficult is the issue of honesty. Being honest—to yourself and the therapist—can be extremely painful. In fact, your inability to be honest about your own feelings or actions may be one of the reasons you are in therapy. Therapists know this, but they are not mind readers, and after a while your lack of candor may wear your therapist down. Linda Pietrafesa points out, "I'm only able to respond to what people are willing to reveal to me. If I'm working on a behavioral issue and the person says, 'Oh yes, I'm doing this,' but he's avoiding eye contact, I would definitely be able to pick that up. But if a person is used to lying to him- or herself as a style of life, I wouldn't be able to pick it up right off the bat. It would take me a while to know the person, and a willingness to challenge them."

Being overly defensive about your feelings and actions can also impede the process, according to Mogel. "Defensiveness is one of their symptoms and they wouldn't be coming to you if they didn't have symptoms," she observes. "It's layers of an onion in psychotherapy and you're peeling away the onion as the trust grows between patient and therapist." However, she notes that "the more defensive people are, the more boring the session is because you're not talking about the real things." It's not your job to keep the therapist entertained, but it is to your advantage to keep her intellectually and emotionally involved. If months go by and you still don't trust her enough to stop being defensive and start telling the truth, you might need to change therapists.

## Oops, Wrong Therapist

"Ending up with the wrong therapist is sort of like marrying the wrong person," says Mogel. "You can slip into it and then it's going to be really hard to change it." Yet there are certain danger signs that won't show up until you've had a session or two. Consider halting your treatment if the therapist:

- Is consistently late to appointments or cancels them
- Seems distracted or fatigued
- Can't remember the discussions or issues of prior sessions
- Seems too emotionally involved in your issues
- Talks excessively about her own problems and experiences
- Insists that you need more therapy if you don't want more
- Indulges in any type of sexual touching, innuendo, or overture

Sex between therapist and client is strictly taboo, and there are laws to reinforce this. But in a relationship that is by its nature so intimate, how can you tell whether the therapist is trying to seduce you or is merely being supportive? Be wary of a therapist who gives you longer than the scheduled hour or doesn't mind if you're late paying the bills, says Mogel. "If they're too helpful, like finding you a decorator," it could be a sign the therapist wants to be your friend (or more) rather than your counselor. Any time a therapist starts offering you special favors, the professional boundary has been breached and you should seriously consider changing therapists.

Go with your gut feeling. Therapy is a service you are paying for, and you don't have to continue with someone you don't feel a rapport with. You needn't provide a long-winded explanation to the therapist or feel apologetic about your decision to end the treatment. Just tell her, "I need to get input from someone else." No ethical therapist will pressure you to stay in a situation against your will.

If you believe that what a therapist is doing may be unethical or unlawful, it is your responsibility to report it to the clinic director, HMO, or local licensing entity.

## Cozy Couch or Pin Cushion?

The relationship with your therapist is unique. On one hand, she needs to create an environment that feels safe, nurturing, and accepting. On the other, she must challenge you to face those aspects of yourself that are at least partially responsible for your predicament. There are times during therapy when you might want to yell at your therapist or bolt from the room. Does that mean you have a lousy therapist? Probably not. More likely, you have reached a point in therapy where a painful growth spurt is about to occur, when you must face the stumbling blocks that have kept you from living a reasonably content life.

One mistaken assumption people often bring to the therapeutic relationship is that it is value neutral—that is, they assume the therapist's office is a place of total acceptance where the patient can spill her guts, confess behavior that is cruel or downright despicable, and the therapist will condone that behavior by never challenging it. A good therapist is value neutral about a patient's *feelings*, helping that patient to explore the roots and causes of a feeling without judgment. However, that therapist will challenge *actions* if they are hurtful, irresponsible, or illegal, and will encourage the patient to take a good hard look at himself with the goal of replacing harmful actions with productive ones. After all, that is one of the goals of therapy. Before dumping your therapist, ask yourself if the criticism you feel is about your feelings or your actions. The difference may be the difference between an effective and ineffective therapist.

People go to therapy because they are in pain and want the expertise of a professional to help them define their feelings, establish goals, see why they fail to reach those goals, and find workable solutions. The therapist *will* apply her values to that process. As psychotherapist Frank Pittman wrote in an article for *Psychology Today*, "Most psychotherapy is about values—about the value dilemmas of sane and ordinary people trying to lead a life amidst great personal, familial, and cultural confusion. The therapists who do psychotherapy effectively do so because they understand value conflicts and they convey, without having to preach about it, values that work." Some therapists achieve this by offering straightforward advice, while others prefer a more subtle approach, slowly nudging the patient to "discover" certain truths on his own. Either way, says Pittman, "psychotherapy involves applying the value system of the therapist to the dilemmas of the clients." That being the case, you may want to discuss your values while you are establishing your goals with your therapist. For instance, if you are going to therapy because you're struggling in your marriage and want to consider all options, including ending it, you may not want to engage a therapist who is strongly opposed to divorce.

Values—whether they are based on a personal sense of right and wrong or on a set of traditional beliefs—are integral to a normal person's psychological makeup. Part of therapy is learning to clarify and live by those values. When people live by their values, they have less conflict. It is a prickly process for most of us. A good therapist will help you get there as gently as possible but won't let you be a slacker. If your therapist's office is a cozy place to complain but the sessions continue for months with no end in sight, and you are no closer to your goals than you were at the beginning, it may be time to end therapy or find someone who is more effective. A therapist worth her salt will not let you drift along aimlessly. She will either offer to refer you to a colleague with a different approach or suggest that it may not be the right time in your life for therapy. In the end, you will need to be responsible for your own growth. It's up to you to find the most effective therapist and to evaluate and reevaluate along the way.

**REALTOR**

## ALWAYS ON THE SUNNY SIDE

In most cities, the Sunday paper, local magazines, bus benches, and even theater programs are full of ads placed by Realtors looking for new business. The ads have an eerie sameness—the faces staring out of them tend to look a little too eager, the smiles a tad too radiant, the eyes a little too bright with hunger. Everyone has heard about the big commissions Realtors earn, so it's no wonder they are practically jumping out of their billboards to grab your business. What many people don't know is that the commission is all most Realtors earn; they make no other salary. A star agent in an upscale market can become very wealthy selling real estate, but many Realtors are middle-income folks who get into the field because they like houses, enjoy interacting with people, and relish the freedom the job allows them. Whatever type of agent you choose to work with, the key to success is understanding his priorities and limits, and making sure he understands yours.

### Behind the Scenes:
### Working Hard for the Money

Satisfying customers and gaining their trust is how Realtors build a loyal clientele, but it has become more challenging in this age of

Internet access. Because it's so easy for people to view homes on-line and drive to open houses themselves, Realtors must prove that they are more than just neighborhood tour guides. According to Rhonna Robles, who has been selling real estate in Dallas for 26 years, "The biggest misconception of people who have not used a Realtor before is that they can do all this themselves and save the commission. If you have a good Realtor, they're going to save you money. They're going to help you get what you want and get a better mortgage. They really earn more than they make."

To convince consumers of this, the Realtor must woo her clients with a menu of skills and resources the average citizen does not possess. She must negotiate the deal, explain the legal transactions, and recommend home inspectors, appraisers, mortgage brokers, and the like. She must be patient, diplomatic, and acutely observant. Says Robles, "A lot of times I can tell what a client wants before the client himself knows, because I see how they physically react when we go in someplace. By the end of the day I may say, 'You keep telling me you like old houses, but the ones you get excited about are the new ones.'"

The majority of buyers and sellers hold nine-to-five jobs, so the Realtor must work evenings and weekends to be available whenever a client has time to view a home. A good Realtor is aware of every new listing and is prepared to swoop a prospective buyer into viewing it before another Realtor gets there. It's a constant hustle, and throughout all the excitement, disappointment, and emotional turmoil, the Realtor must remain upbeat and smiling.

Depending on the location and the housing market, the real estate business ranges from competitive to cutthroat. Each year, hundreds of new agents are licensed in every major metropolitan area. Seventy percent of these newbies will take down their shingle after only one year. The survivors are those who have the best general knowledge of the field and the neighborhood, who follow through, and who have enough drive to compete with established Realtors. Perhaps most important, successful Realtors have good working relationships with other Realtors. The field may be competitive, but there is also a lot of "I'll scratch your back if you scratch mine." Says Robles, "You want someone who's not just a shark, someone who's a really nice person and who the other agents are going to want to work with so you can get the inside scoop. When the market's hot, it's important to know about things before they hit so your client has a little more time to mentally prepare. Sharks may be tough negotiators, but in a hot market you don't need a tough negotiator. You're just trying to get a house and you're going to pay over asking price anyway."

Word-of-mouth recommendations account for 60 percent of an agent's clients, so it's crucial that she maintain a superior track record and a reputation for being honest, accessible, and eager to please. That means going the extra mile to deliver service. With just a bit of knowledge about how Realtors and the real estate transaction work, the ball is always in your court.

## Are They Worth the Commission?

People are sometimes taken aback when they learn that Realtors typically charge the seller a 6 percent commission. That's $18,000 for a $300,000 home. In a hot real estate market, homeowners chafe at the number, reasoning that the Realtor is merely juggling offers, signing some papers, and collecting a check. Why not just sell the home yourself and pocket the $18,000? Meanwhile, sellers in a slow market worry that they're getting too little for their home in the first place and wonder if it might not make more sense to stick a "For sale by owner" sign on their front lawn and do the legwork themselves.

There are pros and cons to selling a home yourself. Actually, there's just one pro: you get to keep the commission. The cons mostly have to do with your knowledge of the real estate industry (or lack thereof), your time, and your ability to negotiate. The typical real estate transaction has the potential to cost naive sellers thousands of dollars, because buyers undoubtedly *will* be using an agent, and that tilts the playing field in their favor. Any number of expenses and events are negotiable—closing costs, appraisals, the items that will stay in the house, the date the new owner will take possession, repairs, and much more. If you don't know what's negotiable, you won't know what to ask for.

Of course, if you have the time to research the process and you live in an area where the housing market is fairly healthy, there is nothing stopping you from listing your home yourself and hiring a property attorney to handle the contract. There are books and Web sites aplenty to help you through the process.

Understanding how the commission is handled may help you decide whether or not to go it alone. In most cases, the seller's agent and buyer's agent split a 6 percent commission. Each agent then splits that 3 percent with his or her parent company. (The cost of advertising and marketing the home comes out of the money that goes to the seller's company.) This means that an agent who sells a $300,000 home makes $4,500, not $18,000. It's still $18,000 out of your pocket, but it sheds a somewhat different light on value of the work the Realtor will be doing for you.

Is there any wiggle room in the commission? Sometimes. If you're a seller in a sluggish market, you might want to find an agent who is willing to pay an extra half percentage point to the buyer's agent in order to spur interest in your house. If you're a seller in a hot market, you might offer your Realtor 5 percent instead of the standard 6 (or even less, depending on the asking price of your home). "I'm more apt to negotiate if it's a big transaction and they're going to sell their house and buy one from me," says Rhonna Robles.

The general perception is that Realtors are rolling in money during a hot market, but that is not always the case. Yes, the Realtor will make more on the commission when a house sells, but a hot housing market is usually a tight housing market. There are fewer homes to divvy up among hungry Realtors. Most real estate transactions involve people who are selling a house and buying another one, which means that your Realtor undoubtedly has clients who are in the buyer category. This can translate into months of unpaid work for the Realtor for that particular client. In a hot market, it's not uncommon for 10 Realtors to bid on a single house; nine will walk away with nothing. A 5 percent commission on the sale of your house might sound just fine to a Realtor whose client roster happens to be heavy with buyers.

## Connecting with a Realtor: Buyers and Sellers

How do you find a Realtor whose style and expertise fit your needs? Whether you are buying a house, selling one, or both, a good start is to ask a few friends or acquaintances who have recently trod this path. If you don't have any personal recommendations, call an established real estate agency and ask for the names of Realtors who specialize in your chosen area of town. You can also attend a few open houses and evaluate how the attending agent shows the home, deals with potential buyers and other Realtors, and answers your questions. For more information on a particular agent's experience and focus, check their Internet house listings. They usually post a brief biography along with the ads.

Once you have narrowed your search to a few individuals, the interview process begins. Realtors expect to spend an hour or so chatting with potential clients on the phone. Be sure to ask about:

**CREDENTIALS.** Realtors are either agents or brokers. An agent must be eighteen years old, a high school graduate, and have passed a written exam on property laws and real estate transactions. A broker is licensed by the state real estate commission and allowed to open his own agency. Your agent or broker should, ideally, be a member of a professional group such as the National Association of Realtors, which has strict ethical guidelines. The letters after some Realtors' names refer to their specialties. For example, CRS stands for Certified Residential Specialist, ABR stands for Accredited Buyer Representative, and SIOR stands for Society of Industrial and Office Realtors. Ask about these designations, as they may apply to your situation. Of main interest to you, the potential client, is that the Realtor is a professional who keeps up with trends in the field.

**EXPERIENCE.** Here is a list of questions you should ask your Realtor regarding his experience.

- How many years have you been in the business?
- Which companies have you worked for? (They should be companies that are well respected in your area.)
- Is real estate your full-time occupation or just a sideline?
- What branch of real estate is your special focus?
- Are you very familiar with the market in my area of interest? (Note whether he can easily answer questions about average home prices, how long homes stay on the market, neighborhood services, shopping, schools, transportation, crime, and safety issues.)
- Do you know of any houses in my price range that are currently for sale in my target area? (He should be able to comment on this immediately, without having to go check on his computer.)
- Are you aware of the location of liquor stores, bars, convenience stores, and government agencies? What impact do these operations have on the neighborhood?

- What can you tell me about financing, loan programs, and insurance?

**PROBLEM SOLVING.** The Realtor will be your trusted advisor throughout the process of buying or selling your home. Ask how she handles snags that come up along the way: credit difficulties, inspection problems, multiple offers, or paperwork snafus. Ask if she is willing to be present during all transactions (the answer should be yes). You might want to make an "I'm most nervous about————" list before phoning the Realtor so you won't forget to ask those questions. You'll want to know how the Realtor might handle the situations you feel least confident about; graceful problem solving skills can save you heartache and disappointment.

**TECHNICAL SAVVY.** The Realtor you choose must have Internet access to e-mail, current databases, and the Multiple Listing Service (MLS, the bible of available houses). He must have a cell phone. If you happen upon a throwback who doesn't believe in such things, beat a hasty retreat.

**REFERENCES.** Ask for at least three. They should include people who have successfully bought or sold a home with this Realtor, as well as at least one who is a professional in the field—for instance, a lender or mortgage broker. Query these folks about the Realtor's performance, and be specific:

- Did the Realtor give solid business advice?
- Did he return phone calls and deliver important information promptly?
- Did he negotiate effectively on their behalf?
- Was there anything particularly skillful or creative in his approach to problems?
- Was there any area where he could have done better?

**PERSONALITY.** "The most important trait in a Realtor, and a lot of people bypass this, is that it be someone you like and have a rapport with," says Jim Lee, who has been selling real estate in Knoxville, Tennessee, for 26 years. Depending on your personal style, you may feel most comfortable with someone who is laid back or someone who is more assertive and direct. Just remember that the Realtor's style will be carried into the negotiations. While you're chatting, be sure to notice how well he listens to you. Most people can get a sense of this over the course of a half-hour conversation. If you don't feel as if you're being heard during this first interview, it's doubtful things will improve later on.

Most Realtors will want you to sign an exclusivity contract. This is fair, but not for more than 60–90 days. If the Realtor says his company's contract is for six months and it's nonnegotiable, politely decline and look for someone else.

## For Buyers Only

Unless you are working with an exclusive buyer's agent, the Realtor you engage has a legal responsibility to the seller, not to you. Her chief goal must be to get the price and terms the seller wants, even if she is supposedly negotiating on your behalf. This means that unless the sellers give their permission, the Realtor is not allowed to disclose personal information that might give you an edge—for example, revealing that the sellers are in the midst of a divorce. Your Realtor's commission is based on the sale price of the home, so it's natural to assume that she has a vested interest in parting you from as much money as she can. How are you going to trust someone with so many incentives in the other direction?

In reality, the situation is not as unfairly skewed as it seems. The money the Realtor stands to earn by advising you to increase your offer by, say, $5,000 is pretty small potatoes—about $75. It's hardly worth alienating you over that amount if you really disagree with her advice. After all, she is counting on you to recommend her to your family and friends so she can broaden her turf.

However, there is no disputing the fact that she *will* be a dual agent representing both you and the seller, so be prudent in your negotiations. Don't fall for the standard line, "What are you willing to pay?" That information will go straight back to the seller, guaranteed.

If the conflict of interest doesn't sit well with you, you can always engage an exclusive buyer's agent. In most cases they earn a percentage of the commission, just as regular agents do. The main difference between the two is that the buyer's agent has a legal responsibility to the buyer, not the seller. She can (and should) dish all the dirt about the seller's circumstances, but she is not allowed to tell the seller any confidential information about you. Another advantage to using a buyer's agent is that they routinely show homes that are for sale "by owner" or "by builder," which seller's agents often neglect to do.

A buyer's agent will ask you to sign a contract just as any agent will. The same rules apply—don't agree to an exclusive arrangement for longer than 60 to 90 days. Read the fine print carefully, and pay special attention to the payment options—for instance, will you owe the Realtor a commission if you buy directly from a homeowner? How much will that commission be? The contract is negotiable, so take your time and ask all the questions you like, of the agent and of any other knowledgeable folks you have access to.

## For Sellers Only

There are a few things to be particularly aware of if you are choosing a Realtor to help you sell your house. First on that list, obviously, is the person's salesmanship. A good way to evaluate the skill of a few Realtors is to go to some open houses without letting on that you're searching for a Realtor. Lurk around for a while and see how they relate to the public. Are they warm and natural, putting people at ease? Do they try to find out what the buyer is looking for so they can tailor pertinent information? Do they know how to emphasize the home's strengths, pointing out areas that a buyer might not have noticed? Do they show a general knowledge of structural and inspection issues that would lead a buyer to trust them? Do they seem genuinely enthusiastic about the property? It takes a clever person to point out the details and promise in a home, particularly if it has been well lived in. A sagging red velour couch or mustard-colored carpet can be off-putting, and the good Realtor will know how to guide the buyer's eye to the finer points. That's the person you want.

Another strategy for finding a Realtor to market your home is to drive around your own neighborhood and look at the For Sale signs. You'll usually find the same few Realtors' names again and again because they tend to specialize in certain neighborhoods. Not only do you want to see the names, you also want to see those "sold" signs.

As you narrow your search for a Realtor, be sure to ask about the following issues.

**MARKETING.** The Realtor should be able to give you, in writing, the marketing plan for selling your house. The plan should include how and where it will be advertised, whether open houses are part of the plan, and when the home will be shown. (Only about 1 percent of homes are sold through open houses, so private viewings are essential.) The plan should also give an estimate of how long the Realtor believes it will take your home to sell. If the home does not sell within that period, what changes in strategy will the Realtor suggest?

**COSTS.** Will the marketing plan include advertising expenses that must be paid by you? (This is not usually the case, but it doesn't hurt to ask.) If so, agree on a budget. Find out if there are any other costs that may come up in the negotiation process, such as repairs or closing costs paid by the seller. If you are not willing to incur any additional costs, make sure the Realtor knows that at the start so the costs are not used as a negotiating tool.

**THE NEIGHBORHOOD.** A good working knowledge of the neighborhood is just as essential when you are selling as when you are buying. That information should include the average price of homes selling in your area and the average length of time on the market. Find out the difference between the asking price and the actual selling price of recently sold homes. Ask the Realtor how many homes in your neighborhood she has closed on in the last three months. If the answer is zero, there better be a good reason before you select this particular Realtor.

## Do You Want a Star, an Eager Beginner, or Someone in Between?

When you're cruising your target neighborhood you might notice one name that seems to appear on every other sign. This person could be either an extremely hardworking agent or a "star" Realtor who actually has very little to do with his clients until the final negotiations are in play. Opinions differ on whether these stars are worth hiring on the basis of their reputation, especially if you are buying rather than selling a home. For sellers, hiring someone who moves a lot of homes has obvious advantages. If nothing else, his track record makes him a known quantity. However, if you are buying a home and are going to be handed off to the star's assistant throughout your weeks or months of house hunting, hiring the star might not be the right move.

Agents everywhere agree that the relationship between client and Realtor is intense. Says Rhonna Robles, "When you're dealing with large amounts of money, you get to know a lot about a person very quickly. A lot of times you know things that their friends don't even know." If you crave the clout of a star but don't feel comfortable enough with him to share that level of intimacy, you would do well to interview a few other agents before making your decision.

Another element to consider is whether the Realtor is working for a large company. That can be important in a hot market, because your agent can describe the type of home you want to his coworkers and, ideally, get a heads-up on a great house before it ever hits the Multiple Listing Service. (The larger the company, the more likely it is that one of those agents will be listing a suitable home.) Even in a slow market, says Robles, "good things still fly off the market, so I always want to let the other agents know what I'm looking for."

Sometimes people find themselves clicking with a young, relatively inexperienced agent. Should experience trump rapport? Not necessarily. Young agents with fewer clients may be able to devote more time and energy to helping you. If they are working at a well-established agency, they are probably being mentored by a more experienced agent who will make sure all the details are handled properly.

---

### PHRASE BOOK

Although a good Realtor will explain the process in detail, it helps if you walk in the door understanding the basic terms of a real estate transaction. Here are the top 10:

**ADJUSTABLE RATE MORTGAGE (ARM):** A loan in which either the interest rate or the length of time the loan is agreed for can change. First-time homebuyers beware: an ARM can be seductive, as you can get in a home at a lower monthly mortgage only to have that mortgage suddenly dramatically increase when interest rates go up.

**AMORTIZATION:** A payment plan on your house loan that allows equal payments over a finite period of time (typically 15 and 30 years). The initial payments primarily cover the interest on the loan and the balance of the payments cover the principal.

**BINDER:** A preliminary agreement or "offer to purchase" on a property that is accompanied by "earnest money." Beware—the earnest money is forfeited if the buyer doesn't go through with the deal.

**CLOSING COSTS:** The numerous expenses and fees incurred by both buyer and seller during a real estate transaction. Who pays what is often negotiable, but the seller always pays the Realtor's commission.

**CLOSING DAY:** The date on which the seller delivers the deed and the buyer pays for the property.

**DEED:** A written instrument, drawn up according to the laws of the state, that formally transfers title to a property from one owner to another. The deed is legally binding, and once it is sealed and accepted, it supercedes all other agreements.

**EQUITY:** The actual value that the owner has in the owned property. Equity is what is left after any outstanding loans or debts are subtracted from the current value of the property. As the mortgage is paid off, equity increases.

**ESCROW:** A special trust account set aside by the lender in which the homeowner may deposit money to be held to cover specific anticipated expenses such as taxes or insurance premiums.

**POINTS:** Points are part of the credit the lender is extending to the borrower. One point is 1 percent of the total loan paid upfront. More than one point can be paid, they *are* subtracted from the principal, and either the buyer or seller can pay them. Note: HUD (U.S. Department of Housing and Urban Development) loans prohibit the buyer, but not the seller, from paying points.

**PRINCIPAL:** The portion of the loan that pays off the actual cost of the house and does not include interest. (Interest goes to the lender.)

**TITLE:** The actual document that proves ownership of a given property.

## Magic Words and Deeds

Most real estate agents love their work, despite the unconventional hours and seesaw income. "I feel real good about what I do because most of my clients, whether they are buyers or sellers, end up happy at the end of the transaction," says Jim Lee. He finds it especially satisfying to work with first-time buyers because "the house is kind of like a toy to them. It makes a change in their lives, usually for the better." Rhonna Robles is equally enthusiastic. "The thing I enjoy most is that I get to meet people I would never have met otherwise and become friends with them. I'm a typical co-dependent: I want to help everybody."

The best way to capitalize on these good vibrations is to begin your relationship with a discussion of the real estate market in general, so you have realistic expectations. If you're moving to a new city, your Realtor can be a great asset in helping you find a neighborhood that suits your lifestyle and budget. Before your first meeting, try to prioritize the elements you most desire in a house. If you are married, attempt to find common ground with your spouse about the basic must-haves—one story or two, big yard or small, number of bathrooms and bedrooms. The more specific you are, the easier it will be for your Realtor to find you a house you will like. Make a list of these items and keep a copy for yourself. You may revise it after you've seen a few homes, but it's a jumping-off point.

If you are selling, the most salient point is price. The Realtor will show you a list of comps—the prices of homes comparable to yours that recently sold in your neighborhood—and will suggest a price based on those and on the condition of your house. It is crucial that you take this advice to heart, because the first two weeks a house is on the market are when you stand to make the most money. After 30 days, you are almost certain to get less than your asking price. Even if your house could have sold for $50,000 more last year and you're kicking yourself for waiting to sell it, do not let your emotions undermine the process. Your Realtor knows what price is right *today*. You should also discuss which items you would be willing to use as bargaining chips in the negotiation—perhaps you wouldn't mind parting with the Sub-Zero refrigerator, the patio furniture, or a custom dining table.

A good Realtor will offer suggestions on what you might to do spruce up your home. Most people expect to clean, perhaps paint a few rooms, and clear out some furniture. Don't take offense, however, if the Realtor asks you to go a bit further. "People have huge collections of family pictures, dolls, model cars, whatever," says Jim Lee. "I always suggest that they get that out of sight, because buyers get all wrapped up in looking at their stuff and forget to look at the house." In addition to being a distraction, too many personal items make it hard for potential buyers to imagine the home as theirs, not yours.

If you are buying, the most important thing you can do to

win the Realtor's enthusiasm is to get prequalified for a loan. "A lot of people kind of fight you on that, especially first-time buyers," says Lee. Getting prequalified proves that you're serious and settles the matter of what you can afford. Most Realtors have mortgage brokers they like to work with, and this can be a boon if your credit isn't perfect or you happen to be between jobs. Whatever your situation, tell the Realtor about it so he can take the approach that is most likely to succeed.

Once the process begins, observe the following rules to keep the relationship with your Realtor on track:

- Agree in advance on how often and through what form of communication you will be checking in with each other.
- Return phone calls promptly.
- Have information and paperwork ready at the agreed-upon time.
- If you change your mind about something—anything— related to the process, tell the Realtor immediately.
- Be on time for appointments.
- Give specific feedback about properties, how the process is going, and what you need.
- Be fair. Don't blame your Realtor in slow economic times if your home isn't selling; set specific timelines for reevaluations.

## Absolute No-No's

Trust is a two-way street in your relationship with your Realtor, and rule number one is remaining loyal. "I refuse to deal with people who work with more than one Realtor at a time," says Rhonna Robles. "What I see happen is that the Realtors all find out and they feel used, so that person always receives the worst service." What else will antagonize your Realtor? Disrespect, lack of clarity, and deviousness. To avoid trying your Realtor's patience:

**DON'T TREAT THE REALTOR LIKE YOUR PERSONAL ASSISTANT.** "Some people are very rude about my time," says Rhonna Robles. These are the folks who call at midnight or 6 A.M., demand instant information whether or not it is necessary, and in general ignore common rules of courtesy. "They don't understand that I'm working and I have other clients and a home life. People like that will probably not get treated very well, and if I can't treat them well, I won't work with them."

**DON'T HIDE CREDIT PROBLEMS IF YOU ARE BUYING A HOME.** The Realtor will earn nothing unless you eventually purchase a house. If you will not be able to qualify for a loan, you are exploiting the Realtor and making him work for free.

**DON'T EXAGGERATE THE AMOUNT YOU WILL BE ABLE TO PAY.** Sometimes people purposely lie about their financial situation, but more often they don't actually know how much they can afford until they go through the loan prequalification process. Many first-time buyers are also unaware of the closing costs associated with buying a home. An agent will probably be willing to show you a few houses on the basis of your word alone, but don't expect her to launch an all-out search until she is certain you can afford what you say you can.

**DON'T EXPECT THE REALTOR TO MAKE RIDICULOUSLY LOWBALL OFFERS.** "A lot of first-time buyers think if somebody's asking $150,000 for a house they can buy it for $100,000, which is typically not the case," says Jim Lee. Lowballing can alienate the seller, who may take it as an insult and refuse to look at any other offers from you, even reasonable ones.

**DON'T WAFFLE TOO MUCH ABOUT THE SORT OF HOUSE YOU WANT.** There's an old saying: buyers are liars. It's not meant as an insult so much as a comment on buyers' notoriously fickle nature and lack of self-awareness. "They'll tell you they absolutely will not buy a two-story house and then they'll buy a two-story house," says Robles. No one will blame you for adjusting your goals, especially during the first few weeks of your search, but too many changes over many months will signal that you're either not serious about buying or not able to make the commitment.

**DON'T ARGUE EXCESSIVELY IN FRONT OF THE REALTOR.** When husband and wife disagree about the type of house they want, the unlucky Realtor can find herself playing therapist/referee while still trying to find that perfect home. "I've witnessed horrible fights before. It's awful," recalls Rhonna Robles.

**DON'T INSIST ON AN UNREALISTICALLY HIGH SELLING PRICE.** It's very common for homeowners to balk at the Realtor's suggested selling price, but it's not as if he's plucking a number out of thin air. If you feel he is really off base, get another opinion. Always keep in mind that pricing your house correctly will get you more money in the long run than pricing it too high and having it go stale on the market.

**DON'T CONCEAL YOUR TIME FRAME.** In an effort not to appear desperate and vulnerable in a negotiation, some people don't tell the Realtor their true time frame. This can come back to haunt you, because it means your Realtor may not devote as much energy to you as she would if she knew you have only, say, two months to sell your home and buy a new one. If you ask your Realtor not to tell potential buyers about your time frame, she is legally obligated to obey. Buyers who are concerned about confidentiality should use an exclusive buyer's agent.

## Time's Up

You are not the only one who should be on good behavior during this journey. The Realtor is also expected to be available, to return phone calls and e-mails promptly, to have paperwork prepared by deadlines, and to give you honest, sound advice. Violations of these courtesies are definitely reasons to seek another Realtor. In addition, there are some red flags particular to the industry that should make you reconsider your affiliation with this person:

- The Realtor continues to show you properties over the price limit you have set.
- The Realtor consistently tries to talk you into properties you are not interested in ("It has such potential!").
- The Realtor grumbles when you haven't made an offer by the third or fourth house (first-time buyers should view at least ten homes).
- The Realtor tries to pressure you by telling you there is another buyer out there who wants to make an offer on the same house. (In a hot real estate market multiple offers are common, so don't fault the Realtor if this is the case.)
- The Realtor consistently embellishes details on prospective houses to get you to view them ("beautiful wood paneling" turns out to be the inexpensive plastic stuff).

These are the cheap tricks of someone who is more interested in making a commission than in satisfying your needs. Don't fall for them.

## House Beautiful

The best time to buy a house is when you're not in a big hurry. That may not always be possible, especially in a hot real estate market. Most markets are not red hot, however, and if you don't get the first house you make an offer on, there will be another. Try to enjoy the process. Get your creative wheels turning— what color would you paint that room? How would the light change if you took out that wall? How would the yard look with a row of tulips along the fence? Would you feel comfortable walking your dog alone at night in this neighborhood? Take the time to dream a little and try on the different homes you look at. You've got your Realtor to do the hard stuff.

**GENERAL CONTRACTOR**

PLAN THE WORK AND
WORK THE PLAN

When people hire a general contractor to build or remodel their home, they're usually thinking "dream house," not "compromise house." But unless you have a bottomless bank account, compromises will be made and, quite possibly, tears will be shed. Building or remodeling a home involves skills that most of us rarely tap, such as imagination, spatial imaging, serious budgeting, and restraint. The countless details and decisions can confuse anyone who is new at it, which is why it is so important to hire a general contractor with lots of experience, and to plan, plan, and plan again before you break ground.

## Behind the Scenes:
## Diplomat in a Hard Hat

Everyone has heard stories about nightmare construction jobs: projects that limp along for months, leaving the owners without a bathroom or kitchen; workmen who brazenly walk out in the middle of the job; landscaping destroyed and yards left looking like craters of the moon. At some point in the telling of these tales, the listener inevitably asks, "Who was the contractor? Did you sue?" General contractors, who reap the financial rewards of these projects, must take the blame when anything goes wrong. Needless to say, they have their own side to these horror stories. Before allowing anyone to tear down a wall or install a new door, you need a basic understanding of how the construction business works.

Think of the construction site as a stage. Homeowners are one set of actors, and their motivations are generally known to everyone involved. They want their home built exactly as they envision it for the most reasonable cost possible, and they reserve the right to change their minds. Homeowners, however, rarely think about the motivation of the rest of the cast—the general contractor and his various crews. Framers and roofers may come and go, but as soon as they leave the stage, homeowners tend to forget they exist. Meanwhile, the general contractor's main motivation is not to please the homeowner (although of course he would like to do that) but rather to keep his crews busy at all times, either on this job or another one. Most general contractors, if they are good, will be juggling several projects at once. The exception is the contractor who oversees extremely high-end, multimillion-dollar homes, in which case building one or two a year might be sufficient to keep everyone happily employed.

Paul Hafenbrack, a Pittsburgh contractor for 27 years, explains it this way: "The important thing in general contracting is to be productive. You have to make money. That means you have to get in, do your work, get it right, and get out. The biggest problem for any contractor, and one they try to avoid passionately, is change. Change costs money and wastes time. Change means indecision. While you're waiting for them to develop a new plan, it's on your dime."

Any remodel or new construction requires multiple crews of subcontractors for tasks such as pouring the foundation, framing, drywalling, plumbing, electrical work, roofing, painting, flooring . . . it can go on and on, depending on the type of home. Some workers are able to perform more than one task, but every job will entail at least several different crews. "If you've got good, all-around guys that are knowledgeable in all areas of the trade, it's important that you keep them busy," says Hafenbrack. The general contractor moves his crews from one site to another as their turn comes up. Too large a time gap between jobs, and the crew members will have to find work with another general contractor, leaving yours in the lurch.

The homeowners' desire to get the house they want, even if it means waiting a few weeks for the right kitchen tile, often ends up at odds with the contractor's need to keep his men busy and keep his different projects on schedule. If the homeowners order the production to stop while they wait for the tile, the crew must be put to work on another job, and they won't be coming back until that other job is complete. Hence crews that vanish for weeks at a time; hurried, perfunctory cleanups; blown budgets as homeowners scramble to find any tile that will be in stock when the tile crew is available; and apocryphal tales of bad contractors.

But let's back up a minute. What, exactly, *is* a contractor? He (or she) is a person who holds a license allowing him to perform a particular trade, such as plumbing, electrical work, or carpentry. A *general* contractor is someone whose license also allows him to obtain permits for the projects that require them, such as home additions, and to subcontract with tradesmen for particular parts of the project. General contractors organize and oversee large construction jobs that involve a variety of trades. They will usually do part of the work themselves and hire others for tasks that are not in the general contractor's area of expertise. When a contractor is "licensed and bonded" it means that he carries insurance that covers his work and the work of the people he hires. Always use a licensed and bonded contractor.

General contractors oversee a project from start to finish. The good ones have cultivated a group of talented, reliable tradesmen and have a broad understanding of building materials. They negotiate for materials, order and deliver supplies, make sure the workmen stay on task, handle complaints, and schedule the inspectors. If something doesn't turn out right, it is the contractor's responsibility to make good on the work.

It is also the contractor's responsibility to collect money from the homeowner—always a calculated risk. "Nine times out of ten, general contractors will build with their own money to start," says Paul Hafenbrack. Typically, the contractor will work the first month, buying the supplies and paying subcontractors out of his own pocket. At the end of the month he'll submit a bill. "The owner is supposed to pay you within the next thirty days, but they don't always. The thing about it is, you take the risk in order to keep the work. If you've got a good crew of guys, you want to keep them busy."

The cell phone has been a great boon to people who are building or remodeling a home. If you're not wealthy enough to command your contractor's full attention, at least you can usually reach him via his cell phone. Likewise, he can reach you, and ask you one more time to select that kitchen tile. It's a close bond you'll be forging with your contractor, and the more you know about what he needs, the more enjoyable that bond will be.

## Are You Really Ready to Build?

Every contractor can tell you about marriages that cracked under the strain of building or renovating. You will need to do intensive work to prepare for the project, but equally important, you should take a little time to prepare yourself psychologically for the marathon to come.

**CLEAR YOUR CALENDAR.** Having your household interrupted for a lengthy period of time is no trivial matter. Make sure all family members are prepared and that other high-stress events, such as extra work projects or major medical procedures, won't be occurring at the same time. You want to enjoy the fruits of all this labor and not end up divorced and using your lovely new tiles to make mosaic ashtrays at the local psych ward.

**DEVELOP A PLAN TO ACCOMMODATE THE DISRUPTION TO YOUR HOUSEHOLD.** If you are not going to have a workable kitchen for a month, how are you going to prepare meals and clean up? Will sleeping arrangements need to be altered? How will you store and arrange your belongings so that they are easy to access? Having a plan for all these details can greatly reduce stress once you're in the thick of the work.

**WORK OUT YOUR BUDGET AHEAD OF TIME.** "Before you even come to a builder, you should go to a lender and get prequalified. Then you're not disappointing yourself and not deceiving the builder," says Hadley H., a general contractor in Northern California for 35 years. Make sure your budget is realistic for your project by researching materials and the type of job you need done. Most of the large home-improvement stores, such as Home Depot, employ people who can tell you about materials and labor so you know the range of prices to expect.

Most projects don't go exactly as planned, and there will undoubtedly be unforeseen problems such as termites or dry rot, so prepare to spend 10–20 percent more than the estimate for the total project. In order to account for that, make a list of first and second choices. For instance, if you love the cherry kitchen cabinets but suddenly discover that the subflooring needs to be replaced, what less-expensive wood cabinets could you live with instead? Planning ahead like this can keep you from spiraling ever upward into the cost-overrun zone.

**PLAN REMODELING ACCORDING TO PROPERTY VALUES IN THE NEIGHBORHOOD.** Remodeling your home is an investment in its future value upon resale. Some homeowners have been shocked when they haven't taken into consideration the average home's value in their neighborhoods. If you spend $100,000 to create a showpiece home in a modest area of town where none of the surrounding homes come close in value, you will never recoup your investment when you sell.

## Architect or Draftsman?

Architects and contractors often come across as unwilling conjoined twins. Each wishes he could get along without the other, but they can't undo the bonds that tie them. Architects get frustrated with what they regard as contractors' nit-picking about the details of the plans, while contractors bemoan architects who either don't provide enough detail or deliver incorrect instructions.

"It all comes down to money," says Paul Hafenbrack. "The owner will say to the architect, 'Here's $5,000. That's all I can afford to spend on a design.' When the $5,000 runs out, that's when the drawings stop." The drawings will cover the foundation and framing, perhaps, but not details about how to construct things such as windows. Hafenbrack explains, "Every time you get drawings, you get elevations and plan views of what they want to build. Then they'll circle areas that point you to a different page where they show a close-up detail of how it should be constructed." If you haven't paid enough for those details, there will be no extra page, and the contractor will have to make it up as he goes along. He won't appreciate that. "If you're good at what you do, you can figure it out. But the thing is, you didn't get hired to design it, you got hired to build it."

The better route is to pay more for complete drawings. If your budget is tight—and even if it isn't—Hadley H. strongly advises homeowners to consider using an architectural draftsman instead of an architect. "Architects run off their egos a lot of times. They'll design a house and just overkill it tremendously with structural requirements that are not necessary for single-family residences. It runs up the bill for the architecture and it runs up the cost of the house." According to Hadley, draftsmen are not only less expensive, they are often a better choice for home design. Contractors are familiar with draftsmen and can point you to those whose work they feel might be a good match for you. You will want to hire one with plenty of experience and visit some of the houses the draftsman has designed.

Whether you use an architect or a draftsman to design your house or renovation, order the most detailed plans you can possibly afford. There is no better use of your money, and you will see a return on it as soon as you meet with the contractor. "The planning and design is everything," says Hafenbrack. "If you go to a general contractor and say, 'I want to build this house; I've got a complete set of drawings from A to Z and all the colors are picked,' that guy will give you an unbelievably good price because he doesn't have any thinking to do. All he has to do is follow the drawings and build it. He can plug in every contractor one right after the other, and at the end he knows he's making his money, so he's going to give you a good price. If he looks at the plans and sees dimensions missing, no colors, no landscape plan, he's going to pad his price because he knows you don't yet know what you're going to do." Having the patience to work out detailed plans with the architect and the courage to write the check is excellent practice for the months ahead.

## Finding a Good Contractor

States' rights are alive and well in the contracting business—each state demands different qualifications to get a license. In California, a contractor must pass a test about the various trades and crafts used in home construction. In Washington, he is interviewed over the phone and must answer a few random questions.

Given such widely varying standards, the shrewd homeowner will do a lot of research before hiring. "They should check the contractor's reputation, how long he's been building, and where he's built," advises Hadley H.

Locating a good contractor is not unlike locating a good lawyer or doctor, with one fortunate exception: you can see samples of the finished product ahead of time. You may not be able to accurately gauge the pain or price you will pay for that product (intense grilling of former clients helps), but it's easier than trying to determine how your leg will feel and function after a surgeon operates. If you have noticed homes in your neighborhood that appeal to you, whether they are remodels or new construction, don't hesitate to ask the owners all about their experience with both architect and builder. They will probably be thrilled to repeat the saga in excruciating detail, and that is to your benefit. If they took photos of the process, examine them closely (many people like to keep an album of before-and-after shots). It's a good time to talk about things such as how well-organized the site was, how thoroughly the crew cleaned up, and whether the contractor was easy to communicate with.

Friends, neighbors, and colleagues are another source of referrals. Most will be happy to let you tour their home to investigate the contractor's work. Inspect the craftsmanship carefully. Are corners on the woodwork exact? Is there evidence of sloppiness, such as visible glue or messy caulking? If something doesn't look well-finished, you will probably want to look elsewhere.

Sometimes the best referrals are not personal but come from professionals in related fields. Architects, home design centers, and stores that sell building materials all work closely with contractors and usually have reputable people to suggest. You may also get great referrals from tradesmen who have done work on your home already. Chances are, if you had an excellent electrician rewiring the attic or a talented finish carpenter refinishing your deck, he will have some sound recommendations for a general contractor.

Once you have a list of several potential contractors, start calling them. Make note of how long they take to return a phone call. Busy contractors may not call back the same day, but if a few days turn into weeks, take heed. The purpose of your initial phone call is to establish some rapport with the contractor, make sure that he handles your type of work, and explain what you need done. One of the most important questions to ask is when he would be able to start work on your project.

Try to narrow your choices down to three contractors who will come out and look at the site, review your plans with you, and give you an estimate. Three estimates should be enough for you to get a rough feel for what the project will cost. It takes many hours to draw up an estimate, and contractors rarely charge for the time, so they appreciate the playing field being small enough so that they have a reasonable chance of getting the job. (Beware of new contractors who may lowball an initial bid and then sock you with price overruns later; the lowest bid is not necessarily the best.)

Getting an estimate doesn't in any way obligate you to hire a given contractor. It's all about establishing trust at this point. If you did your homework and have detailed drawings in hand, the process will go much more smoothly. As you are discussing the project, quiz the contractor about the quality of his work and his style of doing business. Equally important, pay attention to how well you click with him. It is essential that you feel comfortable enough to talk frankly about the work and the crews.

The following list of questions should help you get the information you need.

● **ASK IF THE CONTRACTOR IS LICENSED AND BONDED AND ASK TO SEE HIS LICENSE.** Later, you can call the Better Business Bureau to find out if the license is legitimate and if there have been any complaints against this person.

- **ASK WHAT TYPE OF INSURANCE HE CARRIES.** You want to be sure that he carries workers' compensation and liability so that any injuries on the job do not become your problem.
- **ASK THE CONTRACTOR HOW LONG HE HAS BEEN IN BUSINESS AND ASK TO SEE EXAMPLES OF HIS WORK.** He may be able to refer you to sites where you can view the work for yourself, or he may carry a portfolio of prior projects. In either case, you want a solid history.
- **ASK FOR THREE REFERENCES FROM OTHER CLIENTS.** Be sure to call those clients and get as much detail as you can about how the contractor works and the quality of his work. Ask about timeliness and cost overruns. If they will let you view the project, so much the better.
- **ASK WHAT TYPES OF WORK THE CONTRACTOR IS LICENSED TO DO AND IF HE HAS SPECIALTIES.** Ask what types of jobs he will be contracting out. Sometimes, if your contractor does more of the work himself rather than subcontracting it, it can cut down on costs.
- **ASK GENERAL QUESTIONS ABOUT WORK HOURS AND CLEANUP.** How early will the crews begin work each day, and how late will they stay? Will they work on Saturdays? How do they handle the ongoing mess? What about portable toilet facilities, dumpsters, and so forth?
- **ASK ABOUT CONTRACTS AND WARRANTIES.** The box at the end of this chapter lists items that should be included in every contract. You might show the contractor this list and ask him to comment. Beware of contractors who balk at signing a detailed agreement.

Most contractors are honest and hard-working, but there are a few con artists out there. Things to watch for and avoid are:

- Contractors who drive unmarked trucks or cars and who have post office boxes and answering services but no address.
- Contractors who offer you great deals because they are in the area and have leftover materials or who offer lifetime warranties.
- Contractors who offer suspiciously low bids, particularly without looking at the job.
- Contractors who either don't provide a contract or try to hard-sell you into signing their contract with no comparative estimates.
- Contractors who demand cash upfront or require a large down payment.
- Contractors who solicit work by going door to door (this is not common practice).

Estimates should be delivered to you in writing. They should be very detailed, outlining costs for materials, labor, equipment, fees, overhead, and profit. The contractor typically adds 15 to 20 percent profit for his services. If there are some contingencies, such as a certain price if subflooring needs to be replaced and another if it does not, those should be spelled out. If you have not chosen certain items yet, such as light fixtures, it should be noted so the estimate will change to reflect the actual price when those items are selected. This type of estimate is called a "fixed price" estimate and it is the one most contractors use.

It's often difficult to predict the problems that might be unearthed once work begins, especially if you are remodeling an old house. Older homes tend to be like sweaters: pick at one thread, and the whole thing starts to unravel. Whether or not you think you will run into unforeseen problems, make sure the contractor understands that you must approve any new costs, and that the entire project may not exceed a specific price ceiling.

Estimates are usually negotiable, so don't hesitate to ask how the plans can be adjusted to meet your budget. A good contractor will explain his estimate in detail and may have some creative ideas on how to cut expenses. Once you have arrived at a comfortable place with a contractor and are ready to move forward to the actual work, you will finalize your negotiations by writing a contract.

## Magic Words and Deeds:
## Interviewing a Contractor

Reliable, experienced general contractors are highly sought after. They can often afford to be choosy about their clients, so while you are interviewing them, you can be certain they are closely scrutinizing you. Making a good impression on the contractor involves a number of different elements. The most important, as we've already mentioned, is having detailed drawings in hand when you meet. (If you don't have plans, you will need to work with the contractor and an architect or draftsman to develop them, a process that Hadley H. says usually takes about three months.) In addition to plans, contractors hope to see the following during an interview:

- **CLIENTS WHO KNOW WHAT THEY WANT.** Indecision equals change, and change is bad. The more details you have decided upon the better, even if it's only a general type of decision (for instance, if you know you want granite countertops but haven't yet chosen the slab). There are dozens of items to select—wall and ceiling treatments, paint colors, flooring. The list is very long indeed. Builders expect to help you decide some of these, but the more items you are certain about at the outset, the more confident the builder will feel about taking on the project.

- **CLIENTS WHO DEMONSTRATE KNOWLEDGE OF THE PLANS.** The contractor doesn't expect you to be an expert on blueprints, but he knows it will make his job easier if you understand the basics of what you are asking him to do. Your architect or draftsman should be able to explain the drawings to you so that you feel comfortable discussing them.

- **CLIENTS WHO RESPECT THE CONTRACTOR'S OPINIONS.** "If they're the type of people who think they know more than you do and are very headstrong, they're probably not going to be a good client to work with," says Hadley H.
- **A REALISTIC BUDGET WITH A PREAPPROVED LOAN FROM YOUR BANK.**
- **CHEMISTRY.** "Building a house with somebody is a long-term relationship," says Hadley H. "I try not to work with people I don't like. If you can't communicate with them right from the beginning, chances are you're not going to be able to later on."

## Absolute No-No's: Interviewing a Contractor

A bad feeling about a potential client will prompt most contractors to decline the job. They have a lot of money to lose if a client ends up being difficult, so they are extremely sensitive to their intuition during interviews. A few of the more overt behaviors that cause them to flee:

- **A HUSBAND AND WIFE WHO DISAGREE.** Paul Hafenbrack explains a common scenario that contractors dread: "The husband hires an architect, designs the house, and doesn't get much of his wife's input while he's doing it. When they're starting to build it, the wife comes home one day and says, 'I don't like that. Tear it out.' So now you're at their whim and fancy." If you and your spouse are arguing about the plans on that very first meeting, it's a screaming red flag.
- **CLIENTS WHO SWEAT THE DETAILS.** "If he starts nit-picking little things right off the bat, it's a clue that you probably don't want to deal with him," says Hafenbrack.

- **NERVOUS CHATTER, AVOIDING EYE CONTACT, RUSHING THE INTERVIEW.** All of these are signs of a client who has not thought the project through, who has financial or personal issues that might impact the project, or who may be planning to bilk the contractor.

## The Most Common Mistakes Homeowners Make

Between them, Hadley H. and Paul Hafenbrack have more than 60 years' worth of experience building and remodeling homes. In that time, they have noticed certain stumbling blocks that confound client after client. If you are aware of these when you begin the process, it can save you much heartache and money.

Both men cited their clients' difficulty in envisioning the completed project as a prime source of distress (and change orders) during construction. Most problematic is imagining space. It is nearly impossible for the average person to grasp the way a room will look and feel from blueprints, but according to Hadley, computer graphics and small-scale architectural models aren't much better. He has developed several ways to help his clients overcome this hurdle. If their future house is similar to one he has already built, Hadley walks the client through the exisiting house and asks for feedback on each room—for instance, the client might direct him to make the dining room a few feet longer and the windows a bit larger. If no similar homes exist, Hadley might walk the client through any rooms that are near in size to the ones in the design, fine-tuning the square footage as they go.

Another method Hadley employs is to take the client to the construction site after the foundation has been poured and the floor plan is "snapped" on the concrete (the framer snaps a chalk line marking where each wall will go). Hadley stands on the chalk line that designates one wall and has the client stand on the line for the opposite wall. "When you look at me and I look at you, your eye can define that distance," he says.

Paul Hafenbrack mentions rooflines as another item that clients have difficulty imagining and that sometimes cause disappointment. Again, visiting an existing home with a roofline very similar to the one you're building is the only way to get a sense of how it will really look. Other items that surprise homeowners, according to Hafenbrack: "The view from a window or the shade from a tree that they didn't think was going to affect the sunlight coming in." Frequent visits to the building site, especially when the house is being framed, can help you nip these problems in the bud.

Hafenbrack also stresses that clients should get samples of all the materials and colors they plan on using. Don't just get paint chips, he emphasizes; get samples of the color and finish applied to the material you will be using—wood, plaster, sheet rock, or metal. Hadley cites ceiling treatments as being difficult for clients to envision unless they see them in person: "When you start talking about stairstep ceilings or vaulted ceilings, sometimes they'll know what you're talking about and sometimes they won't." If you are even a tiny bit unsure of what the architect or builder means, insist on seeing a finished example of it, or at the very least a photo.

Finally, Hadley offers this advice to people building a new home: "I think the most common mistake is to get oversold on glitter and not get the square footage you want. You can always come back later and put in the crystal knobs and expensive plumbing fixtures, but if the house is too small, you're never going to be happy with it no matter how much crystal you hang. Add the fancy stuff later. Besides, that way you're not financing it for 30 years. You know what that does to the cost of a $500 chandelier?"

## Magic Words and Deeds: The Job Site

Once the work begins, you will be thrust into close contact with all the players in the production, especially if you're renovating and will be living in the house during construction. The lack of privacy, increased level of dirt and noise, and disruption of your personal space will not leave you unscathed. To keep it all going smoothly, cultivate a professional relationship with the contractors and subcontractors.

- **BE COURTEOUS.** If you are home when workers arrive, greet them. Learn everyone's name and ask how things are going now and then. Compliment and thank the workers if you see a nice piece of finished work. On a lengthy job, offer them coffee and donuts in the morning or a soda or beer after work every once in a while.

- **MANAGE YOUR END OF THE JOB: HANDLING INFORMATION.** Gather all the telephone numbers, cell phone numbers, fax numbers, and pager numbers for you, the contractor, and all subcontractors. Make sure everyone has a copy, and post one as well. Keep an up-to-date file that includes all paperwork pertaining to the job, such as contracts, permits, zoning information, work orders, delivery receipts, and check receipts. Your contractor should have ready access to this file.

- **BE ON TIME FOR SCHEDULED MEETINGS WITH YOUR CONTRACTOR.** Stay abreast of all current activities and take the time to review the work and ask questions.

- **KEEP A WELL-ORGANIZED WORK ENVIRONMENT.** Make sure that there is no clutter in the workspaces when the crews arrive, that utilities that need to be used are accessible, and that anything you promised to be moved by a certain time is indeed moved. Keep your children and pets away from the work areas, as their presence will compromise everyone's safety.

- **PAY THE CONTRACTOR ON TIME.** This will greatly enhance his opinion of you.

## Absolute No-No's: The Job Site

Disorganized, rude, overly finicky homeowners will not bring out the best in their contractor and crews. Work will be perfunctory, and you will receive none of the little perks that a happy worker might throw in, such as special attention to the placement of your wainscotting or an especially fine border on your brick walkway. If your contractor is running behind schedule, as often happens, *you* will be the customer who gets to wait if you are pegged as grouchy and demanding. The following types of clients are particularly irksome to contractors and crews:

- **CLIENTS WHO CHANGE THEIR MINDS FREQUENTLY.** As mentioned earlier, change orders are the bane of a contractor's existence. Women are guilty more often then men, so women who want to get beyond the stereotype should immediately establish themselves as rapid, confident decision makers.
- **WANNABE CONTRACTORS.** Men are the culprits here. Says Hadley H.: "He'll start grilling you about what type of wood you're using, or the mix on concrete. . . . He came to you because he's looked at houses you've built, your reputation is strong, you've been in business for 35 years, and then he starts talking to you like you couldn't build a chicken coop. I've got a short fuse when it comes to people like that."
- **CLIENTS WHO TRY TO RUN THE JOB SITE THEMSELVES.** Men are the main offenders in this case as well, says Hadley. "They'll go on a job site and start talking directly to your subcontractors without going through you. It gets the subcontractors in trouble and screws up the job. A lot of times, the owners have no clue what they're doing."

- **CLIENTS WHO DON'T PAY ATTENTION DURING MEETINGS.** "Getting them to stop what they're doing, listen to you, and check out what you're talking about is unbelievably difficult with some couples," says Hadley. Children are huge distractions during meetings; keep them out of the room. You are spending large sums of money on this project and will need to focus on what the contractor is saying every step of the way.

- **CLIENTS WHO MAKE CHANGES WITHOUT INFORMING THE CONTRACTOR.** In a construction project, each element is tied to several other elements. You cannot simply buy a new front door or different cabinets, have them delivered, and expect them to fit. Every change you make must go through the contractor. He may not be overjoyed about it, but he will be far more miffed if you go around him. (They do expect some changes; it comes with the territory.)

- **CLIENTS WHO CONSTANTLY QUESTION THE CONTRACTOR.** You have the right to understand what is going on with your project, but it's best to save your questions for your regular meetings with the contractor. If you quibble over every detail, you'll get a reputation as a know-nothing pain in the butt. You do not want to be completely discredited when it comes to that piece of the project that genuinely needs reworking.

## What If Something Goes Wrong?

The regular meetings you have with your contractor should always include inspections of the segments of work that have just been completed. That way, if a problem is brewing you will catch it immediately. The longer a mistake goes uncorrected, the more time-consuming and costly it will be to repair. For example, poorly routed electrical wiring will be covered with sheet rock, the sheet rock will be covered with wallpaper, and you will then require at least three workers to remedy the situation. If there is a problem with any of the subcontractors, report it to the general contractor and have him handle it.

At the end of the project, the contractor will have you sign a certificate of completion. Do not sign it until you have thoroughly reviewed the project with him, the site has been cleaned up and debris removed, and the work has passed all the required inspections. If anything is subpar or different than you both agreed upon, discuss it calmly with your contractor and give him a reasonable amount of time to respond. If he doesn't present a solution within a few days, send a registered letter outlining your concerns. Refer to the warranties in your contract, and send a copy to the mediator you designated. *(Every contract should contain a clause about mediation.)* Don't delay, but try to keep the relationship civil. It's worth noting that almost 80 percent of construction disputes involve water—leaking through the roof, seeping through the walls at ground level, or condensing on the walls or ceiling. These problems may not be apparent when the house is first completed, so it would behoove you to stay on good terms with your contractor in case they arise a few months later.

If your dispute with the contractor can't be resolved through mediation, you can try sending a letter to the Better Business Bureau, the licensing department that issues contractor licenses, and, as last resort, a lawyer. Be aware, however, that court costs can be prohibitive—a minimum of $1,000 a day for at least several days, plus out-of-court fees and expenses. With your bank account already an arid wasteland, a legal battle with your contractor may be out of the question. Your best hope is to carefully screen the contractor before you hire him so you never even have to think the word *lawyer*.

## Homeland Insecurity

"General contracting is a risky business," reflects Paul Hafenbrack. "Every time you meet someone, you rely on first impressions. I've gotten to the point in this business, after 27 years, that I can look at a guy and know exactly where he's coming from." Most homeowners don't have the luxury of all that experience, yet construction is even riskier for them. Obsessive planning and staying alert and involved throughout the process will help make it less wrenching and more rewarding. A solid allegiance to your palette wouldn't hurt, either. "Make color decisions ahead of time," implores Hafenbrack. "What kind of brick, what color mortar, what kind of mortar joint? What color trim do you want on the boards up by the roof? What kind of ceramic tile in the bathroom? What colors? What brand?"

Wait—where are you going? We need to discuss gutters!

---

### THE CONTRACT

The contract between you and your general contractor can't be too detailed. If he uses a standardized form, you are entitled to add any other information you deem pertinent. You should clearly write "N/A" in any of the areas you will not be using. Anything that is of concern to you should be written into the contract, and both parties should initial every item. The contract covers costs, conduct, and work expectations. It should include:

**GENERAL INFORMATION.** The date of the contract; the address where the work is to commence; name and address of the property owner; the name, contact information, and license number of the contractor; a copy of the contractor's insurance policy; a copy of the property owner's insurance policy.

**THE EXPECTED START DATE AND COMPLETION DATE.** This section should detail disclaimers for unavoidable problems such as inclement weather or goods not delivered as promised by outside suppliers.

**A DETAILED DESCRIPTION OF THE WORK THAT WILL BE DONE.** The description should include all charges for labor, materials, delivery costs, permits, taxes, and inspections; it is also prudent to add a list of the work that is *not* to be done.

**A DETAILED LIST OF THE WORK THAT WILL BE SUBCONTRACTED OUT.** This should also include all the subcontractors' names and business information and note that the general contractor will be responsible for the hiring.

**A LIST OF ALL THE NECESSARY PERMITS AND AN ASSURANCE THAT ALL WORK WILL BE UP TO CODE.** This should detail who is to get the permits and how they will be paid for (either in advance by the owner or added to the final bill).

**A LIST OF ALL THE MATERIALS TO BE USED.** This should include as much detail as possible including sizes, colors, models, prices, and brands. Delivery dates for all items should be designated if possible.

**A CLAUSE CONCERNING CONTINGENCIES AND ALLOWANCES.** This section covers those unforeseen problems that may arise and how they are to be handled and paid for.

**AN EXPLANATION OF ALL GUARANTEES AND WARRANTIES.** This list should outline how work and materials are guaranteed and by whom, and how problems will be remedied. Naming a third party who will solve disputes is recommended.

**AN EXPLANATION OF CHANGE ORDERS.** This explains the procedures, how the homeowner will be charged, and how the work schedule may be affected if the owner makes any changes to the work or materials that are not outlined in the original contract.

**A DETAILED LIST OF EXPECTATIONS CONCERNING THE PROPERTY IN GENERAL.** This should include any kind of preparations that are necessary such as moving furniture or tree and plant removal, what items (such as appliances) should be saved or discarded, details about cleanup and hauling, and concerns about damage to the property not related to the construction. All of these items should spell out who is responsible for them and what should be done. There should be a statement that the contractor is responsible for any damages to your property.

**A DETAILED LIST ABOUT WORKER CONDUCT AND EXPECTATIONS.** You should know what the work hours are and if the crews will work weekends or holidays. You should designate a place for workers to park and to store tools and materials, and they should know if they can use your bathroom or your telephone. You should also tell them if they are allowed to bring a dog on your property (it's not uncommon for construction workers to have dogs with them) or if it is a problem if they play a radio. They should not drink during working hours.

**A SCHEDULE OF WHEN AND HOW OFTEN YOU WILL MEET WITH THE CONTRACTOR.** It is extremely important to meet regularly with your contractor so that you stay fully informed of the progress of the work and communication is open and ongoing.

**ANY SPECIAL INSTRUCTIONS CONCERNING PETS AND CHILDREN.** Although it is generally your responsibility to keep your pets and children safe when there are workers present, workers need to know about their presence, what gates must be kept closed, etc. If a worker leaves a gate open that was specified in the contract to be kept closed, the contractor is liable for the vet bills if Sparky gets hit by a car.

**A RELEASE OF LIEN CLAUSE.** This is an extremely important item that releases the homeowner from having liens placed on his property by disgruntled subcontractors if they have not been paid by the general contractor.

**AN OUTLINE OF THE PAYMENT SCHEDULE.** Most homeowners have a schedule whereby they pay for segments of the job upon completion. You should agree with your contractor as to how much will be paid for each portion and when it is to be paid. It is typical to pay 10 percent of the total cost at the start of the work. You may also agree to retain a certain portion of the payment until the work is completed. It's also wise to include a clause for "seasonal holdbacks"—payments to be held back if work is forced to stop due to severe weather and must be completed at a much later date. Additionally, you may want to have a termination clause that allows you to cancel the contract after segments of the work are complete if for some reason you do not want to continue.

**A DESCRIPTION OF YOUR CANCELLATION RIGHTS.** You may cancel the contract without explanation for an agreed upon grace period after you have signed it. However, you do have to notify the contractor in writing before the grace period has elapsed; if you feel, for any reason, that you might want to cancel the contract, it is best not to start any work during this grace period.

**THE SIGNATURES OF BOTH THE CONTRACTOR AND THE HOMEOWNER.**
Take as much time as you need to read and consider the contract before signing it to make sure that it addresses all your concerns. It doesn't hurt to have a friend who has been through construction or a renovation review it with you. She might have experienced something that you can gain from and want to include. Once you sign the contract and your grace period has passed, it is legally binding.

**LAWYER**

# DID YOU HEAR THE ONE ABOUT THE HAPPY ATTORNEY?

Quick, name the workers with the highest rate of depression. Could it be policemen? Psychiatrists? Dentists? No, it is lawyers. According to research done at Johns Hopkins University, lawyers have a greater rate of depression than people in any of the other 104 fields studied. Another survey found that they were nearly four times more likely than the general population to be depressed. When the American Bar Association looked into the problem, it discovered that a full 75 percent of its members experienced "high strain" in their jobs.

The lawyer's state of mind is not on the radar of most people seeking legal counsel. They are concerned with their own troubles, and understandably so. We rarely need an attorney when things are going well; it's when our world begins to crack apart that we call a lawyer. In fact, making that call is usually the turning point that shifts a conflict into high gear. By seeing an attorney, we are admitting that something has failed, and we are taking that failure public. That is why, when we find ourselves sitting in an attorney's office for the first time, we are often awash in feelings of anger, confusion, guilt, or fear—emotions a psychologist may be equipped to deal with, but most lawyers are not.

There is a large gulf between the things people expect of their lawyers—emotional support, justice, and financial rewards, to name a few—and what a lawyer can actually deliver. Combine that with the confusing fees they charge and the legalese they spout, and it's not unusual for *everyone* to be depressed when all is said and done. However, if you know what to expect from a lawyer, you can walk away not only satisfied but also having made a new friend. And lawyers are very valuable friends to have.

## Behind the Scenes: The Fighting Life

As a group, lawyers are in the unenviable position of being mistrusted by most of the people who hire them. They bombed in the most recent Gallup poll on honesty and ethics—only 17 percent of those polled believed lawyers had a high standard of ethics. Yet despite their reputation for being sharks, many lawyers enter the field out of a passion for justice and the desire to help people. (Many others are liberal arts majors who can't think of another way to make a living.) Money plays a role—lawyers are among the highest paid workers in the United States—but it is not always the deciding factor. There are easier ways to make money. Every law student is aware of the long hours and high pressure demanded by law firms and the high burn-out rate among lawyers, but they keep applying to law schools anyway: applications were at a 20-year high in 2002. In the end, it takes more than money to lure bright young men and women to the field of law. It takes a measure of idealism. The moment they are out of law school, however, that idealism is put to the test by the relentlessness of the work and the day-to-day drudgery of practicing law.

"In order to get ahead in a big firm, young lawyers really need to focus their energy and put in the hours," says Lenny Sparks, a 30-year-old attorney profiled on wetfeet.com. "The length of the workweek varies by city and firm, but attorneys do work a hell of a lot compared to other professionals." Sparks routinely puts in a 60-hour week. That's 12 hours a day, not unusual for the field. And the hours aren't just long, they're often boring. "A lot of lawyerly tasks are incredibly tedious," states Garrick Tolderry, another young attorney profiled on wetfeet. "People focus on the glamorous aspects of the job—making deals, questioning witnesses, discovering evidence—but the truth is, that makes up a small percentage of what I really do." Still, the intellectual challenge and the desire to help people keeps 29-year-old Tolderry logging 50 hours a week.

Check back with these young men in 10 years and their views might mirror those of Marilyn Sullivan, who has been practicing law since the 1970s. "As is the case with many well-intentioned lawyers, my reason for entering the profession was to assist others with legal crises. But it is impossible to tap any humanistic meaning from the adversarial nature of litigation," she writes on her Web site. Of her years in the legal trenches, she says, "Feelings of loss and depression followed my biggest trial wins. Despite an enviable victory rate, I felt unsuccessful and depleted." Although her clients were glad when she prevailed, it was a mixed blessing for them as well. "They achieved their goal. But the winning felt hollow. Getting there robbed them of valuable resources: a wealth of precious time, energy, and hard-earned money. . . . The legal system depletes energy and money without restoring them." Eventually, Sullivan switched her focus from litigation to dispute resolution, and now feels she is "making a truly meaningful contribution to law—and society."

Such heartfelt confessions are rare for attorneys, particularly in a public forum like a Web site. Yet according to attorney Carey Bennett McRae, thousands of lawyers struggle with similar inner conflicts. McRae has pinpointed attorneys as a growing clientele for psychotherapists, and is working toward a degree in psychology so he can help other lawyers cope. In an article he wrote for the psychology journal *Counseling Today*, McRae outlined the typical attorney's trajectory from impassioned law student to burned-out practitioner.

Upon entering law school, says McRae, the eager student willingly gives up a normal, balanced life to focus on the unrelenting demands of his or her professors. (As rigorous at it is, the standard law school curriculum offers no courses on how to deal with the psychological needs of clients.) The work is painstaking and difficult, but the rewards seem worth it: pursuing justice, fighting for the rights of fellow citizens, and earning a decent salary.

The first stumbling block occurs when the newly minted attorney gets a job at a law firm and discovers that, in the real world, justice takes a back seat to deal making. "The modern legal system is not as concerned with who ran the red light [so much as] with who had insurance," writes McRae. While Marilyn Sullivan may embrace conflict resolution as a good alternative to the battlefield of litigation, McRae has found that many young lawyers resent having to replace the good fight with the neatly crafted compromise.

That disappointment can be overcome, but it is only the beginning of the lawyer's struggles. There are the brutal hours, the five- to ten-year trudge toward attaining partnership status, and the intense competition that goes on among attorneys. Other than becoming a partner, there is little feedback for doing good work. "The legal world delays gratification. It is not uncommon for a lawyer to spend several weeks on a court brief and not hear a result for over a year. Cases drag on for years, even decades." Finally, there is the emotional strain of being in a profession that is reviled by the general public. It's no wonder so many lawyers adopt "maladaptive patterns for handling stress"— drinking, drug abuse, and indulging in other over-the-top behaviors that support the lawyers' credo of "work hard, play hard."

The combination of overly stressed attorney and scared, confused client sets up obstacles before the two ever meet. In order to handle the high pressure of their jobs, attorneys frequently put up emotional barriers between themselves and their clients. According to Norm Hulcher, whose Web site is devoted to helping attorneys warm up their chilly client relationships, "The professional detachment that lawyers invoke to shield themselves from their clients tends to contaminate a whole firm." As a result, the entire staff may view a new client as "one more file, one more headache, one more person to bitch at them." Before you ever get in to see the attorney, you may get the distinct impression that you're not particularly welcome. "Most people's expectations for law office courtesy and service are pretty low. Many legal consumers go into a matter *expecting* to be ignored and jerked around."

Not all attorneys are dismissive, exploitive, or burned-out, however. Many are well-adjusted, empathetic, and get great satisfaction from their work. Suzanne Spillane, a Los Angeles attorney specializing in business law and artists' rights, says, "I love to litigate and I like helping people. The fact is, people sue other people, and for the most part litigation sucks. You're in a conflict, it's stressful, and there's money at issue—your livelihood, in most instances. People are going to ask you mean questions and they're going to look sideways at you and stick their tongues out at you, so to speak. What I say to my clients, assuming that I'm comfortable enough with them, is, 'I'm not going to lie to you. It sucks. But my goal is to make it suck less and to get you what you want.' And when you can make it suck less and get them what they want, it's great."

The low expectations people have of lawyers works in Spillane's favor. "When clients find out that you're passionate and you actually care, they're amazed. When you call them out of the blue—'Hi, just checking in, nothing's going on'—they're so happy."

Whether they are satisfied or stressed out, all lawyers went through a grueling experience at law school; all deal with stiff competition; all have felt the sting of public ridicule; and most are overextended. Their state of mind will almost certainly have an impact on the quality of the work they do for you, so pay attention to it during your initial consultation. Notice the way the attorney treats his staff, whether he looks tense or haggard, and how well he is able to concentrate on what you are saying. If you're feeling comfortable with him, you might ask why he decided to become a lawyer and what he likes and dislikes about his job. His response may reveal crucial information. If nothing else, your interest in him as a human being will set you apart from other clients.

## Your Side of the Desk

It's not a law that lawyers must sit behind huge mahogany desks, but it might as well be. They all seem to hire the same decorator, one who is big on dark woods and intimidation. The office walls are lined with framed diplomas; the bookshelves are packed with thick, leather-bound tomes. There is no comfy sofa, no box of tissues like there is in the therapist's office. Overall, the atmosphere is not exactly conducive to difficult confessions. Yet when you walk through those doors, you must be prepared to tell all. If you are not honest it can have a devastating effect on your case, so before the initial consultation you might want to do a little soul searching. Think about all the facts the lawyer needs to know, and if you find yourself recoiling from some of them, ask yourself the following:

- **ARE YOU WORRIED THE LAWYER WILL JUDGE YOU NEGATIVELY?** Lawyers see it all, so it's unlikely your behavior will shock him. Swallow your pride and disclose everything. You have a lot to lose if you hold back.

- **ARE YOU CONCERNED THAT CERTAIN INFORMATION WILL DAMAGE YOUR CASE?** It will be far more damaging if that information is discovered by your adversary and your lawyer is caught off guard.

- **DO YOU BELIEVE THE LAWYER IS ONLY ENTITLED TO KNOW WHAT YOU WANT HIM TO KNOW?** When you hire a lawyer, you have to trust him enough to give him what he asks for, even if you feel it is irrelevant or too personal. The information is confidential, and the two of you together will decide what will be made public.

- **ARE YOU RELUCTANT TO TALK ABOUT A PAINFUL SITUATION?** If you don't want to recite a traumatic series of events, try writing it down. It's helpful to the lawyer if you tell your tale in chronological order (if you don't remember exact dates, estimate). Include only the facts, not your feelings. The attorney can then ask you questions if he needs more information.

- **ARE YOU BLINDED BY YOUR NEED FOR REVENGE?** According to Marilyn Sullivan, "People aren't able to see clearly because the primary motivation is to get the other person." Editing information to strengthen your case can easily backfire. Again, writing down the facts before you meet with the lawyer might help you stick to the whole truth.

---

### THE ATTORNEY-CLIENT PRIVILEGE

The attorney-client privilege was first used in Elizabethan England in order to encourage clients and attorneys to be entirely truthful with each other. Although the details vary slightly from state to state, the general outlines of the privilege are constant.

- The attorney-client privilege exists between the client and his or her attorney and all members of the attorney's law firm, including staff members. The attorney and his or her staff are not allowed to disclose any privileged information to anyone other than the client, including spouses and family members. The attorney and staff are even forbidden to acknowledge that the client has hired them.

- The privilege exists whenever a client and his or her attorney have a communication for the purpose of seeking, obtaining, or providing legal service to the client. It does not extend to other areas. For example, if you tell your attorney about a business opportunity that has nothing to do with your case, that information is not privileged.

- Neither the client nor the attorney can be compelled to disclose privileged information against the client's wishes.

- The client holds the privilege. Only the client, not the attorney, has the authority to waive the privilege.

- The privilege can be automatically waived in some circumstances, for example, if the client discloses the information to a third party or discusses the information in a location without a reasonable expectation of privacy.

- In most states, the attorney-client privilege extends to communication in person, over the telephone (land line, cordless, or cell), via fax machine, e-mail, or the Internet. This area of the law is still evolving, however, so check with your attorney.

- The attorney-client privilege may not be used as a shield for a contemplated future crime or fraud.

## Choosing a Lawyer

The bottom-line criteria for choosing an attorney is to pick one who is experienced and specializes in your situation. Although you may be tempted to select a family friend because you want someone you can trust, it is far better to hire an attorney who is familiar with your legal issue. Not only is the experienced specialist more likely to get better results, he may also save you money in the long run, writes attorney Richard H. Garrison in his *Client's Guide*: "A $50/hr. lawyer who will earnestly and energetically spend weeks learning about, researching, analyzing, and working on your problem to find a solution is no match for a $400/hr. lawyer who understands the problem, correctly diagnoses it and provides a practical and economical solution in 20 minutes." Don't assume that an attorney who *isn't* a specialist in your area will necessarily volunteer that fact if you don't ask about it. He may want to branch out to a new field and use your case for practice.

There is no shortage of specialist attorneys in most cities, so your challenge will be to narrow the field. The number you interview depends on your stamina and the urgency of your situation. For recommendations, ask friends, coworkers, your dentist or doctor, or anyone whose judgment you trust. Your state bar association will have a referral list organized by specialty. The *Martindale Hubbell Law Directory* and *Who's Who in American Law*, both available at your public library, can also point you toward the right attorney.

In your addled or enraged state of mind, you may want to hire the first lawyer who pounds the desk and declares, "You're right! We'll sue the pants off them!" To avoid making too rash a decision, you need to be clear on what you should reasonably expect from a lawyer aside from commiseration:

**CLARITY.** In all but the most complex situations, the attorney should be able to explain the legal issues in plain English so that you fully comprehend them.

**COMFORT.** You should feel at ease with the lawyer, not intimidated by her. While it may be appealing to hire a "pit bull" who can scare the daylights out of your adversary, that pit bull should not terrify *you* to the point that it would be difficult to speak up for what you want, share information, be truthful, or disagree with his strategy. Avoid lawyers who assume a lofty, godlike air or who rush through their explanations so quickly that you feel like a dunce in their presence. You cannot afford to be intimidated by your lawyer because it could prevent you from being candid or asking questions, which ultimately could hurt your case.

**FORTHRIGHTNESS.** The lawyer should plainly explain his fees, his opinion of the merit of your case, what your case is worth, any conflicts of interest he might have, and anything else that could impact the outcome of your case or the amount of money you will be spending to pursue it.

**OPTIONS.** After your attorney reviews your case, he should present you with all the options you might reasonably take, whether or not he endorses them. He should also explain the risks of going to trial versus settling out of court.

**A PLAN.** The attorney should present you with the strategy he deems most likely to satisfy your needs, bearing in mind any limitations you have set (such as money, time, or energy you are willing to devote to the issue). The plan should include a time frame.

**EXPERIENCE.** To determine an attorney's experience in your particular field, review the questions in the "Phone-Screening a Lawyer" box later in this chapter.

Everyone wants his or her attorney to be a perfect combination of experience and cost-effectiveness, and to that end Richard

Garrison suggests selecting someone who has made partner within the last several years. "Lawyers in that category share many or all of the following characteristics: (1) have about ten years of legal experience; (2) tend to be flexible, imaginative, energetic and eager to please clients; (3) service relatively small client lists and appreciate the importance of new clients and new matters for existing clients; (4) have lower billing rates than 'senior' partners; and (5) can draw on the wisdom of more experienced lawyers in the firm when necessary."

## Lawyers' Fees

Lawyers' fees strike fear into the heart of the average citizen. Hourly rates of $150–$300 are standard for attorneys but surreal to most people, and the idea of being charged every time you call for a brief update can make your blood boil. There are ways to control attorney fees, but it's crucial to do it at the beginning of the relationship. In some states, the law requires the fee structure to be spelled out in a fee agreement, and you should insist on such an agreement whether or not it's the law. Talking to a lawyer about his fees might make you uncomfortable, but it's better than waiting to review the bill.

Lawyer's fees fall into three basic categories: flat fee, hourly rate, and contingency fee.

**FLAT FEE.** The lawyer will work for a specific set fee. Flat fees are usually used for simple cases. Be sure to ask whether expenses such as photocopying, messenger services, and so forth are included in the flat fee.

**HOURLY RATE.** The lawyer will bill you by the hour, and the hours will usually be split up into tenths (six-minute segments). Therefore, if you phone a $150/hr.-lawyer to deliver a two-minute piece of information, you will be billed $15. However, many attorneys are not strict about this. Ask about it at your first meeting to put your mind at ease. Attorneys may also charge different hourly rates for work done in and outside of court.

When you hire an attorney to work by the hour, experience clearly is a major factor. For routine cases, a less-expensive attorney might work out fine. The more complicated the case, the more important it is to have an experienced attorney, even if he charges a high hourly rate. Of course, high fees alone don't guarantee top-notch work. You will still need to interview the lawyer and check his references. Attorneys who charge by the hour should give you a range of time they feel the case is likely to take. You may also be able to negotiate an hourly fee structure that includes a maximum you will pay for the entire project.

**CONTINGENCY FEE.** The lawyer will work for a percentage—usually one-third—of a sum of money awarded by the court. Contingency fees are the norm in cases where an individual, insurance company, or corporation is being sued for a large amount of money, for example, personal injury and property damage cases. If the client doesn't win the case, the lawyer gets nothing. Clients, however, must pay expenses whether or not they win. It is important to set up the agreement so that the contingency fee is calculated *after* expenses have been deducted from the award, ensuring you a larger portion of the money.

Fees vary according to where the attorneys are located (urban lawyers are more expensive), whether or not they are partners, and the number of years they have been in practice. In firms with nine or fewer lawyers, hourly rates average about $180 for partners, $140 for associates, and $72 for paralegals. Young lawyers with three or fewer years' experience average about $120 an hour, while those with 21 years or more take in around $200. Attorneys who specialize in complex criminal cases, corporate litigation, trusts, and estate work often charge $300 an hour or more.

There are several areas in which law firms sometimes try to overcharge their clients. One is expenses. These should be itemized on bills that you receive from the attorney on a regular basis. When you are interviewing attorneys, ask them whether photocopying, word processing, legal research, messenger services, faxing, and meals will be included in the hourly rate, flat fee, or contingency agreement. If they intend to charge you for some of these items, find out what their rates are. Some firms charge 25 cents a page for in-house photocopying—400 percent more than your local copy shop. Not that they should be the cheapest place in town, but they shouldn't gouge you, either.

Another way lawyers stuff their coffers is by padding their hours or charging you a partner's rate for work done by an associate or paralegal. There is no way you can be absolutely sure who is doing what for how long, but you can bring the topic up in your initial consultation by asking pointed questions such as:

- How much of the work will you be doing?
- Who else in the office will be working on my case?
- How many hours do you estimate the case will take?
- Who will be working on the different aspects of my case?

Questions like these will let the attorney know that you will be paying close attention to his bills when they arrive. You may also learn that the attorney doesn't plan to pay your matter much personal attention, in which case you might decide to choose someone else.

Some lawyers will try to include a "minimum billing units" clause in their agreement with you. For example, a lawyer who bills you in units of one-tenths of an hour (six-minute segments) may state that his *minimum* billing unit policy is two-tenths of an hour. That means instead of $15 for your brief phone call, you will be billed $30—two-tenths of an hour. Keep an eye out for this tactic when you look over the fee agreement.

Finally, it is not unheard of for lawyers to bill clients for the time they spend preparing bills *and* the time they spend later arguing with clients over them! Make sure your fee agreement includes a clause prohibiting this nonsense.

---

**THE HALT FEE AGREEMENT**

HALT: The Organization of Americans for Legal Reform has a Web site that includes a "Model Client-Attorney Agreement." This fill-in-the-blank template lists all the pertinent information you will need to craft an equitable fee agreement with your attorney. For simple legal matters, you may not require such a detailed document, but it is still valuable as a checklist for items and events you might not otherwise anticipate. HALT's Web address is www.halt.org.

---

## Phone Screening a Lawyer

Before scheduling a consultation with a lawyer, conduct a phone interview. The following questions will help you determine if the lawyer is a good fit for you and your situation.

- What sort of cases do you specialize in?
- How many cases have you worked on that are similar to mine?
- How long have you been practicing law? Are you a partner in this firm? If so, when did you become a partner?
- Will you be handling the work on my case yourself, or will you be using associates and/or paralegals?
- Is there any reason that my case might present a conflict of interest for you?

- May I have the names and phone numbers of clients for whom you have provided legal services similar to those I need?
- What is your fee structure?
- Is the first consultation free?
- What information and documents would you like me to bring to the first consultation?

Keep notes of these phone interviews, or, better yet, tape record them (ask the attorney permission first). Some of the information might be too confusing for you to grasp as you're scribbling notes, names, and phone numbers. Any electronics store will have inexpensive gadgets you can easily attach to your phone and a tape recorder. Besides, you're about to enter a world where every word counts—you might as well get into the spirit of it.

## Magic Words and Deeds: Working with Your Attorney

The best time to arrange your meeting with an attorney is late in the week and late in the afternoon. Lawyers are rarely available in the mornings anyway, because that's when they have court appearances. If you insist on a morning meeting, the lawyer may have to cancel it. Lawyers also have filing deadlines, which means they must prepare legal documents and deliver them to the court before it closes, usually around 4:30. Documents typically must be completed before 2:00 to allow time for delivery.

"The question is, how much of the attorney's time are you going to get? How at ease is he going to be? How willing to chat with you?" says Suzanne Spillane. "If I were going to have an appointment with an attorney, I'd want it to be on a Friday afternoon. Courts tend to be dark on Friday, so there are no filing deadlines. And the attorneys are going into the weekend, so they're a little less stressed."

Before your meeting, ask the attorney which documents and information he will need. Write a chronology of the events that are relevant to your case as well as a list of questions. Bring two sets of these documents, one for him and one for yourself.

The following words and deeds will help keep the relationship running smoothly during the first meeting and beyond.

**DEFINE YOUR EXPECTATIONS.** After you have explained your case to the attorney, tell him the results you would like to achieve and ask if he feels they are realistic. Ask how long he thinks it will take to settle the matter (or go to trial).

**ASK THE ATTORNEY WHAT HE WILL EXPECT OF YOU.** In addition to legal advice, you need an advocate who shares your philosophy and approach. For instance, a divorce attorney may want you to embark on a long and bloody legal battle that could jeopardize your children's emotional well-being. A personal injury attorney may expect more of your time and energy than you are willing to give. If an attorney's approach feels wrong, look for someone else.

**ASK THE ATTORNEY IF THERE IS WORK YOU CAN DO TO HELP WITH THE CASE.** Acquiring information, photocopying, and drafting simple documents such as letters will not only save you money, it will also send the message that you are an active participant in your case.

**USE E-MAIL.** Attorneys are notorious for not returning phone calls. E-mails are a terrific substitute, enabling you to transmit information without wasting his time and your money.

**TELL THE LAWYER IF YOUR SITUATION CHANGES.** Things that may seem unrelated to the case, such as selecting your child's summer camp, selling some property, or changing jobs, may turn out to have an impact. Run it past your attorney before you do anything.

**KEEP YOUR WORD.** If you agree to do something, follow through. Provide the information he requests, make the phones calls he asks you to make, keep your appointments with him, and be on time. If you are unable honor a commitment, tell him as soon as possible.

**ASK QUESTIONS ABOUT ANYTHING YOU DON'T UNDERSTAND.** Keep asking until you do understand it. Even apparently simple issues can have far-reaching implications.

## Absolute No-No's

"I hate lawyer jokes. Totally hate them," says Suzanne Spillane. "People blame the problems of the legal system on lawyers, and we're not responsible for them. More often than not, it's the clients who want money that they don't deserve. Behind every lawyer, there's a client." Obviously, the wise client does not break the ice with a new lawyer by telling a lawyer joke. Other behaviors to avoid:

- **DON'T EXPECT THE LAWYER TO ANSWER YOUR QUESTIONS INSTANTLY UNLESS THE MATTER IS VERY SIMPLE.** If you're in the office as opposed to having a phone conversation, it means your case is probably too complex to respond to immediately.

- **DON'T DO ANYTHING REGARDING YOUR CASE WITHOUT FIRST RUNNING IT BY YOUR LAWYER.** Nothing. At all.

- **DON'T LEAVE IMPORTANT INFORMATION ON VOICE MAIL OR WITH THE ATTORNEY'S ASSISTANT UNLESS IT'S AN EMERGENCY.** Fax it, mail it, or e-mail it.

- **DON'T CALL OR E-MAIL THE ATTORNEY EVERY TIME A TIDBIT OF INFORMATION POPS INTO YOUR HEAD.** Consolidate them.

- **DON'T MAKE GRATUITOUS JABS ABOUT LAWYERS' FEES.** Example: "So, how much did you bill me for that Christmas card you sent?"

- **DON'T LIE, WITHHOLD INFORMATION, OR TWIST THE FACTS.** "When you're not getting the complete story, you're going to smell it," says Suzanne Spillane. "You're going to say, 'Wait a minute. If this person isn't investing all their knowledge in me, how can I dive into this hook, line, and sinker?' Of course you're going to do your best for them, but in terms of emotionally connecting with them and standing in front of a speeding bullet for them, you're going to hesitate."

---

### PHRASE BOOK: LEGALESE AND LATIN

Legal documents are laced with Latin terms, making them difficult for the average citizen to comprehend. The problem is exacerbated by lawyers' generally awful way with words. To the outsider, their hair-splitting run-on sentences seem created for the sole purpose of confusing people and ensuring more work for themselves. To lawyers, it's a matter of making sure every angle is covered.

The following list of common Latin phrases will help you decipher legal documents, but you may still need a strong cup of coffee and a lot of time.

**AFFIDAVIT:** A written statement made or taken under oath before an officer of the court or someone else authorized to certify the statement.

**ALIAS:** A fictitious name.

**BONA FIDE:** Without fraud or deceit.

**CAVEAT EMPTOR:** Let the buyer beware.

**DE FACTO:** In reality.

**EX OFFICIO:** By virtue of one's office.

**EX PARTE:** In proceedings, when the party against whom they are brought is not heard.

**EX POST FACTO:** After the event.

**FACTUM:** An act or deed.

**FIAT:** Let it be done.

**HABEAS CORPUS:** A procedure for obtaining a judicial determination of the legality of an individual's custody.

**IN CAMERA:** In private.

**IN LOCO PARENTIS:** In place of a parent.

**INTER ALIA:** Among other things.

**IPSO FACTO:** By that very fact; thereby.

**MENS REA:** Mental element or intent required for the commission of a criminal act.

**NON SEQUITUR.** It does not follow.

**OBITE DICTUM:** An incidental statement.

**PER ANNUM:** Annually.

**PER DIEM:** Daily.

**PER SE:** By means of itself.

**PRIMA FACIE:** At first sight; on the face of it.

**QUASI:** Nearly; almost.

**QUID PRO QUO:** Something for something.

**SINE DIE:** Without time.

**STATUS QUO:** The conditions that existed.

**SUBPOENA:** A writ issued under authority of a court to compel the appearance of a witness at a judicial proceeding.

**VERBATIM:** Word by word, exactly.

## The Worst Offenses

Wouldn't it be nice if you had a crystal ball that could reveal exactly what your lawyer would do to annoy you? The next best thing is a *Consumer Reports* survey, and fortunately the magazine conducted one in 1996. They found there was a big difference between the way people perceive lawyers in nonadversarial cases (estate planning, tax preparation, and so forth) and those in adversarial cases (such as insurance claims, divorce, child custody, and personal injury). People whose cases were adversarial were more likely to be dissatisfied, probably because the emotional and monetary stakes are so much higher. Both groups, however, agreed that the following behaviors disturbed them the most.

## TOP SIX COMPLAINTS ABOUT LAWYERS' BEHAVIOR

1. Didn't promptly return my phone calls.

2. Didn't pay adequate attention to my case.

3. Didn't explain how long the process might take.

4. Didn't accurately predict the outcome.

5. Didn't seek my opinion on how to proceed.

6. Had a conflict of interest.

Not returning phone calls is easily the most common criticism. Unfortunately for their clients, good lawyers are often busy. If you need to speak with the attorney and he won't return your call, arrange a phone appointment with his secretary. Otherwise, rely on e-mail.

Complaint number two is similar to the phone call lament but harder to pin down. How much attention is enough? It probably varies from client to client, and you won't know if you're going to feel slighted until you're in the midst of it. However, going over your expectations with the lawyer at the beginning can give you a realistic sense of his commitment to your case.

The rest of the problems might be avoided if you ask about them at the first meeting:

- How long do you think it will take to resolve my case?
- What is your track record on cases like these? (No lawyer can accurately predict the outcome of every case. The best indicator is his track record.)
- Will you consult with me before taking any action?
- Do you have any conflicts of interest?

Take notes as your lawyer is answering these queries, not just to keep him honest but to do the same for yourself. If the lawyer tells you something you don't want to hear, writing it down will prevent you from deceiving yourself about the conversation later on.

## How Do You Say "You're Fired" in Latin?

If you're lucky, the groundwork you do when first hiring a lawyer will save you from ever having to fire him. However, the day may come when you realize that the relationship no longer works and is causing you damage. A great many people fear firing their lawyer because they fear lawyers, period—and not without reason. Attorney Richard Garrison writes, "Consider for a moment what you know about lawyers in general and yours in particular. You probably will agree that your best interests are served by minimizing the number of serious arguments you have with such people."

If you do decide to fire your attorney, plan your moves carefully. Are you in the middle of a legal matter? Switching lawyers at this time can be particularly expensive and risky because whoever else you hire will need to play catch-up on the case. One option is to choose another lawyer from the same firm to be the "lead attorney" on your case. You may even be able to renegotiate your fees, as the change will probably cause you delays and extra work. Asking to switch attorneys will certainly catch the attention of the firm's senior partners, who might want to adjust the fees to mollify you.

If you can't select another lawyer within the firm, start looking elsewhere. Before you let the old lawyer go, make sure the new one is committed to the case and familiar with the details. The good news is, you don't have to fire your old lawyer yourself. The new lawyer will do that for you.

## Hire a Lawyer, Make a Friend

Lawyers' sensitivity about their profession can work in your favor. You can make a positive impression simply by walking into the attorney's office without a chip on your shoulder. Choose your lawyer carefully, and after you hire him, give him your trust and a fair chance to prove his worth. Most attorneys want to have a long-term relationship with you. That is where new work and client referrals come from, but more important, it is where lawyers get their emotional rewards. If you form a bond with your lawyer, he may be the first person you call when trouble strikes. "You want to be able to pick my brain when something bad happens to your family, or you get divorced, or whatever," says Suzanne Spillane. "You don't want to foreclose that opportunity because you're so jaded about lawyers."

**LOCAL POLITICIAN**

# SERVING THE NATION, ONE COMPLAINT AT A TIME

"Politicians," said Abraham Lincoln, "taken as a mass, [are] at least one long step removed from honest men." Not much has changed since he delivered that speech in 1837, least of all the popular opinion of public servants. We mock them from afar, cluck over their incompetence or corruption, and don't bother to vote because the choice often seems to be between Sleepy and Dopey. But love them or hate them, our politicians' decisions influence our lives, and the ones who have the most influence don't live in Washington. They live right in our own neighborhoods. The mayor and city council, along with the various commissioners they appoint, control the roads, schools, libraries, power and water, the police force, and the fire department. Your day-to-day existence is defined by these services, so it behooves you to know how to contact the people who command them.

## Behind the Scenes: New-Fangled, Old-Fashioned Politics

City council members are your most direct link to the forces that govern your town. Who are the people on your city council?

"We're regular citizens like everyone else," says Chuck Mosher, who has served on the city council of Bellevue, Washington, for six years. Like many smaller cities, Bellevue has a part-time council. "We're paid part-time but we're expected to be on duty 24 hours a day. The people I know who are in city offices are not partisan, but we have a strong sense of wanting to serve the public and do what's best in representing our constituents. It really is a sacrificial situation."

Ted Hackworth, who has served on Denver's city council for 22 years, is in it for much the same reason—to be connected with his community. "I'm close to my constituents. We're not talking as strangers, we talk as friends. That type of responsiveness is not something you see with a state legislator or congressional representative. When I first got on the council, the councilmen used to carry a bucket of asphalt and a shovel in the back of their cars. If someone called in and said, 'I've got a chuckhole,' you went and filled it." Personal chuckhole filling is a thing of the past, but the accessibility of your city council is not.

The most popular form of contact with politicians—the personal letter—also happens to be one of the most powerful if it's done right. The hierarchy of effectiveness, from most to least, is:

❶ Personal visit

❷ Personal letter

❸ Phone call

❹ Mass mailing

❺ Petition

❻ E-mail

❼ Electronic barrage

Personal visits make the most impact on a politician, but you will need to invest a fair amount of effort in order to hit your mark (see "Magic Words and Deeds: Meeting with a Politician," on page 211). Letters written by people who are informed about the cause and have a personal stake in it are also extremely effective. Mass mailings are much less so. Politicians figure, often correctly, that signing a preprinted postcard doesn't indicate a very deep level of commitment. Some politicians will even have staff members call a few of the constituents who have mailed in the postcards and query them about the issue. If they seem ignorant, the mail-in campaign loses a lot of its impact. Petitions fail to impress politicians for much the same reason. It takes about 30 seconds to read and sign a petition, so those signatures don't indicate a deep level of commitment on the part of the signees.

Phone calls can be effective *if* you are skilled at communicating verbally. Can you state your case succinctly, come across as well-informed, and not get flustered when Ms. Councilwoman comes on the line? Are you good at answering questions on the fly? Do you know the issue inside and out? If not, you may be better off writing a letter. Even if you're brilliant over the phone, it's wise to send a follow-up letter so the politician has something to keep on file.

E-mails are iffy and should only be used as a last resort, for example, when you learn about an issue mere days or hours before your representative must vote on it. Perhaps the most detested form of communication is the electronic barrage, an orchestrated event where constituents e-mail, fax, and phone their representatives on a prearranged day to make a point. People often resort to this tactic out of frustration, but it is debatable how well it works. Rather than convincing a representative, the e-barrage often infuriates them and their staff and makes them hostile to the cause.

### FINDING THE RIGHT REPRESENTATIVE

People usually contact politicians when they want to change an existing policy, weigh in on an upcoming issue, or get some help with a grievance. The first step in the process is identifying the right person to contact, which depends on the issue itself. Does it relate to a federal, state, or local situation? Your librarian can direct you to the correct official, or you can use the Web:

- Federal representatives: www.senate.gov or www.house.gov.
- State representatives: Type in "state of (your state)" on a search engine to locate the state Web site, which will list all relevant information.
- Local representatives: Type in "city of (your town)" on a search engine. All medium-to-large cities now have Web sites that list city council members (or aldermen, as they are called in some places). Most cities are divided into districts, wards, or boroughs, and the citizens of each district elect a council member to represent their interests. To find your council member, locate the district you live in on the map provided by the Web site, and see who represents it. Smaller cities that are not divided into districts have council members who are elected "at-large," meaning they represent everyone. The Web site will list a street address, phone number, and e-mail address for your council member.

## Magic Words: The Letter

The first place representatives look when a letter arrives is the return address. They want to make sure you live in their district and can vote for them. So whatever you do, put a return address on your envelope and the stationery you use. And if you're considering an anonymous complaint, forget about it. It will immediately get tossed in the wastebasket.

*Do not write about more than one issue per letter.* The whole point of writing is to go on record and have your letter tallied and placed in the appropriate file. Staff members don't always bother to Xerox letters that deal with more than one issue.

Before you write, take a few minutes to think about what you want from the politician. For instance, do you want him or her to:

- Support or oppose particular legislation?
- Make a public statement in support of or opposition to an issue?
- Tell you where he or she stands on an issue?
- Solve a problem (for example, restrict noise or pollution from a nearby factory)?
- Fulfill a request (for example, install speed bumps on your street)?
- Investigate a trend (for example, a rise in home burglaries in your neighborhood)?
- Provide you with information?
- Speak at an event?
- Go on record as supporting a group you're involved with?

The more specific you are, the more satisfaction you're likely to get. If possible, offer one or two solutions to the problem rather than just complaining about it. Try to keep your letter to one page, and never go longer than two. For good results:

❶ Use letterhead stationery or type your name, address, phone number, and e-mail address (if you have one) at the top of a blank page.

**2** In the upper left-hand corner, type the date followed by the representative's title, name, and address.

**3** Write a topic line. (If you are writing a national representative about a particular bill, be sure to include the bill number [Senate bill: S. _____; House bill: H.R._____.]. Include the bill's popular title as well, if there is one.)

**4** Write the salutation, using the person's correct title.

**5** Immediately say what you want the politician to do.

**6** Give your reasons.

**7** Personalize it. Tell how the topic has affected you or someone you know.

**8** Include any quotes or information about the politician that implies he or she agrees with you, either in principle or regarding your specific topic. The more knowledgeable you are about the representative's position, the better.

**9** Mention other people who share your view. It doesn't have to be an organized group; the most important thing is that these other people live in the politician's district and can vote for him or her.

**10** Make it clear that your vote depends on this issue (if it does).

**11** Conclude with a question that demands a specific reply. This leaves them on the hook and makes it harder for them to send back a form letter.

**12** Sign off cordially, and copy the letter to anyone who might conceivably care.

The sample letter below addresses a local issue.

CLAIR S. CITIZEN
460 ANDOVER ST.
SMALLVILLE, FL 07123
000-670-5233 E-MAIL: CCITIZEN@000.COM

May 5, 2005

Councilmember Jane Smith

(Representative's Address)

Re: Dangerous left turns from Maple St. onto Sage Blvd.


Dear Councilmember Smith,

I'm writing to request that you install a traffic signal at the corner of Maple Street and Sage Blvd. The heavy flow of traffic down Sage has led to dangerous conditions at the intersection, especially during morning and evening rush hours. Parents taking their children to nearby Mossman Elementary School tend to cut across the intersection too quickly, endangering pedestrians, many of whom are also children. Last month I personally witnessed a near-collision, and I have since decided to take an alternate, less convenient route to the school to pick up my own kids. I've spoken to many parents and neighbors about the problem and even brought it up at the last P.T.A. meeting. Everyone agrees that the intersection is a disaster waiting to happen.

In the newsletter you sent to my home several months ago, you talked about the safety of our children being a number-one priority. I think you would agree that the traffic hazard at Maple and Sage endangers everyone, children and adults alike. This situation is extremely urgent to me, and your response will affect the way I vote in the next election.

Can you help us alleviate the traffic hazard at Maple and Sage? Perhaps a traffic signal could be installed or a crossing guard hired for the peak school hours. What do you think is the best way to resolve this?

Best regards,
Claire S. Citizen

cc: Mayor William Steckel
Lillian Willco, Producer, CLCK News
Mark Engram, Editor, Smallville Courier

The mayor, the producer, and the editor may not respond to your letter, but if there *is* an accident at Maple and Sage someday, one of them might remember your warning and give the problem more attention than it would otherwise have received.

Do not give a copy of your letter to others in your neighborhood and have them sign their names. "It doesn't help if you have fifteen people writing the same letter," says Bellevue councilman Chuck Mosher. "You think of it more as a machine as opposed to individual taxpayers presenting their thoughts and ideas. If it's obvious that it's an individual who's concerned about a fairly clear-cut issue, we would be more inclined to help."

## Magic Words: The Phone Call

In general, phone calls are not as effective as letters, but if you're more likely to pick up the phone than sit down and write, here are a few pointers.

**BE WILLING TO TALK TO A SUBORDINATE.** Although phone calls are usually easier to arrange than personal meetings, there is a chance you won't get through to the representative and will instead speak with a staff member. Do this graciously. It is the staff member who will tally your opinion and eventually put you in contact with the representative.

**IF YOU END UP SPEAKING WITH A STAFFER, LET THE PERSON KNOW THAT YOU ARE A REGISTERED VOTER IN THE OFFICIAL'S DISTRICT.** Then briefly state the issue and your opinion, backing it up with a few good reasons. Say thank you and good-bye, unless the staffer seems interested in prolonging the conversation.

**KNOW YOUR TOPIC.** There is a good chance the representative and his or her staff will already be aware of the issue, so be prepared to discuss it and answer questions. Listen to what the representative has to say and respond honestly. Don't be taken aback if he or she challenges you; after all, this is a dialogue. If you can't present evidence supporting your case, maybe you should write a letter instead.

**THANK THE POLITICIAN OR STAFF MEMBER FOR HIS OR HER TIME.** If possible, follow up with a brief note of thanks, and again mention what you would like the representative to do.

One word of caution: do not get into the habit of calling the representative's office all the time. Council members and their staffs are usually overworked, and if you get to be a nuisance they might stop taking your calls.

## Magic Words and Deeds: Meeting with a Politician

If you really want to make an impression, nothing beats a personal visit. It's best to bring a friend or two along for the occasion; three people per visit is a good number. You probably won't have much time—maybe as little as five minutes—so it is essential to be prepared.

The advice in this section also applies to speaking at a city council meeting. These meetings typically reserve a period of time for citizens to present their concerns, usually about three to five minutes for each person. You will be speaking before an audience as well as the entire city council, so it's crucial to be well versed on the issue when you step up to the mike.

Whether you are going to a city council meeting or to a visit with your representative, prepare by clarifying what you want the representative to do. Review the list on page 207 and pinpoint the issue or issues you want to discuss, then research the politician's history concerning these issues. If she opposes your views, be sure not to leave her with any information that could be used against your cause. If she is neutral, be equally cautious. If she supports your issue, tell her how grateful you are and ask if there is anything you can do to help with her efforts.

If you are meeting with your representative, write a one-page summary to leave behind. It should include the same information a letter would, minus the salutation and the line about your vote riding on her response. (It's obvious you care about the issue or you wouldn't be bothering to meet with the representative in person.) If there are additional documents that support your view (research papers, articles, or surveys, for example), you may leave them as well, but the summary should be no longer than one page.

You might be making the appointment with a member of the representative's staff. Be polite even if you want to meet *now* and they can't fit you in for another two weeks. You want these staff members on your side in the future.

On the day of your appointment:

- Arrive fifteen minutes early.
- Look "normal." That means neat, clean, and middle-of-the-road.
- Be prepared to wait patiently. Representatives are busy people

and emergencies come up all the time, so don't get offended if your meeting gets delayed.

- Have several copies of your summary and supporting documents on hand.

- When you get inside the politician's office, be friendly but get to the point quickly.

- Present your case, roughly following the course you would in a letter. Don't forget to offer your ideas and suggestions.

- If the representative is personally involved in the issue, make sure to acknowledge that. "If they were to say, 'I've observed your actions and I know you're environmentally sensitive,' I would pay much more attention to that," says Chuck Mosher.

- Talk about the issue in a positive way. Do not label the behavior of the representative, for example by announcing that you know she's "in bed with the developers."

- Bring graphics. "We had someone who was concerned about a road being built in his area," says Mosher. "He actually put up a diagram of the road and showed why bicycles would not be able to pass in the available lane space. It was very effective in getting us to do what he wanted."

- Be ready to engage in a debate. Answer questions to the best of your ability and back up your position with facts whenever you can. Even if the representative agrees with you, he might be eager for fresh ammunition he can use to defend the issue to his opponents.

- Show what you know. It's possible that you will be more informed about your topic than the politician is. It doesn't mean he's ignorant, it's just that politicians have dozens of issues on their plates at a time.

- Ask where the representative stands on the issue. Even if you think you know, make sure he hasn't changed his mind. If he has, ask why.

- Be interested in him. Thank him for anything he has done that you approve of (you'll know about it from your research). If there is an upcoming campaign, inquire as to how things are going.
- Thank the representative for hearing you out, whether or not he agrees to do what you ask.

After the meeting, write a thank-you letter and be sure to include any additional documentation you promised to send. Then wait and see what the person does, and be prepared to follow up with more letters, phone calls, maybe even another visit. The more difficult, controversial, or expensive your proposal, the longer it will take to be resolved.

## Absolute No-No's

"I'm a taxpayer! I have rights, too!" True, but politicians don't want to hear about it. Whether you are writing, phoning, or sitting in their office, avoid the following behaviors.

**DON'T REMIND POLITICIANS THAT YOU PUT THEM IN OFFICE AND THAT THEY ARE SUPPOSED TO REPRESENT THE WILL OF THE PEOPLE.**

**DON'T USE NEGATIVE, AGGRESSIVE BEHAVIOR.** Chuck Mosher recalls a city council meeting where a man who was concerned about city growth stood up and announced, "You stupid people better stop this now, or we're going to be mad at you." A number of people in the audience clapped and cheered. But instead of intimidating the council, this type of bullying "elicits the opposite response," says Mosher. "We're almost ready to do it whether you like it or not. We'll show you who's in charge."

**DON'T MAIL LENGTHY DOCUMENTS WITH A LETTER, AND DON'T BRING A HUGE SHEAF OF DOCUMENTS TO A MEETING.** If there is a lot of documentation available on the topic, provide a list and offer to send the representative any item he requests.

**DON'T LIE.** Being caught in a lie will destroy your credibility and damage the credibility of everyone who backs your cause.

**DON'T THREATEN THE POLITICIAN WITH PETITIONS, A GRASSROOTS CAMPAIGN AGAINST HIM, LETTERS TO THE EDITOR, AND SO FORTH.** Unless you are wealthy or otherwise powerful, your threats won't mean much.

## There's a Limit to Their Powers

City council members can accomplish many things, but they must work within certain limits. For one thing, they must have a name attached to a request in order to act on it. "People want to object to what a neighbor is doing, but they don't want to be identified," says Denver city councilman Ted Hackworth. "They want you to take care of it, to be the complainant so that they don't have to get personally involved. I try to encourage them to stand up for their rights." And then there are those folks who think council members are all-powerful. "I had a lady who took her kids to the park and they got bitten by mosquitoes. She wondered what I was going to do about that," he recalls. It seems that there are a few Sleepy's and Dopey's out in the general population as well as in City Hall.

## IRS AGENT
## A KINDER, GENTLER AUDIT

There is nothing more likely to send our hearts going pitter-pat and our minds conjuring dreadful fantasies than a letter from the Internal Revenue Service. Similar to the guilty assumptions we make about speeding when a police car appears in the rear-view mirror, we automatically assume we've done something wrong if the IRS contacts us. And truth be told, many of us have fudged . . . just a little . . . maybe on that gas or entertainment deduction. Yet even the fudgers among us are not without recourse should the IRS come to call. Times have changed since the days when the "taxman" relentlessly pursued the average citizen. There's a new IRS in town, an IRS determined to sheathe its mighty powers in a cloak of gentility. The agency's newfound manners have made taxes and audits a lot more tolerable for everyone.

### Behind the Scenes:
### Know Your Opponent

Sometime in the year 1996, Congress became aware that the IRS needed a serious face-lift. There had long been a stream of complaints: the system was inefficient and poorly managed; its technology was prehistoric. Its lack of a modern infrastructure made it unresponsive and unaccountable. Congress was also getting uneasy about the fact that the IRS agent, a public servant after all, was greeted with about as much enthusiasm as a rattlesnake might be. Citizens were particularly outraged that individual tax agents could harass them, violate their privacy, and put liens on their property, all without a hint of substantiation. The burden of proof was always on the taxpayer, who was assumed guilty until he could prove he was innocent.

The reaction to all this dysfunction was the formation of the National Commission on Restructuring the IRS. The goals of the commission were to create a more streamlined and efficient IRS that would be sensitive to citizens' civil liberties. This IRS would be courteous and helpful. Employees would be of the highest caliber, governed by a management that was skilled and responsive. These were grandiose plans for a cumbersome bureaucracy, but the commission interviewed hundreds of IRS employees, tax professionals, and ordinary taxpayers to develop a boilerplate for the new and improved IRS. The culmination of all this work resulted in the IRS Restructuring and Reform Act of 1998. Some very concrete benefits have come out of this makeover, particularly for taxpayers facing an audit.

There is now a Taxpayers' Bill of Rights designed to protect your privacy and ensure that tax agents are not abusive or threatening. In addition, there is an independent Taxpayer Advocacy Service (877-777-4778) within the IRS that you can appeal to if you feel you have been treated unfairly or that an IRS ruling will put you through undo hardship. The IRS has set up a user-friendly Web site (www.irs.gov) that offers all kinds of useful information and tips, including all the laws associated with the restructuring and reform act. You can also call the IRS at 800-829-1040 to request assistance in filling out forms and for clarification of the tax laws. The people who answer the phone are, indeed, courteous and helpful, as promised. The IRS even has a mission statement now: "The IRS will provide America's taxpayers top quality service by helping them understand and meet their tax responsibilities by applying the tax law with integrity and fairness to all."

All this warm fuzziness still has at its heart the purpose of collecting taxes. At the time the act was created, it was estimated that the IRS was short $278 million of the taxes it was due for that year. You can bet they want to close that gap. The important thing to remember is that if you must face an audit, you no longer have to greet it with fear and trembling. Your IRS tax agent probably won't bring milk and cookies to the meeting, but you can walk in knowing that you have recourse through the rights of appeal and formal grievance procedures. You have the right to ask for explanations and accountability from the IRS, just as the IRS will ask of you.

## Who Gets Audited?

Your likelihood of being audited is actually quite low. Of the roughly 135 million tax returns filed each year, the IRS audits about 50,000. Of those 50,000, many never reach the excruciating line-by-line, face-to-face interview that is feared by the taxpayer. Most audits are only requests for additional information or clarification of a minor discrepancy, and can be resolved easily through correspondence. Thorough bookkeeping is the best way to keep these inquiries from blossoming into the hated office audit, where you bring your business records to the IRS office, or the hated and feared field visit where the IRS agent comes to your home or office to conduct the audit.

Audits are supposedly selected at random, but there are particular situations and types of tax filings that will increase your chances of being chosen. The following types of returns are at greatest risk:

- Form 1040s that included a Schedule C reporting on gross business earnings more than $100,000. Schedule Cs are filed by sole proprietors of a business; they list the business's income and expenses.

- Form 1040s that include a Schedule A (a list of itemized deductions) that totals more than 35 percent of the filer's adjusted gross income. The IRS is looking for deductions that people don't legitimately qualify for. Large tax deductions relative to income trigger 90 percent of audits.

- S corporations that report payments as dividends rather than as salaries. Sole proprietors sometimes set up S corporations because the dividends they pay themselves in lieu of a salary are not subject to self-employment (Social Security and Medicare) taxes. The IRS is aware of this ploy and on the lookout for it.

- Mathematical mistakes, particularly when earnings don't match the information on W-2s.

- Claiming losses year after year on small, home-based businesses when the filer also works a regular job.

- Sloppy, unprofessional looking returns with incomplete information.

- Not filing a tax return. If you're in a bind and can't make the April 15 deadline, do what millions of others do each year and file an extension.

## Be Prepared

It's never too late to develop good tax habits, and those habits will reap you a world of benefits should you some day get audited. Let the following three rules be your guide.

First, be honest. Claim all your income (including interest on investments; the IRS *will* receive documentation of them) and your business revenue. It is more damaging to lie about income than it is to exaggerate deductions. If you itemize, claim only legitimate deductions. Check with the IRS if you're not sure. For items such as travel and entertainment, automobile mileage, and home office expenses that are allowable in some types of businesses, don't get carried away and claim more than is reasonable. On the other hand, don't under-itemize because you're not sure— you are not expected to pay more taxes than you owe. Laws have changed regarding the receipts and record-keeping required for some deductions; check with an accountant or the IRS if you're uncertain. Also, be wary of tax preparers whose creative ideas for saving you money seem to be borderline illegal. Many a taxpayer has been penalized when these ideas have proven to be nothing but scams. You are still the one who is accountable for your taxes, even if they have been prepared by a professional.

The second important tax habit is keeping good records. IRS agents, like clerical workers everywhere, prefer legible writing and neatly kept records to a shoebox full of crumpled receipts. (Contrary to popular opinion, a shoebox full of receipts will not daunt the agent or make him too weary to continue his work. It will merely provoke him.) Small-business owners are notorious for keeping sloppy records that make them vulnerable in an audit. Save receipts for every business expenditure, particularly those you plan to deduct. Note all deposits and their source. Do not mix personal money with business money in the same account. If you are going to claim a charitable deduction, make sure you have a legitimate receipt for the actual value of the item.

Remember that if you get audited, you may get penalized if you can't show reasonable proof of income, expenditures, and deductions. If you can't provide the simplest form of proof— receipts—there are ways to reconstruct approximate value by getting estimates for a similar item or service or getting duplicate records from a vendor or bank. But why go to all that trouble? It will be easier in the long run, and better for business, to clean up your records now. (The IRS has the right to review tax returns where unreported income is suspected for six years back, so it is wise to save your records for six years and your cancelled checks for seven.)

Last, file professional, complete tax forms. Nothing will cause an IRS tax agent to pounce more quickly than a form that is illegible, incomplete, or mathematically incorrect. Make sure every line is filled out. Write "0" or "N/A" in lines that do not apply. Type the form if you have handwriting that is difficult to read. Check your math twice. Make sure the form is signed. Many thousands of audits have been unnecessarily triggered by bad math or the simple fact that the filer forgot to sign. If you have any entries that are ambiguous or unusual (a very large deduction, for example), attach an explanatory note; most of these notes are accepted on good faith. If you have difficulty getting through the tax process in any way or if your business is complex, do yourself a favor and have an accountant prepare your taxes.

## Magic Words and Deeds

The three habits mentioned in the previous section will not only help you avoid an audit, they will also will make the process go much smoother if you do get selected. If your number comes up, the following advice will minimize your pain and suffering.

**RESPOND IMMEDIATELY TO IRS CORRESPONDENCE REQUESTING AN AUDIT.** The IRS is required to notify you in writing, not on the telephone. If you need more time to prepare for your audit, ask for a later date or even a change of venue. Sometimes these delaying tactics work in your favor because they allow you more time to prepare. Responding quickly to correspondence does not mean that you will be pressured to appear for the audit before you're ready.

**READ WHAT IS BEING REQUESTED VERY CAREFULLY.** Take the time to fully understand what the IRS wants to review. You will want to prepare those documents and those documents only; never let an agent peruse your files. You will also want to present the documents in a very clear manner that is easy for the IRS agent to understand. Offering ambiguous information or more information than is required is always a poor move. You do not want to be questioned in any way that will broaden the scope of the audit. Before the meeting, review your papers once again, comparing what you have prepared against what has been requested.

**KNOW YOUR RIGHTS.** Call the IRS or go to their Web site before your audit. Find out what you have the right to question and how to report the agent if you feel he has treated you unkindly or unfairly.

**BE ON TIME FOR YOUR APPOINTMENT.** It is a good idea to arrive 15 to 20 minutes early so you can review what you have prepared and be relaxed when it is time to begin.

**BE COURTEOUS AND CORDIAL, BUT NOT CHUMMY.** Conduct yourself like a professional at all times but do not get too friendly. Auditors are trained to try to elicit information from people. Some will purposely create gaps of silence in the conversation in hopes that you might offer information that can be used against you in the audit. If you get too relaxed and start chatting away, you might reveal information that will lead to further probing into your financial affairs. Since most audits result in your owing some money, keeping the audit short and sweet may mean keeping more money in your pocket.

**WHEN IN DOUBT, SEND IN THE PROFESSIONALS.** Many people who have been selected for an audit opt for letting their accountants attend the audit instead of attending themselves. This is perfectly legitimate, particularly if an accountant prepared your taxes; that person will need to explain his rationale. Many auditors prefer dealing with accountants because they are fellow professionals in the field and it helps facilitate the process. Having your accountant attend the audit is wise because he will know what the auditor is looking for and can speak his language. The accountant will not be nervous and say the wrong thing, and he will know how to avoid some of the traps an IRS agent might set in order to elicit more information. When deciding whether to have your accountant represent you at an audit, evaluate what is at stake. If you might end up owing a negligible amount of money in taxes, it's hardly worth the expense. If the stakes are higher, go for professional help.

## Absolute No-No's

No one would describe an audit as a magical experience, but there are definite blunders that will break the spell of a short, sweet, to-the-point audit. As stated above, when contacted by the IRS for an audit, respond immediately. Many people have gotten themselves into hot water by not responding at all. Your audit will not go away if you ignore it. Eventually the IRS will come knocking, and it will not be a happy IRS. By ignoring an audit summons, you may have to pay penalties on taxes you don't even owe or risk broadening the scope of the audit because you have aroused suspicion.

When you do attend your audit, never argue and antagonize the IRS agent. They do not want to hear your sarcastic remarks, excuses ("Everybody takes that deduction!"), or demands for your rights as an American citizen. There are procedures to follow when you have a disagreement with the agent, outlined in the next section. Lying is also a very bad idea. If you fear that revealing certain information might incriminate you, you can politely refuse to answer. Simply tell the agent that you're not sure of the information and need more time to prepare it. Arguing and lying are always losing propositions. The IRS may be renovating its public image, but it is still a bureaucracy with enormous powers.

They can seize your assets, attach your wages, and close your business. Don't mess with them.

Finally, do not challenge the IRS with claims that the federal income tax is illegal according to the Constitution. There have been groups and individuals who make these claims (and have convinced naive individuals to join their cause) but they have never been upheld in court. If you legally challenge the legitimacy of federal taxes, the court will actually punish you with a $5,000 frivolous claim penalty that you will have to pay in addition to court costs. Besides, your friends will think you've joined a band of survivalists who are waiting for the world to blow up after the next big computer glitch.

In sum, you want the audit to stay narrowly focused and be resolved quickly. Unless you irritate the agent into a personal grudge match, this is probably his goal as well. IRS agents are not interested in getting as much money from you as possible; they are interested in satisfying bureaucratic paperwork requirements. As long as it looks reasonable on paper, they will go along with it.

## It's Not Over Till You Say It's Over

Before signing off on the auditor's findings, you are allowed to take them home and review them. Do take advantage of this. With findings in hand, you can review every point and even consult your tax preparer to make sure you are not being overtaxed or unfairly penalized. If you have a disagreement with the findings, you can ask to speak to the auditor's supervisor for clarification. If you still don't agree, you have the right to appeal the findings at the IRS appeals office. If no agreement is reached there, you may take your case to tax court. Ideally, none of this will be necessary. If you review the auditor's findings and they appear reasonable to you, the IRS will prepare a document for you to sign, you'll write them a check, and the audit is over.

What if you don't have the money to pay the IRS what it demands? They will probably allow you to work out a payment plan called an Offer in Compromise. Go to www.irs.gov, type "Offer in Compromise" in the search box, and all your questions will be answered.

The important thing to remember about an audit is that it is not an accusation of wrongdoing. It is a request for information. If you keep your emotions in check, don't panic, and handle the request in a straightforward and professional manner, you should have no problems. You may owe some money and, in some cases, you may even get a few bucks back.

## CAR SALESMAN
## LINERS, CLOSERS, AND SUCKERS

Car salesmen are often portrayed as sharks, but selling cars involves more than a blunt attack. It takes cunning, strategy, and teamwork. Don't think sharks, think lions, who must get very close to their prey in order to take it down. One lion will stalk and chase the intended victim, while others wait to ambush it when it is confused and exhausted. Like the hungry lion, the car salesman carefully plots his approach. Every word he speaks has been rehearsed, every movement considered. The plan is to make you feel powerless, panic you into thinking you won't get the car you want, and herd you into the mouth of the waiting "sales manager." Later, what remains of your wallet will be plucked clean by the deceptively mild-mannered "business manager."

Yet your biggest threat at the car dealership isn't the sales staff, it is your own desire. When the salesman sidles up to you and murmurs, "Have you seen that in metallic blue?" your palms aren't sweating because of him. You're scared because you don't trust yourself, and the reason may be that you have walked into this waterhole as unprepared as a baby gnu. You feel weak, trapped. Will you be able to get out alive, or will you cave in to his pressure and your own lust?

There is good reason to worry. If you're not careful, buying a car can cost you thousands of extra dollars in the form of extended monthly payments, unnecessary add-ons, poor value on your trade-in, or a high-interest loan or lease. Your ignorance will cost you more at a car dealership than just about anywhere else, with the possible exception of a funeral home. In fact, car salesmen and funeral directors use many of the same techniques: baffling contracts, confusing lingo, peer pressure, and creating a false sense of urgency about the sale. Fortunately, unlike a funeral, buying a car is usually an event you can plan for in advance.

Knowledge will help you overcome your fear of the salesman and see this transaction for the mind game it really is. To win, you need only be aware of two things: the invoice price of the car and the strategies the salesman will use to overcharge you. Surprisingly, there aren't many variations on these strategies. If you know what to look for, the salesman's moves will be as predictable as a vintage episode of *Wild Kingdom*. You won't get angry, insulted, or intimidated by his machinations, you'll merely smile and play along. And that is how you will walk away with the car you want at a price you can brag about.

## Behind the Scenes: The Clock Is Ticking

Every few years, the Gallup organization asks citizens to rate the honesty and ethics of people in various professions. For the past two and a half decades, Americans have put car salesmen at the very bottom of the list, beneath lawyers, politicians, and even telemarketers. Who are these people we fear and loathe? About 92 percent of them are male. A great many are just passing through the field of auto sales, lured by the possibility of earning a lot of money with a scant amount of training. Chandler Phillips, who spent several months working undercover as a car salesman on assignment for the Web site edmonds.com, found his colleagues to be a dispirited crew: "I was struck by how the other salesmen described themselves in ways that revealed extremely low self-images. Most of them were divorced or refugees from other unsuccessful careers. Others were downright bitter and hostile."

Whether they are morose or upbeat, one common denominator applies: their survival depends on parting you from your money. The typical car salesman is successful only 20 percent of the time, which means that for every ten customers he talks to—often for hours—he will make only two sales. The salesman's take-home pay comes directly from his commission, which is based on a percentage (usually 20–25 percent) of the profit of the sale.

A national survey reported that the average commission is about $250 and most salesmen sell 8–10 cars a month. That means they are earning $500–600 a week, or around $30,000 a year. In order to goose the salesmen along, management usually creates a system of bonuses. It might be a sliding commission scale—the more they sell, the higher their commission percentage will be. It might be a specific dollar amount awarded to the salesman who sells X number of cars in a week, a certain slow-moving model, the most cars in a month, or add-ons such as window-etching or extended warranties.

Car salesmen spend many long hours at the dealership, especially on the weekends, when most cars are sold. Why do they do it? Not for $30,000 a year. Most novice salesmen are led to believe they can earn two or three times that amount if they have the right attitude and tools. More important, they are told they can learn these techniques in a five- or ten-day training period. Knowledge about the dealership's vehicles or about cars in general is rarely a requirement. All you need is the will to sell.

There is one underlying theme to the training programs at car dealerships: do whatever it takes to ingratiate yourself with the customer and get him to buy *today*. Craig Raggio, who sold cars in Northern California for many years, recites the gospel according to car dealers: "Research says, when somebody comes on a lot, they're going to buy a car within 48 hours. That's where the whole bad reputation for car salesmen comes from, the pushy, do anything, keep turning them philosophy." *Turning them* means turning the customer over to another salesperson if the first salesman is getting nowhere. "I might take you over to some guy who just started three days ago and act like he's my superior, like you've moved up a notch," says Raggio. Anything to get you to stay.

Some of the salesman's people skills sound like Dating 101: mirror the customer, copy his body language, agree with his every opinion, flatter him ("That's my favorite make, too. . . . I have that car myself. . . . You live at the marina? I'd love to live there!"). Other techniques hark back to a 1950s sales mentality: pump the person's hand firmly three times when you shake it and remember to say, "Welcome," because it creates a feeling of warmth. Chandler Phillips recalls being instructed to "combine the handshake with a slight pulling motion. This is the beginning of your control over the customer. This would prepare the 'up' [customer] to be moved into the dealership where the negotiation would begin."

It's all about control, of course. Ultimately, you are in control because you can walk out of the dealership any time you like. The salesman's goal, therefore, is to make you feel as if you have no control and are compelled to buy a car right now. As he walks you around the lot, takes you on a test drive, and ushers you into the sales office, he is continually sizing you up to see how malleable you are, how easy to manipulate. In their training sessions or within a few weeks of working on the lot, salesmen learn to poke around for your weak spots and assess your strength.

In the testosterone-rich environment of the average car lot, desk managers are the snarling alpha males. From their offices deep within the labyrinth of the dealership, they crunch the numbers and take most of the profit. (These managers are not the same ones you will be introduced to during your negotiation for a car.) According to Phillips, the desk managers at many dealerships "bully the sales staff, encouraging them to manipulate, control, and intimidate customers." The managers don't hesitate to berate salesmen in front of their coworkers and mete out punishment to poor performers.

The salesman who greets you as you step out of your car is called the *liner* (they line you up for a sale). The sales manager to whom you will eventually be turned over, either on the lot or in the sales office, is the *closer*. The closers have crews of liners with whom they work, playing bad cop to the liners' good cops. During the long hours you spend in the sales office, liners try to establish a bond with you and exploit your empathy in order to prod the sale.

Recently, some dealerships have instructed their salespeople to tone down the hard sell, having finally grasped that today's consumers are aware of car sales strategies and dislike high-pressure pitches. It's all chillin' now at these laid-back dealerships, with bowls of chips on the table and football on TV. They couldn't care less if you buy a car, or so it seems at first. If you tell them that you've done your homework and would like to skip the drama and cut directly to a reasonable negotiation, they will nod wearily and say they couldn't agree more. That may be true, but in the end it doesn't matter. "Today's customers are a lot more informed, but they are still going to go through the same dog and pony show," says Jack McGuirk, who sold cars in Seattle for ten years. The structure of the deal, the hoops they make you jump through, the hours they make you wait, have not changed one whit. You will still end up in a cubicle with the same three players—salesman, sales manager, and business manager—each of whom must scrape for a commission the same way he has always done.

## Shop First, Buy Later

Every savvy consumer spends at least a few hours researching cars before actually buying one. This research can grow into days' or weeks' worth of online detective work, resulting in folders full of printed information. Before you dive into all this, it only makes sense to be sure of the car you want by test driving and inspecting it in person.

On his excellent Web site, beatthecarsalesman.com, former salesman Michael Royce makes an important distinction between shopping for a car and buying one. The great majority of cars are sold on the weekend, so Royce advises people to shop on a weekday or weekday evening when business at the dealership is slow and the salespeople have time to talk with you and take you on long test drives. When you have decided on the car you want and the dealership you want to purchase it from, go back to buy it on the weekend. The more crowded it is, the less time they will have to prolong your negotiation. According to Royce, the time of year you buy isn't as important as the time of month. Dealerships chart sales on a monthly basis, and as the weeks pass, the salesmen become more anxious to meet their monthly quotas so they can earn bonuses. Therefore, you have the best chance of getting a good deal on the last weekend of any month.

Before you go shopping, ask yourself whether you are easily tempted, whether your desire for a new car might lead you to stumble and actually buy one on impulse. If you're weak, take a strong friend along on these shopping excursions. If you trust yourself, you can go alone.

## How Much Do You Really Need to Know Before You Buy a New Car?

The best thing that has happened to auto consumers over the past decade is the advent of Web sites devoted to new and used car sales. The sites break down into three groups: online advertising sites that list cars for sale, such as recycler.com and cars.com; sites that offer buying guidelines, pricing, and reviews, such as kellybluebook.com and edmunds.com; and activist sites such as fightingchance.com, beatthecarsalesman.com, and car-buyingtips. com. The first two groups are fairly easy to use. The latter group has valuable information, but the downside is that some of the activist sites are so jam-packed with data, advice, and warnings that they can be almost as daunting as the dealership itself.

The most effective way to use the Internet for your car search is to target the essential information and compare it on several sites. The must-have info is:

**INVOICE PRICE.** The invoice price is the amount the dealer paid to the manufacturer. You can find it on edmunds.com or autoweb. com, among other pricing sites, or in a *New Car Pricing Guide,* available at newsstands. The invoice price is the same thing as the dealer's wholesale price. When you are negotiating the price of a new car, you can ask to see a copy of the factory invoice, which will show exactly how much that dealer paid for the car. It should be very close to the number you got online. If you are interested in a used car, research prices by following the steps in "The retail value of your trade-in" on the next page.

**DEALER HOLDBACKS.** Dealers get money back from the manufacturers of certain cars after the cars are sold. This money is called a dealer holdback, and it has the effect of lowering the actual wholesale cost of the car. That is how dealers can sell some cars at "below invoice"—after receiving the holdback, they will still make money. If they are getting a holdback, they will require less money from you to make a profit. You can find out if the car you want has a holdback or other incentive by visiting edmunds .com and clicking on "Incentives & Rebates." The dealer holdback may also be called a dealer incentive or dealer marketing support.

**CASH REBATES.** This is money provided to the customer by the manufacturer. Cash rebates are not offered on all cars, but you need to know if one exists for the car you're interested in. This information is listed along with the "Incentives & Rebates" on edmunds.com, or you can call the manufacturer and ask them. You can also ask the dealership, but would you really trust their word alone? Also, some dealerships have been known to act is if they, not the manufacturer, are giving you the rebate. Some have even attempted to withhold it.

**THE RETAIL VALUE OF YOUR TRADE-IN.** The trade-in price of your current car is where dealerships make much of their money. If you must trade it in (as opposed to selling it yourself), make sure you know its retail value. You can find this information on kellybluebook. com and edmunds.com, and do a reality check by comparing prices in your local classified ads or referrering to edmunds.com's True Market Value feature. Naturally, the dealer is not going to give you the full retail price, but you need to be aware of it so you can deal with him from a position of knowledge. Kellybluebook and edmunds offer the price you might reasonably expect a dealership to pay for your trade in.

**YOUR CREDIT RATING.** The super-low-interest loans advertised by dealerships are for people with super-high credit ratings (at least 680). The dealer can get your credit rating for you, but they have been known to lie and say your rating is lower than it actually is. You can get a copy of your credit report, including your rating, online at consumerinfo.com, among many other sites.

## Prep Work: The Four Key Numbers

Once you have gathered the information listed above, you will be able to determine the four key numbers you will work with during your negotiation with the dealership:

- The price you are willing to pay for the car.
- The price you want for your trade-in.
- The interest rate and terms you are willing to accept.
- The down payment.

**THE PRICE YOU ARE WILLING TO PAY FOR THE CAR.** This should be in the range of 2–4 percent over dealer invoice, if the car is not in high demand and there are no dealer holdbacks or customer cash rebates. Dealerships usually strive to make a much higher profit, between 10–20 percent over invoice. At 2 percent on a car with an invoice price of $30,000, the dealer will make $600 and the salesman will walk away with $120–$150. That's fair. If you agree to 4 percent over invoice—$1,200 profit for the dealership—that's quite generous yet still a price you needn't lose sleep over. If there are holdbacks and rebates, apply those to your final price. As a benchmark, use edmunds.com's True Market Value pricing, which takes into account holdbacks and rebates.

As part of the preparation process, you might want to write down the first offer you will make to the salesman, just so it's clear in your mind. On the car with the $30,000 invoice, for example, you might begin negotiations by offering 1 percent over invoice, or $30,300. From that point on, as we'll see later, you can inch your way up.

The more popular the car, the more you will have to pay for it. It's not unusual for people to pay hundreds or even thousands of dollars over sticker price when they're set on having the newest toy on the block. In this case you are at a disadvantage, and your best hope for avoiding financial disaster is to bring along one or two level-headed friends who can reel you in (a necessity in any car deal).

Some consumers become obsessed with getting a car at the lowest possible price in the city. Knowing that the dealer is trying to gouge them ignites a burning desire to beat the pros at their own game. Searching for the lowest of the low prices can lead you to reject a perfectly acceptable deal. What's worse, it means you'll have to spend even more time searching for your new car and haggling with salesmen. Better to decide on a price that's fair to both you and the dealer, and stick to that.

**THE PRICE YOU WANT FOR YOUR TRADE-IN.** This is the soft underbelly of many car buyers—the place they are most vulnerable during the negotiation. It's also the place where dealerships typically make a big profit. They particularly love to see trade-ins on which you still owe a lot of money. The dealership will take your current loan and absorb it into the new loan they're financing for the car you are buying from them. They get that much more on the interest, plus they get to sell your trade-in. "Most people driving down the street are buried in their automobiles," says Craig Raggio. "They owe more on them than they're worth. You'll see dealerships advertising, 'Are you buried in your car? Bring it in. We'll get you out of it.' They will, just to re-bury you in another car."

Whether you owe money on your existing car or it is fully paid, you will make more money selling it yourself. However, if you don't have the time or energy to do that, there are options besides trading it in. You can sell the car later to a used-car dealership like Carmax, which may give you a better price. In any case, you'll be negotiating with a clearer head, which has to work to your advantage. Barter organizations will often accept cars in exchange for trade, and you may be surprised by how much is available through these businesses. Check them out on nate.org, the Web site for the National Association of Trade Exchanges. You can also donate used vehicles to charitable organizations and claim the amount as a tax write-off. This can be a wise move, especially if your car is old. Bottom line: determine a fair trade-in price from your research and do not let the salesman convince you that your car is worth less, no matter how much you long to dump it.

**THE INTEREST RATE AND TERMS YOU ARE WILLING TO ACCEPT.** If your credit rating is good and the manufacturer is offering special low-interest financing on the car you want, there's no reason not to take advantage of it. The only drawback is that the low rates usually apply only to 24- or 36-month loans, which makes the monthly payments too high for many car buyers. If you don't qualify for the low-interest loans, it's far preferable to finance the car elsewhere—your credit union, your bank, your mom and dad. If your credit is so bad that you can't get a loan from anyone but the dealership, do some online homework before beginning your car search. Several Web sites provide auto financing, among them eloan.com and CapitalOneAutoFinance.com. They'll show you how to crunch the numbers so you are prepared for the figures the salesman will thrust at you during the negotiation.

**THE DOWN PAYMENT.** This amount affects your monthly payments; the more cash you can afford to put down, the lower your monthly payments will be.

### FIGHTINGCHANCE.COM

There are many excellent auto Web sites, but if you want to greatly reduce your research hours, visit fightingchance. com. Unique among the Web sites, fightingchance will provide you with an extensive dossier on the new car you want to purchase. The package includes all current pricing, rebate, holdback, and incentive programs; an analysis of how that particular model is doing in the marketplace, including actual transaction prices from across the nation; and a slew of articles about all aspects of the car-buying game. Perhaps most important, the fightingchance package includes the personal coaching services, via telephone, of the car-buying experts who run the site. The current price for this package is $34.95 for the first vehicle and $9.00 for each additional vehicle. You can receive the package through e-mail or U.S. mail. Visit their Web site for more information.

## Price Checking for Your Dream Car

Now that you have gathered all the pertinent information, you have a decision to make. You can either proceed directly to your nearest car dealership or you can phone various dealerships in your general area to compare prices. A number of Web sites make comparison shopping easy by offering services where they forward your request to dealerships you chose. Salesmen from those dealerships then contact you by e-mail or phone to give you quotes. These prices won't necessarily be low, although they will probably be somewhat lower than sticker price because the salesmen know they are competing with other dealerships. (*Sticker price* is the manufacturer's suggested retail price, or MSRP, that is on the sticker affixed to the car window.)

Whether you are calling or using the Internet, be aware that the information you get may be incorrect. "Most management makes you tell the customer you have the car even if you don't, just to get them onto the lot," says former salesman Jack McGuirk. "If they show up and you don't have it, you say the car just sold or there was a mistake on the computer. You tell them, 'But I do have this other car. Why don't we drive it and see what it feels like?'"

This tactic may be infuriating, but nearly all dealerships do it. It's worth noting, however, that the car you have so carefully researched, with all the options you want, may not be available in your city anyway. Craig Raggio explains, "When GM [or any manufacturer] builds cars, the dealers get a certain allotment. They try to get the ones they know are going to sell the best. Somebody will call and say, 'I want a red Corvette with tan leather. Why can't you get that for me?' Well, we can probably find it somewhere in the nation, but bringing it out here? Most dealers don't want to do that. It's not worth it to them. So the main thing is to overcome whatever objections the customer has to the cars you have on the lot." You always have the option of finding a dealership that is willing to order the exact car you want, but you will pay a premium for doing so.

## Buying from the Fleet Manager

Many people boast that they got the best possible deal on their car because they "went directly to the fleet manager." Excellent deals can indeed be had this way. The difference between buying from a fleet manager and buying from a regular salesman is that the fleet manager is authorized to sell cars at low, non-negotiable prices and will not put you through the *Sturm und Drang* described in the rest of this chapter. The fleet manager won't negotiate with you, but if the price he offers is at or below the price your have set as your limit, you will still come out a winner.

Why doesn't everyone buy from the fleet manager? Some people believe they can get the best price only by going head-to-head with the sales team, but the reason most car buyers don't take advantage of the fleet manager is that they don't know he exists. The fleet department is set up to sell multiple cars to businesses. They can also sell to individuals, but they can't publicize that fact because it would put them in direct competition with the salesmen on the lot. Consumers must make the first move by calling the dealership and asking to speak to the fleet manager, who will then meet with you and take you on a test drive. He will offer you a price, and you can either accept or refuse it. You are under no obligation to buy. You can contact the fleet departments of as many dealerships as you like.

AAA offers its members a service whereby they broker the deal with the fleet manager for you. You tell them your desired make and model, and they forward a referral to a dealership whose fleet manager will contact you within 24 hours. He'll give you a prenegotiated price, good for 30 days. You can then go to the dealership and check the car out, just as you would if you had contacted the fleet manager yourself. AAA claims they sometimes get better deals than an individual would from the fleet manager. In any case, having AAA's backing can provide the hesitant buyer a bit more confidence.

For people with an aversion to haggling, buying from the fleet manager can be a very appealing, low-stress option. For those who prefer to negotiate and perhaps secure an even better deal, read on.

## Dancing with the Devil

Few life experiences offer the potential to make you feel like a complete sucker, but it can definitely happen at a car dealership. The first thing to understand is that you are going to be there for many, many hours. Every car buyer should arrive at the dealership equipped with food, drink, and perhaps a good book. They *will* make you wait and they *will* try to squeeze more profits out of the deal any way they can. Don't think for a moment that you can avoid the time trap, because wearing you down physically and emotionally is the cornerstone of the dealership's sales strategy.

The second thing you should understand before embarking on the purchase is the ways the dealership will make its money:

- The price of the car.
- The amount they pay for your trade-in.
- The interest they charge you on financing the car.
- Ad-ons such as warranties, rustproofing, and upholstery protection.

The first three items are included in the basic negotiation. Add-ons, which can cost you hundreds or thousands of dollars more, are sold by the business manager in the finance and insurance office, where you will go after the deal has been struck.

Along with survival supplies, you should bring a file containing printouts from the Web sites mentioned earlier that support the price you want to pay for the car. If the salespeople want to argue about holdbacks, rebates, invoice price, or what people are really paying, it's nice to be able to cut them short by pulling out those documents.

One last thing to keep in mind before stepping onto the lot with the sales crew: Everything that will happen is a performance they have enacted many times before. It feels real to you because you only purchase a car once every few years, and unless you are in the performing arts, you have no experience with play-acting. The salespeople's hemming and hawing, their concern and conspiratorial glances, their sad shaking of the head—it's all pretend.

Now, let's go to the dealership. You have already shopped for your car on a previous day, which means you probably connected with a particular salesman and will be meeting him to negotiate the deal. It's the weekend, and the dealership is abuzz with sell-a-thon energy. You have brought along a friend, your spouse, perhaps more than one other person. *You will not do this alone*. It places you at too great a psychological disadvantage.

The best bargaining position to be in is one where you are only concerned about the price of the car, having decided to finance it elsewhere and sell your current car by yourself. However, if this is the case, you don't want to tip your hand about it. If the salesman thinks you're going to finance the car with him (thus earning the dealership more money because of the interest on the loan), he may be more flexible on the price of the car. The same is true if he believes you'll be trading in your car, which offers him another way to make profits by paying you too little for it. To get your money, the salesman will juggle the four numbers: price of car, price of trade-in, monthly payments, and down payment. Your goal is to take three of them—down payment, monthly payments, and trade-in—off the table until the price of the car has been established.

After greeting you, the salesman will show you to his cubicle and sit you down at his desk. He will then pull out what's called a foursquare, a sheet of paper divided into four equal squares, one for each of the numbers he wants to juggle. After asking for standard information such as your name and address, he will glide to the first really important question: How do you intend to pay for the car? You will tell him that you haven't made a decision on that; you want to keep your options open. For now, you only want to discuss the price of the car. After all, if you can't agree on a price, there's no point in talking about how you're going to pay.

The reason the salesman wants to know how you will be paying is that his next move depends upon your answer. If you need dealership financing, he can steer you into the most seductive of traps: "How much do you want your monthly payment to be?" You do not want to answer that, for several reasons. First, no matter what number you give him, he will respond that it's not quite enough—what's the most you could *really* afford in order to get this car? Second, the monthly payment amount neatly distracts you from the real cost of the car. Suddenly you're thinking not in terms of $30,000 but in terms of a down payment and, say, $250 a month for 60 months. Notice that they always present the loan in terms of months, not years. How many people instantly recognize that 60 months is five years? Five years sounds a lot longer, does it not? Even if you can do the math, there's a tendency to hear only what you want to hear: a monthly payment you can afford.

You are going to avoid all this by politely declining to discuss financing until a price is agreed upon. The salesman may insist that you fill out a credit application anyway, because he wants to make sure you can afford the car. That is not unreasonable. "You'd be amazed how many times people come in—I don't know if they get their thrills off it, or if they're just dense—but they want to buy a car they have no chance of getting," reports Craig Raggio. You can try to work around this by showing the salesman a copy of your credit report and score. If he still insists on your filling out a report, you may have to comply unless you're willing to tell him that you are financing the car elsewhere or paying cash. What you don't want him doing is checking your credit score at this point. Every time someone other than you looks up your credit report, it counts against you, and eventually it will lower your score. (It's okay to let them check your score after you have made a deal and decided to finance through the dealership.)

With the credit and financing issue out of the way for the moment, you are ready to make the salesman an offer, which will be the invoice price (minus any dealer holdbacks), plus a small profit for the dealer. Going back to the $30,000 car we were discussing earlier, that would be an opening offer of $30,300, or 1 percent over invoice price. He'll probably do a spit take, so lean back in your chair. "Sticker on that car is $34,500!" he'll sputter.

"I can come down a little bit, but not that much." Sticker price is as meaningless as its name, "manufacturer's *suggested* retail price," implies. Ignore the suggestion and remind him that your offer is $300 above invoice, which serves him notice that you've done your homework. He will try to argue with you, but hold firm. The game has begun.

A bedrock rule of all negotiations is that he who speaks first after an offer is made is in the weaker position. Therefore, do not speak unless it is to reiterate your offer or suggest that he take it to his sales manager. Be nice, not hostile. He is not out to get you personally, he is just playing his role. For folks who aren't used to negotiating, the gaps in the conversation, filled with disapproving vibes from the salesman, can become very uncomfortable. At moments like this it's helpful to remind yourself that he is a pro and you are a novice, which is why you feel so ill at ease. What you do *not* want to do is raise your offer before he makes a counteroffer. This is a sign of extreme weakness and will signal that you are easily manipulated. Sit calmly, smile, and eventually he will take your offer to his sales manager. Pull out a sandwich and soft drink, open your book, and settle down for a long wait.

## Why Wait?

Contrary to popular suspician, there are some practical reasons for the delays. Behind the scenes, the desk manager is trying to find out if you really can afford the car by investigating everything the salesman has learned about you: where you work, your income, savings, down payment, and so forth. If you will be financing it through the dealership and he has obtained a credit report, he will be on the phone with the manufacturer's financing division, trying to convince them to lend him money at a low interest rate because you have such a sterling credit history. (Later the finance manager will try to sell you that same loan at a higher interest rate.) Also, because your sales manager is working with a crew of as many as 10 salespeople, he may be negotiating with several other parties as well as yours. It all takes time.

The excruciatingly long wait may be somewhat unavoidable given the structure of the dealership, but it works very well to soften up customers, too. Forcing you to wait asserts the dealership's control over you. The salesmen are counting on your getting tired and hungry, which will weaken your resolve. They also hope that during this time you'll be fantasizing about how much you want that new car. Especially important, they use this time to let your original salesman (the liner) cultivate an emotional connection with you. He will usually return from the back room rather quickly, because he doesn't want to leave you alone too long— you might bolt. Then, as you wait for a counteroffer from the sales manager, he will switch the topic away from the car and to more general subjects. "You don't talk about the car deal anymore if at all possible," says Craig Raggio. "You talk about the 49ers. You make them not want to let you down. You're a working man and you're just trying to sell a car here and this is how you feed your family." If you feel yourself getting softhearted, remind yourself that *your* family needs to eat, too. Next month the car salesman may have a different job. You, however, will have those car payments for years.

## The Negotiation, Continued

Eventually the sales manager will return with a counteroffer. By that time, you and the liner are best buddies. "I'm your friend now. It's you and me against the sales manager," says Raggio. "He's the big, bad car salesman guy. But even though you're doing the bonding thing, you don't come in on the customer's side. You don't undercut your manager. You just kind of shut up. That's what's drilled into you; that's the psychology of it."

The first counteroffer the sales manager suggests will probably not be much different than his original offer, maybe just a few hundred dollars less. Don't lose hope; again, this is simply the nature of the game. You will counter his offer with a marginally higher offer of your own, not more than $100. Depending on the volume of other customers that day (recall that you have chosen a busy weekend in hopes of limiting the amount of time they can devote to you), you may have a long wait between each offer. The pressure will increase as they keep urging you to talk about your trade-in or think in terms of monthly payments. Remain strong and stay focused. This is where your friends will come in handy. You will all keep reminding the salesmen that the only number you want to discuss is the price of the car. Finally, you will come to an agreement. As long as you are pleasant and willing to allow the dealer some profit, there is no reason to think it won't happen.

But wait. Whatever you do, don't relax. The negotiations are not over just because you have settled on a price. On the contrary, you are entering round two: the price you will get for your trade-in. By this time, despite your snacks, your energy might be flagging. (Another reason the sales manager takes over in the business office is that he is fresh, whereas the liner gets tired after a while, just as you do.) Don't hesitate to tell the salesmen you need a break. Go for a walk, and take as long as you like. Make them wait for a change.

If you got a decent deal on your new car, don't expect the dealer to be generous with your trade-in. Prepare to hear all sorts of reasons why your trade-in isn't worth very much; assume they are all lies. "I'm going to start dogging that car out," says Craig Raggio. "I'm going to try and drive it down as much as I can. Then the closers will come in and dog it some more. We're going to find every possible dent. A week later, if the car is out on our lot, we'll be telling customers how great it is."

You know what your trade-in is worth, retail and wholesale.

It is up to you to decide how much time you're willing to spend going back and forth, as you did with the new car's price. No one is forcing you to trade in your vehicle. Don't neglect to do the math: take the amount a used car dealership such as Car Max might pay for your trade-in or the price a private party would pay, subtract what this dealer is offering, and add that number to the price you just negotiated for your new car. Now decide whether it's a fair deal, and don't forget, you have other options.

## The Finance and Insurance Office

The sun is setting . . . families are going home to their dinners. But not you. It's time to iron out the financing if you're doing it through the dealership, and to finalize the paperwork if you're not. This takes place in the finance and insurance (F&I) office, sometimes called the business office. It's a separate location from the cubicle where you have been held hostage for the greater part of the day. The change of locale is designed to make you think the negotiations are finally over. Wrong.

The business manager, often a woman with a soft-spoken, friendly demeanor, is also selling you products. For one thing, she's selling you an interest rate on the loan if you are financing through the dealership. Regardless of her protestations, these interest rates are negotiable, even if your credit is not perfect. If you cannot come to an agreement about interest with the business manager, you're free to walk out.

The other products for sale in the F&I office are add-ons, the warranties and options that can seem relatively inexpensive in comparison to the amount you just spent on the car. The fact is, all these extras can be purchased at a lower cost from other sources. You should not buy them from the dealer, particularly at this point in the proceedings, when you are bone tired and in no shape to make rational decisions. You might try telling the business manager at the get-go that you are not going to purchase any add-ons; it may slow her down, but probably not, as she is working on commission.

Extended service warranties are big profit makers in the F&I office. Do not purchase a warranty from the dealer even if you are buying a used car (extended warranties are usually pointless for new cars). Instead, research service warranties online; you'll get a better deal and quite possibly more extensive coverage. Warranty Direct, Warranty Gold, and Warranty-by-Net are three sources recommended by expert Michael Royce. Other add-ons that you will be urged to purchase include:

- Window etching
- Window tinting
- Paint protection
- Rustproofing
- Fabric protection
- Undercoating
- Alarm system
- Insurance

Last but not least, take a close look at the other miscellaneous fees that may show up on the final invoice. These will include license and sales tax (check with the AAA or Department of Motor Vehicles before you buy the car to make sure they are charging you correctly) and items such as the dealer prep and destination fees. Destination fees are charged by the manufacturer to deliver the car to the dealership. They are legitimate, but check with one of the online sites to make sure the dealer isn't overcharging you.

The dealer prep fee is legal, but it can run to hundreds of dollars. Dealer prep is the time spent taking the protective plastic wrapping off the car, putting in fuses, and test driving it to make sure everything's working. According to Jeff Ostroff of carbuyingtips.com, this prep work usually takes about two hours and often is paid by the manufacturer anyway. He strongly suggests refusing to pay the dealer prep fee. "Often it's permanently printed on the buyer's order to make you think it's mandatory," writes Ostroff. "But many people make the dealer remove it by adding a credit on the next line. So if you see a $500 dealer prep on the form, have them add a $500 credit. If they won't budge you need to decide how badly you want that car."

As the clock strikes midnight, the business manager will finish her sales pitch and you will finally sign your name for the last time. With that, the car is yours.

---

### YOU OWN THE CAR ONLY WHEN YOU DRIVE IT OFF THE LOT

No matter who has signed what at the dealership, *you do not legally own the car and are not responsible for it until you drive it off the lot.* This is true in all fifty states. Although many states have three-day Right to Rescind (buyer's remorse) laws, these usually do not apply to motor vehicle sales or leases. Contact your local AAA or state attorney general's office to check the laws in your state.

---

## Magic Words and Deeds

Your head may be reeling from all the previous advice, but after all, this is a costly purchase. Here are a few more pointers to remember during the negotiation.

- **BE PREPARED TO WALK OUT.** This is by far the most important weapon you can bring with you.

- **MENTION OTHER DEALERSHIPS DURING THE NEGOTIATION.** This works best if you have already checked the prices at other dealerships, because you will transmit more conviction when you counter their offer with, "Maybe I should go back to Crazy Moe's. They seemed eager to work with me." If you haven't checked prices, it helps to at least know the names of other dealerships.

- **IF YOU GET TIRED OR CONFUSED AT ANY POINT DURING THE PROCEEDINGS, EXCUSE YOURSELF AND TAKE A BREAK.**

- **BE AWARE THAT SALESMEN SOMETIMES LEAVE ON THEIR TELEPHONE INTERCOM SO THAT THE SALES MANAGER AND OTHERS CAN EAVESDROP ON THE NEGOTIATION.**

- **PAY ANY DEPOSIT BY CREDIT CARD, NOT CHECK.** Dealers generally request a deposit of $500–$1000 for cars they must order from the factory. If they try to pull something funny when the car arrives, such as raising the price or adding more fees, you can dispute the deposit if you charged it. Do not pay a deposit unless you are absolutely sure you will buy the car.

## Absolute No-No's

Whether you are in the trenches of a negotiation or just shopping around, maintain control by revealing as little about yourself as possible and reining in your emotions.

- **DON'T GIVE THE SALESMAN YOUR DRIVER'S LICENSE.** Most will insist that they need to make a copy of it before they let you test drive a car. That is not true; there is no law that requires it. Some dealers use the card to run a credit check on you. Some use it as an excuse to temporarily "misplace" your license, thus holding you hostage at the dealership. To avoid an argument, bring your own copy of your driver's license, on which you have written: "Dealer: Do not use this information to run a credit check on me." There is an FTC law forbidding dealers to run unapproved credit checks, and the fine can be as high as $2,500. (If you are in the process of actually negotiating, they may insist on running a credit check.)

- **DON'T REVEAL INFORMATION ABOUT YOUR JOB, LIFE, BACKGROUND, OR FINANCIAL SITUATION BEYOND WHAT IS NECESSARY.** The more they know, the more they can use to manipulate you.

- **DON'T START TALKING JUST BECAUSE THE SILENCE OR THE SALESMAN'S FACIAL EXPRESSIONS OR BODY LANGUAGE ARE MAKING YOU UNCOMFORTABLE.** Being able to endure silence signals power.

- **DON'T ANGRILY ACCUSE THE SALESMAN OF LYING OR BAIT AND SWITCH.** You can calmly point out that he is doing these things, but getting angry is a sign of weakness. It's better to laugh, signaling that you are on to his game and it's not going to rattle you.

- **DON'T INSULT THE SALESMAN.** He has feelings, too. Experts claim that, to a small degree, your rapport with the salesman does affect the deal you will get.

- **DON'T BE TOO ENTHUSIASTIC.** This is easier said than done if you're really excited about the car, but it's crucial in convincing the salesman that you can and will walk away from the deal if it's not right for you.

## Into the Sunset

Some people love new-car smell and nothing can take its place, not even very realistic "new car smell" spray in a spanking-clean year-old vehicle. Before you allow yourself to be dazzled by this year's model, consider what the salesmen think of new cars. "I never buy a new car," says Jack McGuirk. "You lose thousands." Craig Raggio agrees. "The minute you drive a new car off the lot, the thing's depreciated 30 percent. I would buy a really new used car, one with under 10,000 miles on it. I would go into the dealership with the invoice, and for a big-ticket item give them $1,000 over invoice. For a smaller ticket item I'd give them $500 over invoice, and that's it."

McGuirk offers one more word of advice for car buyers: "Don't ever buy a first-year model car. Generally they have problems. Wait until the second or third year."

For all the anxiety of researching a car and doing battle with the salespeople, the thrill of owning a new (or nearly new) vehicle cannot be denied. In spite of his own considerable cynicism about car dealerships, Craig Raggio believes that at a certain level you have to love the car, not just the deal. "If somebody's going to buy a $30,000 vehicle, they're better off buying a $33,000 vehicle if it's going to be what makes them happy." As long as you know that you are the one calling the shots, there's no reason why you shouldn't drive away smiling.

## AUTO MECHANIC
# IN SEARCH OF A FEW GOOD MEN

Most drivers would agree that what lurks beneath the hood of their car is about as familiar as the first photos sent back from the Hubble telescope. It's sort of a landscape, but one lacking any point of reference. Since the 1980s car engines have become increasingly sophisticated, with computerized systems that make it difficult to repair the engine without special equipment. The average person who loves to tinker and has a basic understanding of motors can no longer make a common-sense diagnosis when something starts to shudder or grind. The result is that all of us, male and female alike, are now at the mercy of professional mechanics and the repair shops where they work their magic.

Finding a good mechanic can definitely try the souls of mortal men. It's common knowledge that the car repair business is one of the most dishonest, and consumers walk into repair shops fully expecting to be ripped off. Every year, the Better Business Bureau is flooded with thousands of complaints about unnecessary or incompetent repairs. Undercover investigations by consumer groups have proven that as many as 40 percent of both national franchises and independent repair businesses engage in routine dishonesty. When confronted with their lies, the shop managers inevitably issue bland statements such as, "Our technicians are some of the finest," or, "We stand behind our work." No one would expect the managers to fall on their swords in shame, but the lack of acknowledgment or remorse shows how endemic dishonesty is to the car repair industry.

Trading in the BMW for a horse and buggy is hardly a practical remedy to the problem. Developing trust in your mechanics is the obvious solution, but first you have learn how to recognize the ones who might be trustworthy.

## Behind the Scenes:
## The Smell of the Grease, the Lure of the Fib

Most mechanics are drawn to the work because they love cars and are challenged by what makes them go. Regardless of the quality of their character and their business practices, they enjoy problem-solving and take genuine pleasure in turning the wheezing jalopy you brought to the shop into a sleek and humming road warrior. Mechanics regard themselves as professionals, and those who are experienced can make more than $100,000 a year. Like all professionals, they want to be respected for their expertise. They resent having to argue and convince customers to allow repairs that they, the pros, deem necessary and correct. The honest mechanics are forced to deal with the fallout from the conniving mechanics, and that can take its toll on a group of guys not famous for their people skills. Some mechanics complain that the stress of dealing with customers is so high that it creates burnout in the field.

Mike Burke, owner of Hilltop Service Station in Seattle, Washington, says that today's mechanics are a different breed than earlier generations: "Thirty, forty, fifty years ago it used to be that mechanics were the guys who never really figured out what they wanted to do. They had a knack for turning wrenches and fixing things so they became mechanics. Modern cars, with all the electronics and really fine tolerances, require somebody with a high intelligence level as well as the understanding that he will require ongoing education."

As cars become more high-tech, mechanics are almost as challenged as consumers to keep up with the changes. A competitive mechanic today will have completed courses offered by the National Institute for Automotive Service Excellence (ASE) and will prominently display the certificates in his office. A master technician will have completed all eight areas of expertise. (Look closely at the certificates if you see them; you don't want a mechanic who has received honors only in air-conditioner repair to take apart your transmission.) The certifications are only good for five years, which forces the technician to stay up-to-date on the latest automotive technology if he wants to remain certified and on top of his game.

Yet certification alone doesn't guarantee that the mechanic is top-notch, warns Julie Hanson, Burke's executive assistant. "They also have to have some experience with cars. A good mechanic is smart and will remember the idiosyncrasies of particular cars. It takes training, and being tenacious and stubborn." Adds Burke, "And being calm and having a heck of a good memory."

Why would someone who prides himself in his work take advantage of you or cheat you? Why would a business that depends largely on personal referrals and repeat business take the risk of alienating customers through poor or dishonest service? The answer is complex. Like many businesses, independent repair shops have taken a beating over the past decade. Mom-and-pop shops such as Hilltop, where the owner has a personal relationship with his customers, are fading fast. Says Burke, "Our focus is providing good service for the dollar spent here. Nobody's getting rich at Hilltop. There's not a lot of fat in the industry, period. The profit margins are much smaller than they were years ago. But we do pay everybody here a living wage."

Repair shops that are not independent are either associated

with a dealership or are franchises of large national chains. The mechanics who work at the franchises are often poorly paid and don't have a face-to-face, ongoing relationship with their customers. It is common for the parent chain to offer mechanics and managers incentives for selling services. This leads to a competitive culture that relies on convincing the customer to buy unnecessary services and repairs, some of which are never even performed. In this climate, the honest souls are often afraid to speak out. It's an easy leap from, "He's going to need that service at some point anyway," to, "He needs that service right now." Because the customer is in such a vulnerable position—his car is broken and he doesn't know what's wrong with it—garages are breeding grounds for manipulation and dishonesty. The independent repair shop is also in a precarious position when competing with national chains that offer speedy service and lower prices. The temptation to get into the unnecessary repair game as a means of survival is very strong. When a Midas opens right across the street, the mechanics in a small, independent shop start sweating lug nuts.

And what about incompetence? There are also lots of honest mechanics out there who make honest mistakes. As mentioned earlier, cars are getting increasingly complex. If a repair shop does not employ master technicians or have the latest equipment, it's going to be difficult for them to correctly diagnose your car's problem. As in human ailments, a single symptom can have a number of different root causes. It's not uncommon for two auto technicians to give you two very different explanations for why old faithful is on the verge of collapse. And because diagnosing a problem can take a lot of time (time customers don't like to pay for), mechanics will often give a quick and dirty diagnosis to get you in the door, only to sock you with a whopping bill later, when they have taken a closer look and discovered the real problem.

With dishonesty on the left and incompetence on the right,

it's easy to feel paranoid about car maintenance and repair. But even though statistics show that up to 40 percent of garages will take you for a ride, that still leaves 60 percent that will give you an honest deal. With some forethought, you can find them.

## A Little Bit of Car Knowledge Goes a Long Way

Although no one is safe from being scammed by a mechanic, certain people are widely regarded as pigeons. Women have always been thought of as the most vulnerable group, and that still holds true. The complexity of engines has somewhat leveled the playing field between males and females (now *nobody* understands cars), but because safety and reliability are such emotional issues for women, they remain more susceptible to scare tactics. If you are elderly, a minority, or appear to have a lot of money, you may also be targeted. Anyone who breaks down while out of town is a pigeon deluxe.

The dishonest mechanic is looking for someone who seems to know little about his car and appears easy to manipulate. By doing a bit of homework, you can set yourself apart from this group. Show the mechanic you know your stuff by following these steps:

**READ YOUR CAR'S MANUAL.** No one will quiz you on all the details, but you should know how to work everything and understand the fundamentals of your vehicle's maintenance. Pay particular attention to where the fluids go and where the fuses are housed. New cars often come with a video that demonstrates the various features; they are a painless way to absorb information.

**FOLLOW THE MANUFACTURER'S RECOMMENDATIONS.** Every car comes with a schedule of routine maintenance to be performed at particular mileage intervals: change the oil every 3,000 miles; check the transmission, brakes, belts, coolant system, and so forth. If you follow these recommendations and keep good records, not only will your car run better, but you are also less likely to be pressured into buying these services when you don't need them. Shady mechanics are fond of urging routine maintenance on anyone who crosses their threshold. "The manufacturer recommends that you change your belts every 30,000 miles," they'll declare, or, "Lucky for you, we're running a special on flushing the coolant system this week." A scare tactic or two will typically follow. If you know that your routine maintenance is up to date, you can say no thanks and stop the manipulator in his tracks. Check your maintenance calendar and records before going to the repair shop. It's a good way to judge the honesty of the mechanic.

**DON'T WAIT UNTIL YOUR CAR BREAKS DOWN TO FIND A MECHANIC.** Because many people find dealing with car maintenance about as rewarding as a broken toe, it is very common for folks to put it off altogether until their car breaks. A dishonest mechanic will exploit your desperation if you take your car in for the first time under these circumstances. Do your homework up front and find a mechanic before you need him. Instead of pulling into the nearest garage when you need a tune-up, take the time to locate someone you could trust your car to should it need major work. Establish the personal relationship now, and it's like money in the bank later.

## Finding a Good Mechanic

Finding a mechanic before disaster strikes obviously gives you the luxury of shopping around. Your first challenge is to select a few repair shops to visit. A friend's recommendation is helpful, but consider the source. Is the friend car-savvy, or at least somewhat sophisticated about service in general? If not, he could be having a lovely experience with a mechanic who is very graciously ripping him off. Also, does your friend have the make of car that you do, such as Japanese, German, or American? That's important for any type of complex repair. An excellent resource for information about repair shops in your community is cartalk. com's Mechan-X Files page (www.cartalk.com/content/mechx/), which features more than 16,000 mechanics recommended by listeners of *Car Talk*, the National Public Radio show. The listings include names of specific mechanics at each shop, plus customer comments and a rating chart.

Most people assume that independent repair shops will be more likely to offer honest service than dealerships or franchises (such as Midas or Goodyear). This isn't always the case. Besides, there is no law saying you can only have one mechanic. Dealerships are great for routine maintenance, as they have the diagnostic equipment, parts, calibrations, and specifications for your make and model. Obviously, they should be used for any warranty work. They might cost a little more for this type of thing, but they are headache-free and probably won't try to talk you into unneeded repairs (although you should still be vigilant about it). Sometimes the franchises that specialize in mufflers, brakes, or tires can give you very competitive prices for this type of work. They can be iffy if you need a diagnosis, but if your muffler sounds like a dying rhino, it's a no-brainer. Go to Midas and save a few bucks.

When you have selected a few shops to visit, do a visual inspection. Although taking a good look around does not address the nitty-gritty of what goes on under the hood, a business that is well managed and customer-oriented bodes well for providing good service.

- Is the waiting room clean and comfortable? (Give extra points if there is an area for children or free coffee.)
- Does the staff treat you respectfully and acknowledge you when you come in?

- Are the mechanics' certifications prominently displayed? Are there any other "excellence in service" awards displayed?

- Are rows of repair manuals visible? Some mechanics claim that a good shop will have twelve feet of shelf space filled with manuals, and the grimier the better—they're being read.

- Can you see into the garage from the waiting room? Shops that aren't afraid to have you observe the mechanics at work have nothing to hide.

- Is the garage clean and neat? "A clean shop is typically a well-run shop," says Mike Burke. "The technicians are the greatest example of how well the shop does mechanically, and if their own space is organized and clean—clean being a relative thing in an inherently dirty business—that's probably a pretty good visual indication that the work is being done well."

- How do the mechanics interact with one another and management? A happy, relaxed atmosphere is a good sign. Like employees everywhere, a happy mechanic is much more likely to care about his work.

- Is the shop busy? Although you don't want to have to wait many days for a simple repair, a shop that is busy obviously has a loyal clientele.

- Ask about warranties and customer satisfaction policies. The good shops should guarantee their work.

- What is your gut instinct? "If a tow truck driver says it's a good place and you show up and you're getting a bad vibe from the owner or mechanic, move on," advises Burke. "On the other hand, you may get a great sense for honesty and integrity and competence from somebody who is less than visually pleasing—greasy hands or whatever. It's the luck of the draw, and using your common sense and intuition helps to narrow the field."

Budding consumer advocates can supplement their visit to the mechanic with their own test of honesty and competence. This is wise if you fall into a high-risk-for-scamming group (that is, if you are not a white male age 20–60). Unscrew a headlight or remove a fuse, take your car into the shop, and see what happens. If the mechanic genuinely doesn't seem able to find the problem or tells you that you need a $500 fribblewacker to fix it, depart quickly.

Complaints about car repairs top the list at the Better Business Bureau, so go ahead and check in with them before using a particular shop. They'll tell you if customer complaints have been lodged against that business, what the nature of the complaints have been, and whether the shop is properly licensed if licensing is required in your state. A clean record at the shop you want to use will boost your confidence; knowledge of a poor one will spare you a lot of grief.

## Magic Words and Deeds: Talking to a Mechanic

A good mechanic will thoroughly explain what he intends to do and why. If he shows you what is going to take place under the hood, that's even better (never mind that you may be clueless about what he is pointing at). If you're feeling queasy about an expensive repair and would like a second opinion before beginning, a professional will not bat an eye.

The biggest mistake people make when talking to a mechanic, says Mike Burke, is to announce what they think is wrong with the car instead of adequately describing the symptoms. "If their car is having a performance problem, they'll tell us that it's probably the fuel pump or timing, when in many cases with modern cars those are the last two things it's likely to be." So rule number one is to explain, in detail, exactly what is going wrong. Better yet, write it down.

**SYMPTOM CHECKLIST**

- What happens?
- When does it happen?
- How long has it been going on?
- Have you noticed any unusual smells in or around your car?
- Are there any sounds associated with the problem?
- Have you noticed any leaks? If so, where? When?
- How has the problem affected your car's performance?

Mechanics will also appreciate it if you are sensitive to their schedules. "Be reasonable," says Julie Hanson. "Tell us if there's a reason you need your car back at a certain time. Be understanding if that is not possible. On the other hand, if you could go without your car for a couple of days, let us know that so we can maybe give that time to someone else who's in a bigger hurry. Customers are doing each other a favor by prioritizing their needs."

## Absolute No-No's

"If people behave badly, they're going to pay every justifiable cent that we can legitimately bill them for because they're taking additional time," says Julie Hanson. "We won't charge them for stuff that didn't happen, but there's fewer breaks. There's no love. We're by the book." Lovable clients:

**DON'T ASSUME THE REPAIR SHOP IS DISHONEST.** Maybe your experiences with other repair shops have made you justifiably wary, but try to keep an open mind when dealing with a new shop. "We understand when people are afraid, but it saddens and disappoints us that they're afraid of us because they haven't been here before," says Hanson. "That defensive, fearful posture is difficult."

**DON'T DEMAND INSTANT SERVICE.** Says Mike Burke: "They think we can drop everything and take care of their problem immediately, as if they are our only customer and scheduling is for everybody else." Keep in mind that excellent repair shops are probably going to be busy.

**DON'T CALL FREQUENTLY TO CHECK ON THE STATUS OF THE CAR.** "That's not only irksome but it's counterproductive," says Burke. "It's taking time away from actual work to hold their hand."

**DON'T PRETEND TO BE CAR EXPERTS.** This isn't so much annoying as amusing. "We get a lot of people who pretend that they're knowledgeable. It works for about a minute," says Hanson. Even Mike Burke, who *is* an expert, doesn't bother impressing the mechanic if he happens to be out of town and needs his car repaired: "It's not as important to me to convey to a garage that I know something about cars as it is to convey why I'm there, the specifics, the clues for them to figure out how to resolve the problem."

## More Magic: The Invaluable Oil Change

You know you're supposed to get your oil changed regularly, and perhaps you do so, following the manufacturer's recommendations. According to Mike Burke, that may not be good enough. You should change the oil four times a year or every 3,000 miles, whichever comes first. "That last phrase is the most important: *Whichever comes first.* It's the frequency that is key to getting that second 100,000 miles out of an engine." Some manufacturers are currently recommending changing the oil every 7,500 or once a year; Burke says that if you want to keep the engine purring and to avoid big repair bills, you will ignore their advice and stick to 3,000 miles or four times a year. "It's not just the oil. It's the opportunity for the mechanic who's doing the work to spot the hose or belt that's about ready to go, or the bubble in your tire—things that can lead to inconvenient, more costly repairs. The biggest misconception consumers have about car maintenance is that new cars don't require maintenance like old cars. Guess what?

New cars become old cars real quick if they don't receive fundamental maintenance."

---

**GET IT IN WRITING**

Before you give the go-ahead on any repair, make sure that the symptoms are documented clearly, that every item to be examined on your car is documented, and that all the costs, including labor, are agreed upon. If you have been given a cost estimate, make sure the mechanic must consult with you first before authorizing any additional repairs that go over that amount. Get that in writing too. Be sure you understand what parts are to be used in the repair—new, name brand, or reconditioned—and understand the warranties that come with that product. Ask to have the parts that have been replaced returned to you. When the job is done, you should get a completed repair order that describes exactly what work was performed.

---

## Scammin' All Over the Land

If you take the time to know your car and its maintenance schedule, and if you make sure every repair has been authorized by you in writing, you are less likely to be cheated and will have recourse if you suspect that you have been. Auto repair scams usually involve charging you for work that was never done, convincing you to approve unneeded, overpriced repairs, or both. Unethical shops use a variety of tactics to bilk their customers. Beware of:

- Fast talkers who are patronizing and rush you to make a decision.

- Mechanics who show you a "leak" they've discovered that is unrelated to the complaint you've brought to them (sometimes they will squirt oil on parts to create what looks like a leak).

- Anyone who wants you to sign a blank work order, operates on a cash-only basis, or refuses to return the old parts.

- Mechanics who refuse to explain a repair in detail or who refuse to go on a test drive.

- Mechanics who use scare tactics to frighten you into authorizing repairs that you don't feel right about.

Here is a list of symptoms that typically arise when a particular system is faulty. If your car is not experiencing the symptom, chances are you don't need that repair.

- **FLUID LEAKS:** Dark brown oily spots are associated with bad seals and gaskets; fluorescent liquid could mean an antifreeze leak; red oily leaks are usually transmission or power steering leaks; watery leaks usually mean nothing—they are condensation.

- **BAD SMELLS:** Smells like burnt toast are usually electrical, such as a short; rotten egg smells are usually associated with emission controls; dense, acrid odors can mean an oil leak; burning chemical odors can mean overheated brakes or clutch; sweet steamy odors can mean a coolant leak.

- **SQUEALS:** Worn belts of all types.

- **CLICKS:** Loose wheel cover; loose fan blade; stuck valve lifter; low engine oil.

- **SCREECHES:** Usually brake wear indicators telling you it's time for repair.

- **LOW RUMBLES:** Defective exhaust pipe, muffler, or converter; worn universal joint.

- **PINGS:** Usually caused by using gas with too low an octane rating for that car; could be an ignition timing problem.

- **HEAVY RHYTHMIC KNOCKING:** Worn crankshaft, connecting rod bearings, or loose transmission.
- **CLUNKS:** Loose shock absorbers, exhaust pipe, or muffler.
- **DIFFICULT STEERING (PULLING, WANDERING, HARD-TO-TURN STEERING WHEEL):** Poor alignment, underinflated tires, worn steering components, low power-steering fluid.
- **POOR CORNERING AND VIBRATION:** Worn shock absorbers, unbalanced tires.
- **BRAKING PROBLEMS:** Pedal to the floor, vehicle pulling to one side when braking, scraping or grinding when braking indicate a needed repair.
- **ROUGH IDLING, POOR FUEL ECONOMY, STALLING:** Indicates engine repair is needed.
- **ABRUPT, DELAYED, OR SLIPPED GEAR SHIFTS:** Indicates poor transmission performance, but check hoses and filters before going in for the expensive repairs.

These are only a few of the common symptoms of car trouble. For more details, buy a basic car-owner's repair guide. Like home repair guides, these books can familiarize you with the terminology and explain in layman's terms how a car's various systems function.

## I Fell for It—Now What?

You are not completely without recourse if you believe you've been a victim of a scam or an incompetent repair. If you signed off on the repair you will have a more difficult time than if the mechanic performed unauthorized work. You are not obligated to pay for unauthorized work, period. If you signed off on the work but your car is still not running correctly, take the rational approach. Return without delay and calmly explain the situation to the management. The longer you wait, the more difficult it will be to negotiate. If your work order detailed the symptoms of your car accurately and you are still experiencing those symptoms, most shops will try to make the repair right. Get the manager to take a test drive with you. Make sure he experiences the symptom himself. If it's an intermittent problem, you may have some difficulty, but persist. If the shop tries to convince you that it's a completely different problem and refuses to honor the work, get a second opinion in writing and present it to the original shop. If you still don't get satisfaction, make a complaint to the Better Business Bureau. They will advise you on the next steps and tell you if they think your case is strong enough for small claims court. Smart repair shops will try to make good on their work, even if they were dishonest. They still need to stay in business.

## Cruising

Going to the repair shop should not feel like a face-off with the big bad wolf. You deserve a mechanic who likes you and wants to help you, and with a bit of research, you can find one. "Most of our customers have been coming here for years," says Julie Hanson. "We have established a trust relationship. You give us the information and trust that we're going to assess, diagnose, and repair the car properly." She offers this final tip for the most vulnerable consumer, one whose car has broken down out of town. "Tell the mechanic, 'I'm not comfortable dealing with a shop I don't know. How would you guys feel about talking to my mechanic back home about the problem?' Have your original mechanic act as the interpreter of realistic information. If the shop is opposed to that, tow it somewhere else." On the road or in your hometown, a good, honest mechanic will be an ally indispensable to both your pocketbook and your peace of mind.

## NURSING HOME STAFF
## ATTENDING TO THE
## "ATTENDS" GENERATION

*There but for the grace of God go I.* Never will these words ring truer than when you walk the corridors of a nursing home. The line of wheelchairs and the slumped, fragile old folks can be terribly unnerving. Anyone faced with caring for an aging or disabled relative would recoil from placing their loved one in such a place. Yet regardless of our fears and guilty consciences, nursing homes are here to stay, a necessary evil in an age when caring for someone at home has become increasingly difficult.

It is estimated that three out of five people over the age of 65 will need some kind of long-term care, so most of us will be affected personally by the specter of the nursing home. What is one to do? Go to bed with many blankets over one's head? Start stockpiling cyanide just in case? The answer is to be informed, to know your rights as a consumer and an advocate for someone using long-term care, and to learn how to get the most from the care you choose.

## Behind the Scenes: The Kindness of Underpaid Strangers

"If you want a nursing home to be just like the home Grandma has always lived in, it ain't never gonna be that. Because it's not her home. It's one room that she's sharing with a stranger in a facility that's heavily regulated. The way she would have been treated at home, the way she would have been spoken to—it's not the same." So says Stephen H., former chief administrator of a 60-bed nursing home in the Midwest. The high cost of nursing home care naturally leads people to have high expectations, and these are often exacerbated by guilt: "We don't want to put Grandma in, and then if we have to, it had better be perfect." Families demand care as good as or better than they themselves would have provided, but chances are no nursing home will live up to that standard.

Nursing homes are staffed by a variety of professionals: administrators, social workers, doctors, physical and occupational therapists, activities staff, and dieticians. But the heart and soul of a nursing home, everyone would agree, are the nurses and aides who provide the hands-on, day-to-day care for the people who live there. Unfortunately, says Stephen H., "It's a given fact that every nursing home is going to be understaffed. The nursing assistant is going to be horrendously overworked. She may care as much or conceivably even more than you do about your loved one, but in most cases she doesn't have time to do her job at the level she would like to."

In addition to being overworked, most aides are poorly trained. The training they do receive often is not reimbursed and is a financial hardship, because nurse's aides are typically minimum-wage earners. Their brief training period doesn't prepare them for the tough real-life situations they will confront when they're working the floor. The chronic overwork and meager pay become a self-perpetuating cycle that the home cannot conquer, as employees burn out and quit. Most surveys of nursing homes report staff-to-patient ratios that fall below an adequate standard of care. Ideally, there should be one nurse's aid to three clients during mealtime, one to six during non-meal hours, and one to fifteen at night. In reality, it's not uncommon to find a single nurse's aid responsible for 30 people. The understaffing results in a frayed system where nurses don't have time to properly document the patients' condition or medications, and aides barely have time to answer call buttons, feed residents in a respectful manner, or change those who have soiled themselves. Often aides must rouse residents at unreasonable hours for baths or meals because that's the only time they will be able to help them.

It can be a frightening and disheartening picture. On the positive side, the vast majority of nursing-home aides and nurses report that they truly care about the residents they work with. They may be frustrated by poor working conditions and unresponsive administrators, yet they are very clear about how fond they are of residents and how much they worry about their welfare. The dedication they feel toward the residents is often what drives them to come in for another long and grueling shift. Many aides report that nursing-home work has been the most rewarding of all their jobs.

Although staffing shortages are an industry-wide problem, the shortages are much more prevalent in big cities. Nursing homes in smaller towns have better luck holding on to their employees because a large facility will be a major employer in the area. Retaining employees is a key factor in quality of care. Long-term employees know the residents and their families, and that personal bond makes all the difference. The relationships they form with the residents are a morale booster and a comfort to them. In general, fewer mistakes are made at these small-town nursing homes.

It's not only the harried staff that causes family members to worry about nursing homes. The homes often strike outsiders as being too regimented, with little regard shown for individual preferences. Few people realize that nursing homes are the second most heavily regulated industry in America (the nuclear power industry is first). In theory these regulations guarantee that residents will get bathed, fed, and tended to on a regular basis. In practice it can lead to a routine sameness that family members, if not the residents themselves, find depressing.

According to Stephen H., families typically have a harder time adjusting to the realities of nursing home life than residents do. "Once residents are there for 24 hours, they begin to understand the routine. They may not like it, but they tend to be more accepting than the family, who wants everything the way it always was." That particularly applies to their loved one's condition. "Families want to see Grandma as though she's never going to change or get worse. So, because she's worse, it's the nursing home's fault. Yet 95 percent of the time it's simply the course of the disease she's in there for, be it cancer or Alzheimer's or whatever. When you're home with somebody, you don't see it as quickly as you do when you're there only once a week."

Nursing homes are for-profit enterprises. They rely on word-of-mouth to maintain their reputations and keep their beds full. So in spite of the staffing problems that plague the industry, most homes try their best to accommodate the residents and make their stay tolerable. Naturally, some homes are better than others. But as anyone who has been a caregiver knows, it is impossible to provide flawless care 24 hours a day. Sometimes you give the wrong pill at the wrong hour. Sometimes you're late preparing a meal, giving a bath, or getting Grandma dressed. Sometimes, awful as it is, you might even injure her while attempting to move her. There is no excuse for it, but at the same time it is futile to expect the human beings caring for your loved one never to make a human mistake.

What this means for people on the brink of choosing a long-term care facility is that there are pros and cons to every one of them. You must learn how to recognize the signs of both, and try to reach the best in the people you will be depending on for care.

## How Much Care Do You Need?

The first step in finding long-term care is figuring out exactly how much is needed. If your loved one is in a hospital after an illness or accident, there will be doctors and social workers to help you assess his condition. If there has been no medical crisis but you are unable to care for a parent who is "aging out" of independence, the most practical place to start researching facilities is the state agency that addresses the needs of the elderly. This agency is usually a division of your state's Health or Social Services Department. If you're stymied in tracking down the right phone numbers, try a local hospital. They often have volunteers who specialize in dispensing this type of information.

When you have connected with the right agency, the patient—let's assume it's your mother—will be assigned a case manager who will do a thorough assessment of her condition. The case worker will ask about activities such as bathing, dressing, and cooking as well as medical and mental health issues. Then she will let you know what level of care your mom qualifies for, the local services that address those needs, and how they are paid for. Having a firm grasp of your mother's condition will allow you to help her choose her next move wisely, and it may not involve a nursing home after all. There are other options that might provide her the care she needs while still allowing her some independence.

**IN-HOME SUPPORTS.** If your parent simply needs assistance with activities of daily living such as bathing, dressing, shopping, and cooking, she may be eligible for in-home supports through senior services, Medicare, or Medicaid. Your social worker should be able locate the agencies that provide such services and help you figure out funding. Some long-term care plans include in-home supports.

**ADULT DAY CARE.** If your parent cannot be left alone during the day and you must work but otherwise find caring for her at home a reasonable option, consider adult day care. These activity centers provide a social scene, meals, and nurses to watch over the proceedings. Most centers even provide transportation to and from the site.

**RETIREMENT HOMES AND COMMUNITIES.** Not to be confused with nursing homes, retirement communities are private residences within a larger community that provides meals, social activities, nurses (on a limited basis), transportation, and housekeeping to seniors who are still largely independent and do not have major medical issues. Retirement communities are not covered by insurance companies and can be pricey, but they may be cost-effective in the long run when you consider the services that are included.

**ASSISTED LIVING.** Assisted living provides the same services as a retirement community with the addition of having nurses available round the clock, an on-site team to respond to emergencies, and personal assistance with bathing, cooking, and so forth. While they allow more privacy than nursing homes, the "apartments" in assisted living facilities frequently are only a room or studio. Many nursing homes are combining assisted living with their nursing-home services so that residents can easily move to the next level of care when it becomes necessary. Assisted living is funded through insurance and private pay.

**ADULT FAMILY HOMES.** An increasingly popular alternative to nursing homes, adult family homes are a residential service where an individual is licensed to provide care for two to six individuals in her own home. The providers are trained, their homes must be up to state safety and fire codes, and they are regularly monitored by state licensors. Residents have plans of care and the same daily assistance that they would receive in a nursing home. Many providers are licensed nurses. There usually is no on-site medical care, but most providers are willing to accept fragile clients with intensive needs. The advantage of an AFH is the personal touch. Because family life goes on around the residents, they don't suffer the demoralization of institutional life. And because there are only two to six individuals living in the home, personal preferences, privacy, and unhurried care are the norm. Most adult family homes are not equipped to deal with extreme behaviors such as those associated with Alzheimer's disease. They are funded through Medicaid, Medicare, and private pay.

## Finding the Best Nursing Home

If none of the above options will work for your parent, you will need to begin the search for a nursing home. Despite all the horror stories, there *are* nursing homes that provide good care and a safe, nurturing environment. Careful research and continuing advocacy are the keys to finding satisfaction with one of them.

Begin your search by identifying all the nursing homes within a reasonable radius to where your parent lives. (Most homes are in the telephone book; local senior services or government agencies can also help locate them.) Location is important if the resident expects to have visitors—not just the immediate family, but other relatives and friends as well. You want to make it as easy as possible for everyone to visit your parent so he or she won't feel isolated and you won't feel overwhelmed.

After narrowing the search by location, get as much background information as you can on each home. The Web site www.medicare.gov is an excellent resource. It can tell you if the home is licensed, when it had its last evaluation, and what the results were. You can also find out if any violations have been corrected. (They should be!) You want the homes you are considering to have been evaluated within the last year. You can also check with the state ombudsmen program to get an overview of a perspective home and find out if there have been many complaints from family and residents (see box on page 284).

When you have selected a few homes that appear to have a good record, ask about their monthly rates and what forms of payment they accept (Medicaid, Medicare, private insurance, or private pay). Don't assume that the monthly rate covers all services—there may be extra charges for therapies, doctor visits, or special linen or incontinence care.

A common misconception is that Medicare will cover the cost of a nursing home indefinitely. Medicare is, at best, a short-term solution. It is intended to return a patient to the level of health he enjoyed prior to a medical crisis or, if that's not possible, to help him reach a maximum level of functioning. Whichever the case, Medicare will not pay for care beyond 120 days. Medicaid will pay for long-term maintenance care, but only after the patient's savings have been all but depleted. It is up to you to educate yourself about Medicare, Medicaid, and any other payment options, because nursing homes will not necessarily offer the information. (They'd just as soon you install Mom and learn the truth about payments later, when no one will want to move her.) If the home is nice but there is no way you or your parent can afford it, there is no point in wasting your time visiting it.

Before you tour any nursing homes, arm yourself with a comprehensive checklist that addresses all the pertinent issues. The Centers for Medicare and Medicaid Services publishes a booklet that includes a checklist along with information on selecting a home, paying for it, moving in, and more. To get a free copy, call 800-633-4227. Another extremely useful checklist is offered by the Assisted Living Federation of America's Web site, www.alfa.org. Click on "Consumers," then scroll down until you see the link for "Consumer Checklist." The site has much other useful information as well.

## Touring the Homes

Ideally, your research will lead you to several prospective nursing homes. Any home you consider should meet a few basic standards. It should be clean, well lit, and have a warm atmosphere brightened by plants and pictures. There should be no overwhelming odors such as urine or harsh cleaning agents, and no powerful perfumes used to mask odors. The individual rooms should be personalized, have windows, and have a cabinet or drawer where residents can lock personal items. Hallways, bedrooms, and bathrooms should be wheelchair accessible and the bathrooms should have grab bars.

Because the rooms in most nursing homes are small, common areas are extremely important for your parent's well-being. Good homes will have a library, recreation area, and chapel. There should also be areas where residents can have privacy when visitors arrive. The lobby and day rooms should have comfortable places to sit, tables where residents can play games and socialize, and telephones within easy acccess. Some nursing homes have gardens where residents can go outside and some have pets; both are enormously helpful for morale. Exits should be clearly marked and evacuation plans should be posted. Don't be afraid to ask about any of these basic features when you are on your tour.

Last but certainly not least, inspect the dining room. It should be pleasant, airy, well-lit, and clean. Go ahead and order a meal; in fact, sample lunch as well as dinner if you can. Mealtime is the highlight of the day for most residents. You may not be able to afford a home with gourmet cuisine, but you owe it to your relative to sample the fare at each place you visit. While not a deal-breaker, the food should be part of the criteria you use to select a facility.

The physical aspects of the nursing home are the easiest to assess. Less obvious but equally important are the home's staff. Ask questions about staff-to-resident ratios, background checks, training and orientation, and turnover. (Much of this information can be found on the Medicare Web site mentioned earlier.) Administrators may simply tell you what you want to hear, so be sure to keep your eyes and ears open on your tour. Do you see staff members responding quickly to residents? Can you hear anyone repeatedly calling out for help? Does the staff treat the residents with respect and warmth, or are they patronizing and dismissive? Are the residents clean and dressed appropriately? Are there groups of aides congregating in the halls while residents sit alone and isolated? These initial snapshots of how the staff and residents relate to one another are very telling.

Nurses and aides aren't the only ones who will be caring for your relative. Find out whether there are doctors, physical therapists, counselors, and recreation specialists on site. If not, how often do they visit? Do the residents have access to clergy in their denomination, to volunteers, or to pet therapy? Are the administrators readily available if residents have questions? You are looking for a facility that has comprehensive care in an atmosphere that is open and responsive to needs, both physical and emotional.

## Service Plans and House Rules

The biggest fear most people have when they enter a nursing home is that they will stop being "themselves" and be treated as a nonentity. To alleviate that fear, good nursing homes develop a personalized service plan for each resident (it is required by law in most states). The plan should not only address your parent's medical, dietary, and therapeutic needs but it also should document the important relationships in her life, as well as personal preferences including sleeping patterns, food choices, recreation choices, hobbies, and religious activities. The planning process should include the resident and her family; you should not simply be handed a document to sign. Ask the home to see a sample service plan or the blank forms they use to develop the plan. It will give you a sense of how detailed and patient-oriented the facility is.

Any upstanding nursing home will send you away with written material about the facility, including policies and procedures. Review these carefully. Among other things, these documents should address:

- House rules
- Staff conduct
- Safety procedures
- A description of how resident program plans are developed (they should state that resident and family input are included)
- If and under what circumstances physical or chemical restraints are used
- Grievance procedures. The policies should state that residents and families have the right to contact the state ombudsman or other advocacy groups, and they should give reasonable assurance that complaints will not result in retaliation against residents.
- Causes for discharge. Not all homes are equipped to handle certain medical conditions or abnormal or aggressive behavior, and you need to know up front what would constitute a discharge.

## RESIDENT RIGHTS

Residents of nursing homes are guaranteed certain basic rights. The better homes post them, but at the least they should be included somewhere in the home's policies. You should know the basic rights before you scan the nursing home policies:

- Residents have the right to receive information about their own care and diagnoses.
- Residents have the right to participate in all aspects of their care.
- Residents have the right to make choices and decisions about their treatment and activities.
- Residents have the right to privacy in their personal care, which means doors should be knocked on before someone enters, they should not be exposed to public view when dressing or toileting, and they have the right to have visitors without the intrusion of others.
- Residents have the right to confidentiality, which means their diagnosis, treatment, financial, or personal affairs cannot be disclosed to anyone without their permission.
- Residents have the right to be protected from unreasonable transfers to other rooms or locations; if a transfer is deemed necessary for safety or medical reasons, proper written notice should be given (typically 30 days unless there is an emergency).
- Residents have the right to their personal possessions; there should be safeguards against theft and a procedure in place for when thefts occur.
- Residents have the right to complain without fear of retaliation; a formal grievance procedure should be in place.

- Residents have the right to be treated with dignity and respect and to be free of unnecessary physical or chemical restraints.

When you are satisfied that a given nursing home meets most of the important criteria and you're ready to place your parent there, be aware that you will have to continue to be an advocate throughout the person's stay. All but the most costly homes will be understaffed, and the watchful eye of families often makes the difference between good care and borderline negligence.

If you feel that your family member is mentally compromised to the point where she cannot participate meaningfully in her own treatment or make rational decisions, consider filing for legal guardianship through the court or to get power of attorney, if she can still grant it. Without these legal safeguards, you might find yourself cut out of the decision-making process due to confidentiality laws. Just because you are family does not automatically give you the right to direct care or peruse your mother's file. You will need some kind of legal documentation to do so. A substitute decision-maker should be legally in place *before* the move to the nursing home. Finally, before you sign any papers, read the last chapter in this book. The nursing home will require you to select a funeral home before they allow your relative to move in, and although thinking about funerals is undoubtedly the last thing you want to do at this point, later on you might be very glad that you did.

## Magic Words and Deeds

So, Mother has moved in. Her room is decorated, she is participating in therapy, she has begun to know the staff and other residents, and her fury at you is beginning to subside. As a family member, you will have to decide how much participation in her care you can reasonably do beyond this point, but there are several things that will enhance the quality of care.

**MAKE YOUR PRESENCE KNOWN.** Regular phone calls are good, regular visits are better (particularly random, unannounced visits). It is a fact that residents who are visited often and whose family members are involved receive better care.

**CULTIVATE THE DIRECT-CARE STAFF.** Rather than checking in only with the charge nurse or the administrator, make an effort to know the people who directly work with your mother. The aides actually know her, whereas the supervisors typically do not. They will appreciate your questions, your thanks, and your insistence that they be included at planning or problem-solving meetings. They will also be grateful for Christmas cards, a box of cookies, or your taking the time to ask about their families. The best way to ensure that your mother is not treated like a nobody is to treat the people who care for her as if they, too, are somebody.

**ASK QUESTIONS OF A VARIETY OF STAFF MEMBERS.** The nursing staff will know your mother, but does anyone else know her? If they don't, it means she isn't getting out of her room very often. Speak to the activity person, the social services person, perhaps even the staff in the dining hall. They may not have detailed information about her, but some of them should recognize her and know her name.

**BRING MEMORABILIA.** Make sure that your mother's room is decorated with personal photos and memorabilia. If there are public bulletin boards where photos can be displayed, use them. Reminders of your mother's life outside the nursing home will enhance her individuality and are also good conversation starters for staff and visitors.

**ATTEND MEETINGS.** In addition to the individual care plan meeting, be as involved as you can in other meetings the nursing home holds. Some have family gatherings, holiday events, or even positions on the board of directors. Again, your presence will enhance your mother's care.

**VOLUNTEER.** If you have time to volunteer with residents, you'll be providing a vital community service in addition to making your presence known for your mother's sake. Many people in nursing homes receive no visits at all. Their loneliness is profound. If you can visit with folks, bring them treats, or participate in a pet therapy program, you are doing a world of good. Not only will you be improving your mother's care, but you will also be improving the care of the other people you attend to because suddenly there is a pair of outside eyes upon them, and the staff will be aware of that.

**STAY INFORMED AND EDUCATE YOURSELF.** Read the nursing home newsletter, search the Internet to understand the laws and trends that affect nursing homes, contact the state ombudsman program, and join a citizen advocacy group such as the National Citizens' Coalition for Nursing Home Reform. The more you know, the better equipped you will be to act if you see any situations that don't seem right to you or if you need assistance with some aspect of your mother's care. You do not have to become a crusader. You only need to empower yourself.

## Absolute No-No's

Nothing will spoil relationships with the staff faster than a family member who is meddlesome, complains a lot, and micromanages everything. Never forget that when care falls below your standard of excellence, it may be due to circumstances beyond the staff's control. Instead of casting blame, be sensitive to what may be happening at the nursing home. There might be nothing worse to an aide than seeing your angry face looming over her, demanding to know where Mom's other pink sock is after a night of staff shortages and resident emergencies. This is trivial. It infuriates exhausted staff and sends the message that you have no empathy for their situation as workers in less-than-optimal conditions. Although retaliation is against policy, it is not against human nature. You do not want to jeopardize the quality of your mother's care by becoming a known whiner and snoop. As bad as missing socks, overcooked pasta, and crummy bingo prizes may be, you do have to pick your battles. Safety, cleanliness, medical care, and rights violations are where the heart of good advocacy lies.

If you do have a legitimate complaint, do not storm the barricades in a state of anger. Do not sling the arrows of blame. Take some time to formulate the problem in your mind; write it down to clarify it if you need to and say it out loud to know how it will sound to the people from whom you need results. Know what you want the outcome to be before going into the discussion, and make sure it is reasonable. Ask for a meeting to discuss the problem and invite the relevant people from every level of the agency to attend. During the meeting do not blame anyone, but instead ask for suggestions for fixing the problem. If you don't feel you can handle a meeting objectively, ask an ombudsmen to attend with you. You can tell people you are angry and upset, but you can't act that way if you want to get results. Effective advocacy is not about you and your feelings, it's about creative solutions that improve life for everyone.

### YOUR STATE OMBUDSMAN

Under the federal Older Americans Act, every state is required to have an ombudsman program. Ombudsmen are advocates for residents of nursing homes and other long-term care facilities. They can help you locate a facility and advise you on how to get good care. Perhaps most important, ombudsmen are trained to resolve problems with the facility or staff. Most ombudsmen are volunteers, and the training they get varies widely from state to state. The program has had limited success in forcing homes to make drastic overall improvements, but ombudsmen can be invaluable to individuals who want to address a specific problem within a facility. Your ombudsman can accompany you to a staff meeting, help you articulate your frustration, and advise you on realistic solutions. To find out the name of the ombudsmen in your area, visit the Web site of the National Citizens' Coalition for Nursing Home Reform: www.nccnhr.org, or call them at 202-332-2276.

## It's Too Hot, It's Too Cold, It's Rarely Just Right

Nearly everyone who enters a nursing home has some complaints about the facility, particularly when he or she first arrives. When should the family take these laments seriously? According to Stephen H., an effective reality check is to walk down the hall and ask six or seven other residents how they like living there. If several of them volunteer the same critique as your relative—for instance, the temperature at night is too warm—the complaint is probably valid.

Residents often grumble about the quality of the food at nursing homes. Food is an easy target because everyone eats, and mealtime is the main event of each day. If you sample the fare before choosing a home, you will have a basic idea of the quality of the food and will be able to tell if it declines during the time your relative is living there, in which case you can legitimately lodge a complaint.

Another common source of irritation involves activities—the residents either don't like them or complain that the aides don't take them to the activites frequently enough. The only way to ascertain the truth is to drop by unannounced and see for yourself (nursing homes usually print monthly activity calendars). As for the quality of the activities, once again, you should try to investigate this before deciding on the home.

Most nursing-home residents have roommates, and that can be a very difficult adjustment for someone who is accustomed to having her own house, not to mention a private bedroom. Mother might complain that the roommate talks too much, too loudly; watches too much television (too loudly), or has too many (loud) visitors. Before rushing to address these problems, give it a few weeks. She might get used to it and forget all about her complaints. If not, she can eventually change rooms or roommates. One thing is certain about nursing homes: there is consistent turnover.

Theft is a recurring theme at nearly every nursing home, from the most elite to the state-run. Tales abound of seemingly pointless thefts: cheap cotton nightgowns, personal photo albums, even dentures. However, it's not always a case of dishonest orderlies stealing Mom's costume jewelry. Some of these thefts are mere mix-ups. Laundry gets delivered to the wrong room; another resident wanders into a room and walks off with the photo album; Mom leaves her dentures or earrings in a napkin at the dining table and they get thrown out. This isn't to say that theft does not occur, but before marching into the administrator's office, consider the nature of the loss and the various scenarios that might have led to it. Certainly, you should not bring valuable items into the home (a wedding band that stays on the person's finger is an exception). If your mother wants to wear an expensive dress or piece of jewelry for a special occasion, it's best for the family to bring it to her that day and take it with them when they leave.

## The Wheelchair You Push Could Be Your Own

One of the more stressful aspects of placing a relative in a nursing home is the unwelcome glimpse it offers into your own possible future. Not all of us will go quietly in our sleep after a full life where we skied until we were eighty-six. Instead, you may be among the 5 million people in nursing homes when you reach your dotage. While you are still hale and hearty and light-years away from needing to, why not do a bit more research for yourself? Investigate long-term care insurance. Let your children and friends know your preferences for medical interventions and assisted living options. Get your estate in order, appoint a power of attorney, and acquaint yourself with the resources that are out there. If you have the inclination, work for nursing home reform and connect with elder-care advocacy groups. Then, if the time comes when a nursing home is your only option, you can go with grace and know that you did your best.

## FUNERAL DIRECTOR
# HONOR THY FATHER,
# GUARD THY DOLLAR

Three things in life are certain. You know the first two. The third
is that, unless you are prepared for it, your consultation with a funeral director will be the most exploitive and expensive meeting
you ever have. Most people who purchase funerals fall into what
the industry calls the "sudden need" category. This doesn't necessarily mean the deceased died suddenly, it means that you suddenly need to arrange the funeral and haven't planned for it.
People are naturally reluctant to face the impending death of
someone they love; most will delay dealing with it until the last
possible moment, which puts them at a great psychological disadvantage when it comes to negotiating a funeral. That is why
funerals are the third largest purchase the average American family will make, and it is how the funeral industry reaps about 30
billion dollars a year from fewer than 2.5 million deaths.

Consumers of sudden-need funerals are a salesperson's
dream come true. Their ignorance about the industry makes them
extremely susceptible to scams and price-gouging, while grief
and shock make it difficult for them to think clearly. They usually
feel as if they have only one day to arrange everything, which
makes the experience even more unnerving. And funerals are
public events, which means that every decision they make will be

on view for the world to see and judge. It's hard to imagine a more vulnerable consumer, and even harder to face the fact that someday that consumer will be you.

The best time to plan a funeral is before it is needed. Prearranging (not necessarily prepaying) is without doubt the least stressful and most cost-effective way to go. After reading this chapter, you may feel so empowered that you will decide to go out and plan your own funeral. More important, if someone close to you is terminally ill, you may realize that now is the time to begin making arrangements. Perhaps you won't need them for a month, a year, or five years, but when the time comes, you will be glad you acted before the last minute.

To get a dignified funeral at a fair price, you must be aware of your options, the law, and the psychological ploys the funeral director will use to manipulate you. Armed with this knowledge, you will be able to resist the sales pressure and honor your loved one with a dignified funeral that leaves your bank account intact.

## Behind the Scenes: Funeral Homes and Memorial Societies

Why is the funeral business so exploitive? *The American Way of Death Revisited* (Knopf, 1998), by Jessica Mitford, and Darryl J. Roberts's *Profits of Death* (Five Star Publications, 1997) provide the long answers and are fascinating, if infuriating, to read. For our purposes, it's enough to know that funeral homes exploit you because (1) they can; and (2) in most cities there are too many funeral homes for too few bodies. According to a survey compiled by the Funeral Consumers Alliance, many states have two or three times the number of funeral homes they need, and several have four or five times the number. This means that some mortuaries sell only two or three funerals a month. With so few customers, they need to charge you as much as they can get away with. Bigger, well-known mortuaries sell more funerals but charge for the name-brand status.

Lest you think small, family-owned mortuaries will automatically be more understanding of your budget, you should know that many of them have been bought out by funeral conglomerates such as Service Corporation International and Stewart Enterprises, Inc. These funeral homes often keep the family name, but their employees use time-tested, very calculated sales techniques to get you to pay the same inflated prices that the big boys charge.

But there is a bright side to this picture. In response to the outrageous prices wrung from grieving consumers, memorial societies have been established in most states. These are groups of individuals—usually volunteers—who provide consumer information and access to reasonably priced funerals. It costs $10–$30 to join a memorial society, and doing so can save you hundreds, if not thousands, of dollars. Most memorial societies provide a wide range of funeral planning services—price surveys of local funeral homes, casket manufacturers, and crematoriums; guidelines about the paperwork associated with funerals; and legal advice. Best of all, the societies negotiate fair prices with local funeral homes who promise certain rates to their members. Your memorial society will also know if there are any discount funeral professionals in your city. These businesspeople, who typically have offices in mini-malls as opposed to mini-mansions, offer services without the overhead of parlors and chapels.

In general, memorial societies do not sell merchandise, so beware of funeral homes and other for-profit businesses that masquerade as memorial societies by using the words *memorial* or *society* in their names.

**MEMORIAL SOCIETIES AND FUNERAL INFORMATION**

**FUNERAL CONSUMERS ALLIANCE**

www.funerals.org

800-356-5563

Features a nationwide listing of memorial societies, an explanation of how they work, and a great deal of other useful data in a well-designed format.

**THE FUNERAL HELP! PROGRAM**

dragonet.com/funeral/index2.htm

Free hot-line: 757-427-0220.

Along with its online casket catalogue, this site offers a wealth of consumer information in a brief, easy-to-read format.

## The Value of a Loved One

"Guilt is a huge thing when you walk in the door. Huge," says author Darryl J. Roberts, a longtime funeral director who retired and went on to expose industry abuses in his book. "I think it is the most driving factor, along with the inability to think straight. You wouldn't go buy a car the day after your mother or father died—probably not even a refrigerator! And here you are making a decision that's going to cost you anywhere from two thousand to ten thousand bucks, on the worst day of your life."

Funeral directors know guilt intimately and will use it to manipulate you into buying a costly funeral to convince yourself and everyone else how much you cared about the deceased. But this emotional overspending often causes people even greater remorse later on, when they realize they could have spent thousands less, still had a lovely funeral, and put the rest of the money toward their children's education or any number of worthy causes.

Karen Leonard, founder of the Redwood Funeral Society in Northern California, maintains that one cause of overspending on funerals is that Americans confuse money with value: "Here, human worth equals monetary worth." Leonard believes that before any funeral decisions are made, the family should come together and contemplate how best to honor the person who is dying. Even if no one has dared broach the subject before the actual death, it is not too late. There is still time to gather the family together and plan a service that would have real meaning to the person who has died.

"Do you really think your mother would want you to spend $5,000?" Leonard queries. "Possibly she loves her grandchildren more than the funeral director. Could you put up a trust fund for the grandchildren instead of spending it on her funeral? Or you might say to your family, 'Remember how Grandpa would always go to that park? Maybe we could buy a bench right where he used to sit, like he was still there.'" Leonard advises families not to call the funeral home to remove the body until they have taken at least a few minutes to ponder these issues.

This is radically different from the way most people proceed when a loved one dies. Yet thinking through the options *before* you call the funeral home will give you the emotional ballast you need to stay in control of the events rather than becoming overwhelmed by guilt, sorrow, fear, or helplessness. If you and your family and friends can take a look at the money that is available and devote just one or two hours to brainstorming the most meaningful way to spend it, you will have taken charge on an emotional level. More than anything else, that will protect you from the funeral director's tactics.

"It's not an issue of money," Leonard is careful to point out. "You could spend five times more in the name of that person by giving donations, building a park bench, or supporting good works in that person's name."

## It's OK to Take Some Time

The first decision you will face when someone passes away is where to hold the funeral. You need time to make this decision, and it will feel as if you have no time at all. "You put an artificial rush on yourself," says Darryl Roberts. This is the result of our natural desire to put death behind us as quickly as possible. Over the years, the funeral industry has added to the sense of urgency by promoting a "tradition" of funerals that take place within a few days of the death. This works for them on two levels: first, they make more money dealing with grief-stricken customers a day or two after the death; and second, it's more cost-effective for them to move bodies through their establishments quickly.

If your loved one died in a hospital that has a morgue, you can request that they hold the body for another day or two while you make arrangements. The cost may be far less than what you will spend if you choose a funeral home too hastily. Some hospitals ask you to give them the name of a funeral home when a terminally ill person is admitted. Try not to do this unless you have already done some research; don't just pick a name out of thin air.

Unlike hospitals, nursing homes are decidedly *not* accommodating when it comes to holding the body an extra day. They usually make residents designate a funeral home before allowing them to move in, so that the moment the person dies they can have the body whisked away. Understandably, the last thing most people want to do when they are moving Mom or Dad into a nursing home is to plan their funeral as well. Instead, they jot down the name of any funeral home that comes to mind, figuring they can deal with the details later. If you have done this, now is the time to research funeral homes and, if necessary, change the name that is on file with the nursing home.

When a loved one dies at home, you are legally entitled to keep the body as long as you like. If you did not preplan the funeral, try to fight the urge to have the body removed instantly, and allow yourself an hour or so to meet with family members, brainstorm about financial limits, and call a memorial society. Although decomposition technically begins at the moment of death, if you turn up the air conditioner and keep the room cool, the body should be fine for a couple of hours. If you don't have air conditioning, do what you can (shut the drapes, turn on a fan) to keep the room as cool as possible.

## Which Funeral Home?

The best way to find an ethical funeral director is to phone either your local memorial society or the national headquarters at the 800 number listed earlier. It is far more common, however, for people to rely on recommendations from their family or friends. The problem is, the average person plans a funeral only once every 17 years, so he has no expertise. Members of the clergy are more experienced, but they are frequently courted by the funeral industry, which brings their reliability into question. According to a 1994 study by the Interfaith Funeral Information Committee, ministers and priests have been known to accept gifts, charitable contributions, gratuities, and other perks from funeral homes in return for referrals. Funeral directors have also been known to bribe hospital and emergency room personnel to send bodies to their establishments, so be cautious about advice from them as well.

Ideally, you should visit at least two funeral homes to compare facilities and prices. As long as the funeral home does not have possession of your loved one's body, you are in a much better position to negotiate. If you select a funeral home and then decide it's not right after all, don't panic. You can change mortuaries. The law prohibits any funeral home from holding a body hostage for money—that is, refusing to release the body to you unless you pay an extra fee. You need only pay for services they have already performed, such as picking up the body from the hospital. (The cost of these services will be itemized in their general price list.) Simply select another funeral home, sign a form requesting them to pick up the body, and the first mortuary must release it.

If someone dies out of town or in another state, *do not* hire a funeral home in that town to deliver the body to the city where the funeral will take place. You will be charged double—once by the funeral home that transports the body, and again by the funeral home that receives it! Both of these charges are nondeclinable, and both average about $1,000. (*Nondeclinable* means you cannot refuse to pay.) The mortuary located in the town where the funeral will actually take place is the one to call. They will arrange for the body's delivery through a national shipping company at a much more reasonable rate, and you won't be billed twice.

## And Now, Your Choices

What are you purchasing when you arrange a funeral? Aside from the casket, which is discussed in the next section, these are the basic options.

**TRANSPORTATION.** This includes transporting the body to the funeral home, to the chapel (if you're not using the funeral home's), and then to the cemetery.

**EMBALMING.** Embalming is a process whereby the body is injected with a formaldehyde solution that delays the natural process of decomposition *by several days.* It does not preserve the body any longer than that. There is no federal law requiring bodies to be embalmed, regardless of whether they will be buried or cremated. (According to the Centers for Disease Control, no public health purpose is served by embalming.) A few states require embalming or refrigeration after 24–48 hours, or if the body will be shipped out of state. Embalming usually costs about $400. Yet if you choose not to embalm, you will probably pay about that much to have the body refrigerated for the two or three days it takes to arrange the funeral and complete the legal paperwork. If there will be a viewing, it is wise to embalm the body. (Note: Federal law prohibits funeral homes from charging extra to embalm the bodies of people who died from AIDS or other infectious diseases.)

**DIRECT BURIAL.** This refers to a body that is not embalmed and for which there is no viewing or service in the funeral home. The body, in an inexpensive casket, is delivered directly to the cemetery, where there may be a graveside service.

**CREMATION.** Even if all the other elements of a funeral service are identical, cremation is often less than half the cost of a "traditional" (not direct) burial. If you want to display the body before cremation, ask the funeral director about inexpensive wooden cremation caskets or rental caskets. For the actual cremation itself, you can purchase a cardboard or fiberboard casket, a cardboard cremation tray, or a canvas bag to be used in the retort (cremation chamber). If you intend to scatter the ashes, be sure to tell the funeral director, who will have them put through a pulverizing machine that grinds them to a sandlike consistency.

**DIRECT CREMATION.** In this process, the body is not embalmed and is sent directly to the crematorium in an inexpensive container. No service is held in the funeral home or elsewhere prior to cremation. The ashes are given to you in a plastic container or cardboard box, and the rest—purchasing an urn, scattering the ashes, arranging a memorial service—is up to you. Other than medical donation, this is the least expensive option. (Medical donation must be arranged before the person dies.)

**THE SERVICE.** If you belong to a church, synagogue, mosque, or any other religious organization, you might wish to hold the service there. If you are not a member, a local house of worship may agree to hold the service. Fraternal or veterans organizations may also allow you to hold services in their buildings. Otherwise, you can use the chapel at the funeral home, for which you will be charged. Of course, you can always arrange a memorial service without the body present to be held a few days or weeks after the burial or cremation.

**FLOWERS, GUEST REGISTERS, AND STATIONERY (PRAYER CARDS, PROGRAMS, DEATH ANNOUNCEMENTS, ETC.).** Funeral homes will charge more for these items than stationery stores and florists.

**A CEMETERY PLOT, VAULT, OR RECEPTACLE FOR THE ASHES ("CREMAINS").** You will need to visit a cemetery to purchase a plot or vault for your loved one's remains, unless you intend to keep the ashes or scatter them. Cemeteries are discussed on page 309.

## Your Biggest Purchase: The Casket

The casket is a highly emotional purchase. In most cases, it is also the biggest single expense of a funeral, eating up about half the budget. Funeral homes typically charge anywhere from two to ten times the wholesale price for a casket, but fortunately there is a simple way to avoid being ripped off: you can order a casket directly from the manufacturer and have it shipped overnight to the funeral home.

The Federal Funeral Rule, explained on page 301, requires all mortuaries to accept caskets the consumer has purchased elsewhere. The Funeral Rule also prohibits mortuaries from charging you extra for other services if you don't buy their casket. Direct-ordering a casket can save you thousands of dollars, and it isn't difficult or confusing to do. It helps to have access to the Internet, however, so if you aren't computer savvy, find a friend who is.

Even if you don't end up purchasing a casket directly from the manufacturer, knowing the retail price will give you a big advantage when visiting the funeral home. Funeral directors use all sorts of strategies to get you to pay top dollar for their caskets. The most common is the three-level approach: they offer you a choice of modest, medium-priced, and expensive caskets, knowing that most people will choose the middle one. Looking through an online casket catalogue beforehand, even if it's only for a half-hour, will give you enough information to be able to negotiate shrewdly. Also, ask the funeral director about caskets that aren't in the showroom. The funeral home might only be displaying a few of your possible choices.

Caskets come in more than a thousand styles and two basic categories: wooden or metal (steel, bronze, or copper). Most caskets, even those made of metal, will leak within two or three years. There is no such thing as a casket that will ensure your loved one stays unchanged forever or for more than the few months it takes every human body to decompose. There is no seal, no embalming process, no casket or vault that will halt nature's course.

The following Web sites are especially valuable for casket shopping.

- Dragonet.com/funeral/index2.htm. Click "Online Casket Catalogue."
- Casketstores.com
- Webcaskets.com.
- Directcasket.com.
- Funerals-ripoffs.org. This long and passionate site is jam-packed with information but is difficult to navigate. Tucked into its recesses is an ad for the Good Shepherd Funeral Pro-

gram brochure, which features a number of handsome caskets, their wholesale prices (a highly guarded industry secret), and the price for which you can purchase the caskets through the Good Shepherd Program, at a mere $200 over wholesale (not including shipping). You can skip the Web site altogether and call them at 602-303-0857.

### WARNING! DO NOT BUY A "PROTECTIVE SEALER" CASKET

"Protective sealer" caskets are a particularly repulsive offering from the funeral industry. Unnecessary and expensive, it is surprising they have not yet fallen out of favor with the general public. The seal is a neoprene rubber gasket that fits between the lid and rim of the casket. When the casket is screwed shut, it creates an airtight environment. The federal government prohibits the funeral industry from falsely claiming that the caskets can forever seal out water, insects, roots, and so forth. Still, these caskets continue to be sold under the guise of providing a high level of protection.

The truth is a far cry from the sales pitch. Anaerobic bacteria thrive inside these airless coffins, causing the body to putrefy instead of dehydrate. Bloating and liquefaction are the result. Within a month or two, built-up gases from the decomposing body fill the casket and may even burst the seal. In some cases, the gases actually blow the lid off the casket, spewing liquefied body parts all over the crypt. According to the Interfaith Funeral Information Committee, a class-action suit is currently being prepared on behalf of families who were misled about protective sealer caskets. For more information about the lawsuit, call 602-253-6814.

## The Federal Funeral Rule

In 1984 Congress passed the Federal Funeral Rule, which prohibits funeral directors from lying to consumers and claiming that the law requires them to buy certain services or products. At funeralplan.com you can read it in bite-sized pieces that are easy to understand. Here is the rule in a nutshell.

- Funeral homes must provide you with a written General Price List (GPL) of their services when you meet with them in person. The list must identify and itemize all services. The funeral director must give you a copy of the GPL to keep. They are also required to verbally quote their prices over the phone.
- The GPL must include prices for direct cremation and direct burial, the no-frills options that are least expensive.
- Consumers must be told in writing that embalming is not legally required except in certain cases.
- Consumers must be told that it is not necessary to purchase a casket for direct cremation if there will be no viewing or visitation.
- It is illegal to lie to consumers about state and local laws, claiming that those laws require them to buy certain items.
- It is illegal for funeral directors to engage in any and all deceptive practices not specifically prohibited by the Funeral Rule.

You are ahead of the game by knowing about the Funeral Rule, but there's a catch (there is always a catch in the funeral business): the rule is very poorly enforced. It's up to you to make sure the funeral director isn't misleading you regarding the law. When you mention the Funeral Rule to an unscrupulous funeral director, he may claim that *state* laws override it. If that occurs, contact a memorial society in your state. They will tell you about any state laws that conflict with the Funeral Rule. More important, they will steer you to an ethical funeral director.

## Magic Words: Phoning the Funeral Home

The biggest problem most people encounter when they call a funeral home is that they have no idea how much things are supposed to cost. Is $750 a fair price for a 20-gauge steel casket, or is it reasonable to pay $4,000? Should you pay $500 for direct cremation or $2,500? There are astonishing price differences among mortuaries. (With the funeral director, you will only be negotiating the preparation of the body, the casket, cremation if you choose it, and the service. The cemetery arrangements are made separately.)

The Interfaith Funeral Information Committee, a consumer organization, recommends getting a sense of the price range in your area by contacting a local memorial society or phoning ten or more mortuaries in various parts of your community. In a sudden-need situation, you probably won't have the time or emotional fortitude to shop around that much. Do your best, and call as many as you feel up to dealing with. If you are next of kin to the person who has died, you shouldn't have to make these calls at all. Now is the time to ask your family and friends for help.

Many funeral directors will not want to give information over the phone, although they are legally required to do so. According to Darryl Roberts, a typical phone exchange goes something like this:

> **BEREAVED:** "My mother just passed away, and I need to arrange a funeral. She wanted to be cremated."
>
> **FUNERAL DIRECTOR:** "There are many types of cremation. What are you looking for?"
>
> **BEREAVED:** "I didn't know there was more than one way to be cremated."

**FUNERAL DIRECTOR:** "Explaining it over the phone doesn't give you the full idea of what the options are. There are a lot of things to consider. It's really better if we sit down face to face."

**BEREAVED:** "But I don't have much time. How long will this take?"

**FUNERAL DIRECTOR:** "It will take an hour or so. You want to make sure that you give your mother all the thought and care that she deserves, and that she gave you over the years. You don't want to rush this. You don't want to make a quick decision that you'll regret later."

You get the idea. Obviously, the more knowledge you have and the more specific your questions, the more likely it is that you will get useful information over the phone. If you have a fax machine, ask the funeral director to fax you the mortuary's GPL. If you don't, the following list includes the basic items you will need to decide upon. Cross off those you don't want, and as you make your calls, go down the list and fill in the prices. Funeral directors will occasionally bait-and-switch you—tell you a price to get you into the office, then change it once you're there. All such abuses should be reported to the Federal Trade Commission at 877-382-4357.

FUNERAL CHECKLIST

____ Basic professional services (nondeclinable)

____ Transfer of remains to funeral home

____ Receiving remains from another funeral home

____ Embalming, including cosmetology

____ Guest book, program, acknowledgment cards

____ Flowers

____ Casket

\_\_\_\_ Visitation/Viewing

\_\_\_\_ Funeral or memorial service at funeral home

\_\_\_\_ Graveside service

\_\_\_\_ Hearse (transporting body to house of worship and/or cemetery)

\_\_\_\_ Limousine

\_\_\_\_ Service car or van

\_\_\_\_ Direct burial

\_\_\_\_ Direct cremation

\_\_\_\_ Transportation to crematorium

\_\_\_\_ Cremation (the actual process)

The first item on the list, "Basic professional services," is nondeclinable (you can't refuse to pay it) and covers the funeral home's overhead (rooms, furnishings, staff, and consultations). The fee typically runs around $1,000 but can go as high as $2,000, even if you hold the service elsewhere. Your only hope of lowering the professional services fee is to comparison shop and drive a hard bargain.

Be aware that when giving you information about direct cremation, funeral directors sometimes neglect to quote you the cost of the actual event. Under "Direct cremation," the GPL may list services such as retrieving the body, filing legal paperwork, transportation to the crematorium, and perhaps the cardboard box for the body. But it may leave out items such as the cremation itself, storing the body for the three days it takes to get the paperwork done, and the box for the ashes. You have to ask for these costs specifically.

Your best defense is to call three or more funeral homes and visit at least two so that you are able to negotiate. No matter how many you visit (many people can only muster the strength to visit one), read the next section very carefully.

## Come into My Office . . .

What looks like a chapel, smells like a chapel, and feels like a chapel, but is really a sales office? It's the gloomy inner chamber of a funeral home. In *Profits of Death*, Darryl Roberts contrasts a typical sales office to that of a funeral director: "At Slick Jack's Car Emporium, was there a picture of Jesus hanging on the wall above the salesperson's head? Was there a crucifix mounted next to the picture? Were there other religious symbols on the desk? Most probably not . . . the atmosphere is crafted to be quasi-holy, an atmosphere in which you would experience pangs of guilt were you to question the decisions you were making or the price you would have to pay for those decisions."

This atmosphere, combined with the powerful force of the funeral director's sales pitch, is very difficult to resist if you are alone. That is why the first rule of funeral shopping is to take along a strong friend, someone who is not intimately related to the deceased. Studies have shown that it is common for people to go into shock for about two days after a loved one dies. No matter how lucid you think you are, it is best not to trust your own judgment at this time.

The funeral director will probably ask you lots of questions about your loved one. These are designed to put you at ease, win your trust, and gauge how much money you are willing to spend. If you are interested in a very expensive and elaborate funeral, go ahead and tell the funeral director all about the deceased. He will no doubt have plenty of suggestions as to how the service and merchandise can reflect the person's life. If you already have a pretty good idea about the sort of funeral you want, don't spend too much time on preliminary conversation.

"You need to look at it as a business arrangement," says Roberts, who stresses that you should never sign the mortuary's contract while you are at the mortuary. "Go home and read the contract, and only sign it at home. The best thing to do would be to take an attorney with you or let your attorney review it."

Throughout the consultation, he warns, "they're always going to be watching you and trying to pick up on the signals you're sending. Is this a guilt thing? Is it a money issue? Who is the strong person in the family? Often there are three or four people in the room, so they'll be looking for the one who's going to take charge. They'll start talking to that person, but always using the guilt card." At some point, the funeral director might try to separate the "leader" from everyone else. Do not allow him to do this. There is emotional strength in numbers.

## Magic Words and Deeds: Negotiating with the Funeral Director

"Your death is my life." One of Darryl Roberts' funeral-home colleagues admitted to thinking this every time a new client walked though the door. Roberts says, "You don't want to make light of someone's death, but in fact it's true. The death provides life for the funeral director, puts food on his table, pays for his kids' education." Never forget this during your meeting. To establish yourself as calm and well-informed:

- If you are a member of a memorial society, remind him of that fact at the outset. Participating funeral homes also cater to nonmembers, and some have separate written agreements for members and nonmembers.

- Mention that you are meeting with several other funeral homes.
- Make it clear that the deceased and the family have already decided upon the type of funeral they want—cremation, open or closed casket, and so forth.
- Let him known that you have looked at online casket catalogues.

The art of dealing with the funeral director is more defensive than it is offensive, so stay alert for the following guilt-inducing sales strategies:

**"THIS IS YOUR LAST CHANCE TO SHOW EVERYONE HOW MUCH YOU LOVED THE DECEASED."** Here we have the granddaddy of all funeral sales tactics. Guilt over the person's death (no matter how well you cared for him or her in life) combined with the specter of public scrutiny intimidates many grieving families. As was mentioned earlier, you and your family know the best way to honor your loved one's memory, and it might have nothing to do with a funeral.

**"YOUR LOVED ONE WOULD HAVE WANTED IT THIS WAY."** Really? You certainly know the deceased better than the funeral director does. Maybe your grandma would have wanted a $12,000 funeral. Maybe not. If you are clear about this in your own mind before you meet with the funeral director, you will not be swayed by this statement.

**"YOUR LOVED ONE IS NOW DECEASED. THE FUNERAL IS FOR THE LIVING; IT'S REALLY ABOUT WHAT *YOU* WANT. HOW DO *YOU* THINK THIS PERSON SHOULD BE HONORED?"** This approach is used when people arrive at the funeral home with specific instructions from the deceased, usually a request for direct cremation or direct burial with a modest service. If your loved one went to the trouble of telling you his wishes regarding a funeral, he was probably sincere about it. Do not let the funeral director imply otherwise or convince you not to honor your loved one's wishes, unless you have already decided on your own that you want to do things differently.

**"THIS IS A VERY DIFFICULT TIME. LET US HANDLE EVERYTHING FOR YOU."** It would be lovely if during this crisis you could trust the funeral director to look after your best interests. In most cases you can't. Instead, trust the friend you brought along with you to help you make the right choices.

**"THE LAW REQUIRES EMBALMING."** Or the purchase of a casket prior to cremation. Or "sanitation" of the body. Whenever the law is invoked, be careful. Take the contract home and review all such charges. Call the Funeral Consumers Alliance or your local memorial society if you have any questions.

**"DID YOU HAVE A CHANCE TO SEE THE PERSON BEFORE HE DIED?"** This question is intended to put doubt into the minds of people who have opted for cremation or don't want to view the body. It opens the door to a more costly funeral, because viewing usually leads to the purchase of a more elaborate casket.

**"VIEWING THE DECEASED IS A NECESSARY PART OF THE GRIEVING PROCESS. IT HELPS PEOPLE DEAL WITH THE DEATH."** This sentiment is put forth to encourage people to embalm and view the body. Some grief counselors agree that viewing is useful in coming to terms with death, but this is by no means a hard and fast rule. What matters is your family's feelings and religious or spiritual traditions.

**"WHAT WILL YOU BE DOING FOR THE CHILDREN (OR GRANDCHILDREN)? WERE THEY CLOSE TO THE DECEASED?"** Some funeral directors will try to get you to upgrade the service "for the sake of the children," implying that a more elaborate funeral shows the children how much you cared. They also like to stress how important it is for the children to take part in the ritual and view the body so they can process the death.

The bottom line, according to Darryl Roberts: "You need to have some idea what you want, and you need to ignore the funeral director and follow your own wishes totally. Whatever he's saying, just act like he didn't say it and go ahead and do what is best for you."

## Shopping for a Plot

As you did with the funeral home, you will want to shop around a bit for cemeteries if at all possible. If it is a sudden-need funeral, you will probably go to the cemetery as soon as you are finished at the funeral home. Unless you have chosen to scatter your loved one's ashes or keep them in an urn at home, you will need to select a burial plot or mausoleum unit to hold the remains or cremains. Church, private, and public cemeteries are still available in some areas, and veterans and their families may be buried in national or state cemeteries, although some of these are running out of room. Most people, however, end up choosing commercial cemeteries. Here are the options available in most cities.

- **CEMETERIES:** Will accept any type of tombstone, monument, or grave marker.

- **MEMORIAL GARDENS:** Only permit flat grave markers of a single, uniform size.

- **CREMATION GARDENS:** A portion of the cemetery set aside for the burial of urns beneath the ground.

- **SCATTERING GARDENS:** Provided by some cemeteries for people who want to scatter their loved one's ashes.

- **COLUMBARIA:** A vault, room, or wall with niches for urns.

- **MAUSOLEUMS (CRYPTS):** Above-ground tombs.

You will need to decide whether you want to *immur* the casket (or cremains) in a mausoleum or to *inter* (bury) it. In some cases it is less costly to have the casket immurred in a mausoleum, as you don't have to pay for services such as opening and closing the grave (that is, digging the grave and filling it again). As for plots, prices vary from cemetery to cemetery and within each cemetery, depending on the location.

Whether you choose a mausoleum or a plot, you will need a grave marker or monument. You can purchase one either from the cemetery or an outside supplier. Before going to an outside source, check with the cemetery to see if there are any size restrictions and make sure buying it elsewhere will save you money. It is not uncommon for cemeteries to charge as much to install the grave marker you provide as they do to provide and install their own—usually around $500.

Of all the expenses you will incur for the funeral, the grave marker is the only one that will remain on view for longer than a single day. Not surprisingly, the Alzheimer's Research Foundation reports that many families end up wishing they had spent more on the grave marker and less on the casket. Here is your basic graveyard menu.

CEMETERY CHECKLIST

____Plot

____Urn or other receptacle for the ashes

____Opening and closing of the grave

____Grave liner or vault (including installation)

____Installation of the liner (if purchased from an outside supplier)

____Grave marker or monument

____Installation of the marker or monument (if purchased from an outside supplier)

___Perpetual care (maintenance) of the site (usually included in the cost of the plot, but ask to make sure)

No state law requires the use of grave liners or vaults, but most cemeteries insist on them. The chief reasons, they say, are to offer further "protection" from the elements—roots, moisture, and insects—and to prevent the ground above the casket from sinking, causing an indentation in the grass that slows down the cemetery's lawn mowers. "Over time, [a vault or grave liner] will do precious little to protect the remains of the deceased," notes Roberts. Vaults can be extremely pricey—as much as $10,000—or they can cost as little as $200. They are definitely not worth a big investment. To learn prices of the other items, contact a local memorial society, check the Web sites of some of the larger cemeteries near you, or call them and ask.

The oft-repeated wisdom about cemetery sales is that nothing comes for free, not even the free plot they offer if you will pay in advance or buy multiple plots. If you have not yet purchased a plot, chances are the cemeterian will try to sell you two (if the person who died was married) or more (for the entire family). This isn't necessarily a bad thing, as long as you are certain this is where everyone will want to be buried years from now.

## Absolute No-No's

There are only a few absolute no-no's you should keep in mind when embarking on the emotionally draining duty that is arranging a funeral. The most important is not to do it alone, as was mentioned earlier. If you don't have anyone to help you, call a local house of worship and ask them to recommend a funeral consultant. These folks charge an hourly fee to assist with the arrangements and can save you anywhere from 20–40 percent on the final cost. They can be extremely useful to any family that is planning a funeral.

Another thing to avoid—it, too, bears repeating—is waiting until the person passes away to start thinking about the funeral. It will not be easier to plan it then; it will be harder. If you can force yourself (or better yet, ask a friend) to start making phone calls and meeting with funeral directors a few weeks or even a few days before your loved one dies, you will spare yourself some of the stress.

During your discussions with the funeral director, do not mention a specific dollar figure that you have in mind. He will certainly find a way to part you from every penny of it, and perhaps more. Instead, deal with each item—casket, flowers, service, and so forth—individually.

Finally, do not blame yourself for the outcome of this experience, no matter what it ends up costing. The point isn't to walk away rubbing your hands together and chortling, "That was the most kick-ass funeral deal anyone ever cut!" The point is to provide a loving tribute to the person who died and not get mired in the quicksand of guilt, be it guilt about not spending enough or guilt about spending too much. Planning a funeral is one of the most wrenching, disorienting tasks any of us will face. We can only do our best, and then move on.

---

### RECOMMENDED READING

*Caring for the Dead: Your Final Act of Love,* by Lisa Carlson (Upper Access, 1998). Along with essays about the various aspects of planning a funeral, this book includes a state-by-state breakdown of funeral laws. Carlson is director of the Funeral Consumers Alliance, www.funerals.org.

*The Affordable Funeral: Going in Style, Not in Debt : A Consumer's Guide to Funeral Arrangements and the Funeral Industry,* by R. E. Markin (Flaming Hooker Press, 1998). Explains the many details involved in planning a funeral and makes a point of defining funeral terminology, which can cost you hundreds or thousands of dollars if you are not well-informed. Includes checklists and a resources index. Available in bookstores, via online retailers, or on the Funeral HELP Web site (you can download it): dragonet.com/funeral/index2.htm.

## A Radical Old Idea

"Going broke to assure the funeral director that you do, indeed, care, is asinine. Fully 92 percent of all funeral directors surveyed cited Emotional Overspending as the prime reason funerals are so expensive. They should know since they encourage it." So states the Alzheimer's Research Foundation, which conducted a survey of more than 3,700 members of the funeral industry. Across the nation, people are beginning to realize that the costly choices urged on them by funeral directors may not be the best choices for their family. The increased popularity of cremation is testimony to the changes. In 1975, only 6 percent of Americans were cremated; by 2000 the figure had risen to nearly 24 percent. The top three reasons people gave for choosing cremation was that it is less expensive, more environmentally responsible, and simpler.

At the cutting edge of the quiet revolution in funerals is Final Passages, a group working to "reintroduce the concept of funerals in the home as a part of family life and as a way to de-institutionalize death." Final Passages offers guidance in planning and directing your own funeral. This doesn't mean you bury your loved one in your backyard; it means that you, not a funeral director, orchestrates the service and makes the arrangements with the cemetery, casket manufacturer, crematorium, and other providers. It is a return to a truly traditional, very personal way of dealing with death. You can contact Final Passages at www.finalpassages.org or 707-824-0268.

The choices can be difficult and overwhelming, but they are *your* choices, and they extend far beyond those the typical funeral director is likely to offer. Never forget that when it comes your turn to make those final arrangements.

---

### PHRASE BOOK

The jargon of the funeral industry has evolved to shield consumers from the gritty realities of death and from the mechanics of the industry. Below are the most commonly misunderstood terms.

| INDUSTRY TERM | WHAT IT MEANS |
| --- | --- |
| Casket | Coffin |
| Cemeterian | Cemetery operator |
| Coach | Hearse |
| Columbaria | Vaults or walls where urns may be placed |
| Cremains | Ashes |
| Cremation gardens | Area in a cemetery where ashes may be buried |
| Dermasurgeon; demi-surgeon | Embalmer |
| Funeral Director | Undertaker, mortician |
| GPL | General price list |

| | |
|---|---|
| Immur | To place in a mausoleum |
| Inter | Bury |
| Interment space | Plot; grave |
| Memory picture | Embalmed body |
| Opening/closing the grave or "interment space" | Digging and filling a grave |
| Preparation room | Embalming room |
| Remains | Body |
| Retort | Cremation chamber, oven |
| Scattering gardens | Area where ashes may be scattered |
| Vital statistics form | Death certificate |

# ACKNOWLEDGMENTS

This book would not have been possible without the support—emotional, comedic, and literary—of Lani Scheman. Lani helped me write many of the chapters, always delivering excellent work with an occasional raunchy line thrown in to keep me alert. Sadly, those lines had to be deleted from the final draft.

There are many others to whom I am indebted for help on this project. Jane von Mehren, my editor, has been consistently encouraging and gracious, and it is always a pleasure to work with her. The multitalented Betsy Amster is a terrific agent, friend, critic, and cheerleader. Researcher Katy Ngan provided me with the background material for each chapter, meeting every deadline and making the process worry-free. Leslie Moffett transcribed the interviews and managed to stay cheerful no matter how muffled the tapes were. I'm also extremely grateful to the many people who agreed to be interviewed or took the time to e-mail me with their insights and stories.

# INDEX